Routledge R

The Judgment of the King of Navarre

Guillaume de Machaut

The Judgment of the King of Navarre

edited and translated

by

R. BARTON PALMER

Volume 45
Series A

Routledge
Taylor & Francis Group

First published in 1988 by Garland Publishing, Inc.

This edition first published in 2018 by Routledge
2 Park Square, Milton Park, Abingdon, Oxon, OX14 4RN
and by Routledge
52 Vanderbilt Avenue, New York, NY 10017, USA

Routledge is an imprint of the Taylor & Francis Group, an informa business

© 1988 by R. Barton Palmer

Publisher's Note
The publisher has gone to great lengths to ensure the quality of this reprint but points out that some imperfections in the original copies may be apparent.

Disclaimer
The publisher has made every effort to trace copyright holders and welcomes correspondence from those they have been unable to contact.
A Library of Congress record exists under ISBN:

ISBN 13: 978-0-367-17910-6 (hbk)
ISBN 13: 978-0-367-17911-3 (pbk)
ISBN 13: 978-0-429-05841-7 (ebk)

The Garland Library
of Medieval Literature

General Editors
James J. Wilhelm, Rutgers University
Lowry Nelson, Jr., Yale University

Literary Advisors
Ingeborg Glier, Yale University
William W. Kibler, University of Texas
Norris J. Lacy, University of Kansas
Fred C. Robinson, Yale University
Aldo Scaglione, University of North Carolina

Art Advisor
Elizabeth Parker McLachlan, Rutgers University

Music Advisor
Hendrik van der Werf, Eastman School of Music

Guillaume de Machaut

The Judgment of the King of Navarre

edited and translated

by

R. BARTON PALMER

Volume 45
Series A
GARLAND LIBRARY OF MEDIEVAL LITERATURE

GARLAND PUBLISHING, INC.
NEW YORK & LONDON
1988

LIBRARY OF CONGRESS
Library of Congress Cataloging-in-Publication Data

Guillaume, de Machaut, ca. 1300–1377.
   [Jugement deu roy de Navarre. English]
   The judgment of the king of Navarre / Guillaume de Machaut :
translated and edited by R. Barton Palmer.
      p.   cm.—(Garland library of medieval literature ; v.
45. Series A)
   ISBN 0-8240-8638-4 (alk. paper)
   I. Palmer, R. Barton, 1946–   . II. Title. III. Series: Garland
library of medieval literature ; v. 45.
PQ1483.G5A68   1988   88-3786
841'.1—dc 19   CIP

Printed on acid-free, 250-year-life paper
Manufactured in the United States of America

FOR CARLA, CELE, AND COLIN

Preface of the General Editors

The Garland Library of Medieval Literature was established to make available to the general reader modern translations of texts in editions that conform to the highest academic standards. All of the translations are original, and were created especially for this series. The translations attempt to render the foreign works in a natural idiom that remains faithful to the originals.

The Library is divided into two sections: Series A, texts and translations; and Series B, translations alone. Those volumes containing texts have been prepared after consultation of the major previous editions and manuscripts. The aim in the editing has been to offer a reliable text with a minimum of editorial intervention. Significant variants accompany the original, and important problems are discussed in the Textual Notes. Volumes without texts contain translations based on the most scholarly texts available, which have been updated in terms of recent scholarship.

Most volumes contain Introductions with the following features: (1) a biography of the author or a discussion of the problem of authorship, with any pertinent historical or legendary information; (2) an objective discussion of the literary style of the original, emphasizing any individual features; (3) a consideration of sources for the work and its influence; and (4) a statement of the editorial policy for each edition and translation. There is also a Select Bibliography, which emphasizes recent criticism on the works. Critical writings are often accompanied by brief descriptions of their importance. Selective glossaries, indices, and footnotes are included where appropriate.

The Library covers a broad range of linguistic areas, including all of the major European languages. All of the important literary forms and genres are considered, sometimes in anthologies or selections.

The General Editors hope that these volumes will bring the general reader a closer awareness of a richly diversified area that has for too long been closed to everyone except those with precise academic training, an area that is well worth study and reflection.

James J. Wilhelm
Rutgers University

Lowry Nelson, Jr.
Yale University

Contents

INTRODUCTION

LIFE OF THE AUTHOR

After delivering a manuscript containing the works of Guillaume
de Machaut to Count Louis de Male of Flanders, Eustache Deschamps, Machaut's disciple and himself a poet soon to be cele-
brated, dedicated a poem to his master in which he declares:

> All your works are with great honor
> Received by all in many a far-off place,
> And there no one, to my knowledge,
> Speaks anything of them but praise.
> Guillaume, the great lords hold you very dear,
> And take pleasure in what you write.
>   (Text quoted in Hoepffner, *Oeuvres*, I, iv)

Elsewhere Deschamps observes that Machaut "nourished" him and
"paid him many kindnesses"; so perhaps we should consider his
opinion of the older poet's reputation somewhat inflated by
gratitude and personal admiration. But Deschamps is hardly
the only contemporary to offer a positive view of Machaut's
artistic accomplishments. Martin Le Franc terms him a "grand
rhetorician," while Achille Caulier, in the *Ospital d'amour*,
written some eighty years after Machaut's death, praises him
as a "renowned poet" and accords him a place alongside Alain
Chartier, Boccaccio, and Petrarch in a pantheon of vernacular
authors. We may safely conclude from this and other evidence
that Guillaume de Machaut, in fact, was the most famous and
influential poet of fourteenth century France.
In large measure his reputation resulted from his production
of an immense and varied corpus of works, many of which were
composed for the several grand nobles with whose courts he
was at various times in his life associated. As a musician,
he wrote more than twenty motets and a polyphonic setting of
the ordinary of the mass, the virtuosity and innovations of
which earned him the admiration of his contemporaries. Of
musical as well as of literary interest is his large body of
lyric poems, in various fixed forms like the *ballade* and the
virelay; Machaut was personally responsible for the continuing
fashion of this type of poetry (for details see Poirion's work

of 1965, details in Select Bibliography). Finally, following
in the tradition of thirteenth century love poetry, especially
the *Romance of the Rose*, Machaut composed ten long narrative
and didactic poems (*dits amoreux* or "love poems" as well as
others with philosophical or historical themes) and four
shorter ones (which are all concerned with love). These not
only pleased the noble audiences for which they were intended
(the number of surviving manuscripts of the poetry, some beautifully illuminated, testifies to this popularity). His *dits*
also exerted considerable influence on poets to follow, particularly Jean Froissart, Eustache Deschamps, Christine de
Pizan, and the young Geoffrey Chaucer, whose early poetry,
especially *The Book of the Duchess*, evidences a close and rev-
erent reading of the narrative works of the French master.

Because he was a low-born cleric, even though he became a
servant of the well-born and famous, little is now known about
Machaut's life, beyond what has been preserved in various ecclesiastical documents and what the poet reveals about himself
in his own works, especially some of the longer *dits*. From
later documents which detail his appointment to certain benefices, it can be inferred that Machaut was born at or near
the beginning of the fourteenth century, probably in the vil-
lage of Machault in Champagne. Since the same documents fail
to accord him the various titles which would indicate noble
birth, it can also be safely assumed that he was of humble
origin. This social status is consistent with the self-
portrait that emerges from the poetry itself, in which Machaut
often makes his poetic *persona* a humble or even cowardly clerk
who moves somewhat uncertainly among his betters, the butt of
mild class humor. In *The Judgment of the King of Navarre*,
for example, the protagonist, a poet named Guillaume de
Machaut, encounters, while hunting rabbits, a beautiful and
distinguished lady, who later turns out to be the allegorical
character "Good Fortune." Starting to get off his horse,
Guillaume is forbidden from such an unmannerly act of obeisance
by the lady himself; returning her greeting, the poet confides
to his readers that he had learned well how to honor those of
such high station (lines 739-759 of this edition).

Many documents refer to Machaut as "master." This means
that after an early education, probably in the cathedral school
at Rheims, Machaut pursued theological studies at a university,
likely Paris. Though he received the Master of Arts degree,
he did not go on to take Holy Orders, or so it can be assumed,
since he is nowhere referred to as a priest and only served
in the offices, like the canonicate, open to those outside
the priesthood.

Instead his career took another direction, one that per-
mitted low-born clerics, who like himself had the right educa-

tion and social graces, to advance in society. Through circumstances no longer known, Machaut became associated, while
in his early twenties, with one of the most notable grand nobles of the era, John of Luxembourg, the King of Bohemia.
Machaut may have come to John's notice during one of the latter's sojourns at the castle of Durbuy; it is known that John
spent most of 1320 living in his favorite estate in Luxembourg.
A good deal of one of Machaut's earliest works, *The Judgment
of the King of Bohemia*, is set at Durbuy castle, and the unnamed clerk/protagonist describes himself as quite familiar
with those inside. To the modern historian John appears an
extravagant and perhaps unstable figure. To his contemporaries, however, the king's fabled prodigality, the restless-
ness with which he sought to expand and consolidate the lands
under his rule, and his social finesse made him the ideal
ruler. For a number of years, Machaut served John as both
secretary and chaplain (so the ecclesiastical documents assign-
ing him benefices attest) and, according to Machaut's own testimony in *La Prise d'Alexandrie* (*The Capture of Alexandria*),
a poem written many years after John's death, he accompanied
him on a number of his military campaigns in Eastern Europe,
the harrowing details of which Machaut relates. His reward
for faithful service was a number of church offices, obtained
through John's influence with the pope, including that of canon
at Rheims (in which Machaut would continue until his death,
at which time he was buried in the cathedral there). In 1333,
in fact, Machaut's brother Jean (it is unknown if he was
younger or older than the poet) was also provided with a nice
benefice which he received, according to the papal bull, "because of the consideration of our most beloved son, John, King
of Bohemia." Machaut himself is silent about John's activities
during the last years of his life, including a number of disap-
pointing military campaigns during the 1330's and several un-
successful operations to prevent blindness. John died at the
Battle of Crécy (1346) in a final, magnificent gesture of military bravery, a fact to which Machaut never alludes, but the
poet had likely for some years before been more or less permanently resident in Rheims.

During his association with the King of Bohemia, Machaut
began to establish a reputation for himself with both musical
and poetical works. Three of his longer *dits* were certainly
composed and circulated prior to 1342: *Dit dou Vergier* (*The
Story of the Garden*), *Le Jugement dou Roy de Behaingne* (*The
Judgment of the King of Bohemia*), and *Remede de Fortune* (*Fortune's Remedy*). It was their success which quite likely en-
abled Machaut to find other noble patrons after John's death.

In an essay on Machaut's politics, a subject we will consider in more detail below, Claude Gauvard asks an interesting

question about the institution of literary patronage in late
medieval France: "'to retain' a poet, is that not for a prince
at the end of the Middle Ages a means for assuring the prestige
of his court?" In fact, Gauvard concludes, "the true client
is less the poet than the prince" (Gauvard 1982, p. 26; see
also Poirion 1965, p. 196 for a similar view). A well-estab-
lished author, already provided for by a previous benefactor,
Machaut, we may presume, would have been welcome at many a
noble court. Perhaps surprisingly, he did not choose (or was
not asked) to enter the service of John's son Charles, the
Emperor of Germany. Much later, however, Machaut did dedicate
The Capture of Alexandria to him. This same poem indicates
that, sometime after John's death, Machaut entered the service
of his daughter Bonne (Gutha), who was married to John, the
son of Philip VI, and the future King of France. We do not
know whether Machaut served Bonne as he had served her father,
that is, as secretary and chaplain as well as court poet; in
any case, none of Machaut's *dits* is dedicated to her or features her as a character (all the other acknowledged patrons
of the poet figure as characters in works that exalt their
various noble qualities). Their association, however, was
short-lived since Bonne died on September 11, 1349, apparently
of the plague which then swept across France.

    The opening of the *Judgment of the King of Navarre* furnishes
important details about Machaut's activities at that time.
Apparently resident at Rheims, and performing his office of
canon, the poet describes his feelings of melancholy on November 9th and then his reactions to the outbreak of disease (and
other attendant events) during the subsequent winter and
spring. Machaut tells us that, after having made a good confession, he shut himself up inside his house and did not leave
until assured of the disease's passing some months later. As
we will see, the text furnishes an important indication that
these lines were probably written during the epidemic; the
rest of the poem, which features the poet/protagonist's encounter with a court full of allegorical personages and a debate presided over by the youthful King of Navarre, could have
been written immediately after the events Machaut describes
or some time later. It is usually assumed that the *Judgment*
was written without interruption, but this assumption is unwar-
ranted. This means that we cannot be sure whether Machaut
had entered the service of Charles the Bad, King of Navarre,
immediately after Bonne's death or some time later; the latter's presence in the poem--and prominent role as the judge
of the debate--makes it fairly certain that he was Machaut's
patron at the time of the text's composition. Long associated
with the royal house of France (and those, like John of Bohemia, connected to it), Machaut suddenly becomes the servant

of a man bitterly opposed to that house. How did this come
about?

A pretendant to the throne, Charles, who was about eighteen
when he became king on October 6, 1349, pursued interests and
support in Champagne and Brie. He might have seen in Machaut
a Champenois who could be of some political usefulness. On
the other hand, the narrator refers to Charles in the *Judgment*
as a man with romantic interests; the king, therefore, might
well have been more enthusiastic about Machaut's literary abilities (and the prestige he would lend to his court) than the
clerk's political connections. In an uncertain atmosphere of
intrigue among his betters, Machaut, in turn, might have seen
in Charles a useful protector, especially since the poet at
the same time very wisely continued close relations with the
royal house of France. It is during this period that Machaut's
fame began to spread. In his *Meditations* (composed about
1350), Giles le Muisit writes:

> There are now those alive writing pretty verse
> Who certainly don't keep silent as they go,
> One is good Guillaume de Machaut
> Whose works soothe and smell like balm.
> (Text quoted in Machabey 1955, p. 46)

During the decade or so that Machaut was associated with
Charles of Navarre, the king was involved in continuing in-
trigues against the King of France. In the early 1350's
Charles enjoyed a certain popularity among both nobles and
commons because he presented himself as a man tricked out of
his just heritage; John II, then king, attempted to appease
him somewhat by offering him his daughter in marriage. Then
Charles' hostility gradually grew more open, culminating in a
series of negotiations with the enemy English, even to a con-
spiracy with Edward III to divide France between them. But
this alliance fell through, and the English army debarked from
Cherbourg during August, 1355. The following April John II
finally moved against Charles and took him prisoner in a surprise attack.

The next year, Guillaume de Machaut dedicated a long poem
to the emprisoned king, a work entitled *Confort d'ami* (*Comfort
for a Friend*), in which the poet expresses his friendship for,
devotion to, and admiration of the suffering nobleman. Machaut
even assures Charles that he enjoys the sympathy of all his
countrymen. Machaut, it must be remarked, was hardly alone
in his partisanship. The royal government was then troubled
by scandal and inefficiency, having just been humiliated at
the Battle of Poitiers (1356), and even the influential Council
of Reformers had called for the release of Charles, who escaped

from captivity not long after Machaut delivered him his poem.
Supported by many of the people of Paris, Charles, with the
aid of Etienne Marcel, then attempted to foment an uprising
against the young regent. But the coup failed and Marcel was
executed. Charles' fortunes slipped, and Machaut soon broke
off his relationship with him, or so we can assume since no
further mention is made of the king in his poetry.

Instead Machaut re-allied himself with the royal house.
During the winter 1359-60 Machaut lived through the siege laid
to the city of Rheims by the English army and was even required, despite his age, to do some military service. In the
lyric *complainte* "A toi Henri," the poet observes:

> For I was forced to stand on the city walls
> Because they wanted me to guard the gate,
> And I wore on my back a coat of mail
>   (Text in Machabey 1955, p. 51)

In the spring of 1360 the French were required by the treaty
of Brétigny to supply hostages, one of whom was Jean de Berry,
son of King John, and a man who was later to become famous as
a patron of the arts. Machaut, apparently in his service,
addressed a poem of comfort to Jean, who was newly married to
Jeanne d'Armagnac, a work entitled *Dit de la fonteinne amoureuse* (*Story of the Lovers' Fountain*). In the poem, the
clerk/narrator (another version of the Machaut *persona*) becomes
acquainted with a noble lord whose nighttime lyric complaint
he had faithfully copied down. Presenting the nobleman with
a text of his poem, the clerk strolls off with him to a lovers'
fountain where the pair fall asleep and each receives a vision
of a comforting Venus. Fortified, the nobleman asks his new
friend to accompany him to a port where he must embark on a
voyage of separation from his loved one. The characters' real
names are revealed in a closing anagram. The work enjoyed an
immense popularity and exerted a profound influence on the
young Geoffrey Chaucer.

During the later years of his life Machaut was likely in
more or less permanent residence at the canonial chapter in
Rheims. The records of that house reveal that he died in April
of 1377 and was interred alongside his brother Jean, who had
died some years before. In the second of two *ballades* composed
to honor his dead friend and mentor, Eustache Deschamps observed:

> O flower of the very flowers of melody itself,
> So sweet master of such great talent,
> O Guillaume the earthly god of harmony...

> ...For in France and in Artois the death
> Of Machaut the noble rhetorician is deeply mourned.
>   (Text in Machabey 1955, p. 71)

Even more fitting, perhaps, was the indirect tribute paid to
him by poets, both lyric and narrative, as well as by musical
composers who continued to be deeply influenced by his work
well into the next century. (For further details see Machabey
1955, the work on which this brief account is largely based.)

ARTISTIC ACHIEVEMENT

Until quite recently, the received scholarly opinion of
Machaut's narrative poetry--those ten long and four shorter
dits which constitute the bulk of his literary corpus--was, at
worst, dismissive and, at best, unfavorable. As William Calin
points out in an interesting examination of the modern scholarship devoted to the fourteenth-century French poet (Calin
1987), Machaut's narrative verse has conventionally been re-
garded as a stale and unimaginative derivative of the "classic"
texts from the twelfth and thirteenth centuries, especially
the *Romance of the Rose* (for a full history of this literary
tradition, including summaries of important texts, see Wimsatt
1968). Machaut was, in fact, often compared with Geoffrey
Chaucer, his English contemporary, who was praised, in his
later "periods," for exceeding or discarding the very same
literary tradition within which Machaut was said to have remained entrapped for his entire career (see Clemen 1963 for
an extensive development of this thesis, one most damaging to
the international reputation of Machaut as a literary figure).
Even Ernest Hoepffner, one of Machaut's earliest editors and
enthusiasts, echoes these views in suggesting that the French
poet's only originality lay in his creation of literary *mélanges* from poetic motifs and elements of personal experience:

> For, if he found it impossible to extricate himself from
> the domination exerted by the *Romance of the Rose* over
> the era as a whole, he did however succeed in forging
> for himself a certain originality which belonged to him
> alone and for which he was indebted to no one else, in
> that he mixed elements completely personal and individual
> with fiction of an abstract and general kind.
>   (*Oeuvres*, I, ii)

As it turns out, Hoepffner's observation about these poetic

"mixtures" is insightful and will be discussed at greater
length below. For the moment, we may notice his determination
to justify Machaut's achievement according to modern critical
canons of "originality." This determination leads Hoepffner
into what is certainly a grave error: the assumption that Machaut viewed convention, the inheritance of a respected artistic past, as a domination to be overthrown in favor of originality or a personal view of the world and life unaffected by
literary influences.

This notion of artistic originality, of course, is essentially a modern one, which gained currency and shape during
the Romantic period. We should excuse Machaut for not conforming to it since, like his contemporaries, he understood literary production in quite different terms. It happens that Machaut composed a long *Prologue* as an introduction to the collected edition of his works (a piece that, it seems, was written after the corpus of poetry and music was itself completed;
see the section on "Editorial Policy for This Text and Translation" later in the introduction for further discussion on this
point). This *Prologue* is important because, as we shall see,
it furnishes important insights about the nature of love poetry
and the mission of the poet as Machaut conceived them. In
any case, a more historically based criticism of Machaut's
poetry has been developing during the last decade (see Brownlee
1984, Kelly 1978, Palmer 1984, Calin 1974, and Cosman and
Chandler 1978). While this body of criticism does not condemn
Machaut for not conforming to modern notions of literature
and authorial creativity, it does make important use of the
methodologies and insights furnished by contemporary literary
theory. The critical consensus now is that Machaut's narrative
poetry is deeply affected by late medieval ideas about literature and literary institutions (e.g., the patron as both an
important figure in the text and the existential presence whom
the poem's rhetoric is designed to move, amuse, teach, or enlighten). But contemporary scholars have also demonstrated
the subtle and complex ways that Machaut's narrative poetry
engages with the givens of literary tradition and inherited
notions about the poet's role. As Hoepffner recognized nearly
eighty years ago, Machaut's *dits amoreux* are "mixtures," but
only in the sense that all good literature, embodying but also
rejecting the conventions which allow its creation and existence, is an impure combination of the old and the new. *The
Judgment of the King of Navarre*, viewed from this perspective,
is an impressive achievement, one that reflects Machaut's mature and insightful understanding of his own function as court
poet. Despite the recent revival of interest in Machaut, this
poem has been somewhat neglected, perhaps because the "mixture"
it offers is somewhat surprising (even at times outlandish).

Careful study reveals, however, that this poem, more than the
better recognized works of the author, manifests an intriguing
and humorous engagement with the traditions and institutions
of late medieval literature.

Those traditions and institutions, at least as Machaut understood and knew them, do not have to be supplied by (or inferred from) the historical/social context of the poet's practice. Instead, they are embodied in the *Prologue*, which not
only explains how Machaut came to be a poet and musician but
establishes the guidelines for his subsequent practice. This
298 line text is divided into five sections, the first four
of which are cast in the form of *ballades*, while the last is
written in rhymed couplets (a "mixture" which suits Machaut's
production of both narrative and lyric poetry). The first
two *ballades* comprise a dialogue between the poet and lady
Nature, while the second two treat the subsequent dialogue
between Guillaume and Love. The poem concludes with meditations about the craft and importance of poetry.

A prose heading in the first dialogue reveals that Nature,
"wishing more than ever before to make known and exalt the
benefits and honor pertaining to Love," has come to Guillaume
de Machaut in order to commission the composition of some "new
dis amoureus." This task properly belongs to Nature because,
as she goes on to suggest, the act of literary creation forms
part of a great chain of generation:

> I, Nature, by whom all things take form,
> All that there is above and on the earth and in the sea,
> Have come to you, Guillaume, a man I have formed
> For my part, in order for you to create
>> Some new and pleasant love poems.
>> (I, lines 1-5, text from Hoepffner, *Oeuvres*, I, 1)

The creation of poetry, however, depends on more than just a
simple command from nature (something we might understand today
as the emergence of talent). And so Nature lends Guillaume
the services of her three children Meaning, Rhetoric, and
Music, who will supply him with the intellectual and technical
resources for the composition of appropriate verse. In closing, Nature predicts to Guillaume that "your works will be
more renowned than those of any other because there will be
nothing in them to criticize, and thus they will be loved by
everyone" (I, lines 19-21). This prediction seems both serious
and comic, an appeal for renown to which Guillaume the character can respond modestly (he says "I have or will have no wit
or subtlety of mind at all unless you give it to me"), but
which the reader recognizes as issuing ultimately from
Guillaume the poet himself. In any case, the concern for repu-

tation and the attendant desire not to do anything which would
be faulted are important constituents of Guillaume's conception
of the poet's role which are examined and problematized in
The Judgment of the King of Navarre. Guillaume naturally
agrees to Nature's request, promising to dedicate himself to
the task of poetic composition as long as Nature pleases to
keep him alive in this world.

But the proper composition of love poetry requires more
than talent, willingness, and the requisite intellectual or
technical skills. It is perhaps strange that Nature, who asks
Guillaume to write poems about love, does not introduce him
to Love; the latter, overhearing Nature's request, appears to
Guillaume independently, leading her three children Sweet
Thought, Pleasure, and Hope, abstractions which belong traditionally more to the experience of the lover character than
to the poet (though of course in the *Romance of the Rose* the
narrating-I and the experiencing-I are ultimately one and the
same). The connection between experience and the subsequent
creation of poetry is made very clear by Love when she says
that from her children "you can derive great assistance, and
this will help you invent and compose many a pretty poem about
them" (III, lines 17-19). In any case, Guillaume is warned
explicitly to observe the decorum of the love experience, which
depends on the proper attitude toward women:

> But above all else, take care that you are not emboldened
> To write anything full of disrespect,
> And never slander any of my ladies.
> Rather in every case you are to praise and exalt them.
> Know well that if you do otherwise,
> I will most cruelly take away your standing.
> Instead, do everything in honor and thus advance yourself.
> (III, lines 21-27)

Guillaume's reputation and success as a poet, Love suggests,
depend on his avoidance of the antifeminism then still current
among the learned. It is precisely this aspect of his career
which is humorously called into question during *The Judgment
of the King of Navarre*.

Significantly, Guillaume thanks Love for her advice and
help, maintaining that "never has a lover, however much he
was your friend, served you better than will I, with all my
strength, as long as I do live" (IV, lines 18-20). And he
promises to write nothing sad or difficult to understand, only
pleasant and sweet works which will soften and nourish hardened
hearts. This means that he will also "keep himself from finding fault with women" (IV, line 27), a vow he eventually breaks
in the course of the *Navarre*. In the *Prologue*'s closing sec-

tion, Guillaume considers the importance of the mission which
has been entrusted to him; music and poetry, he maintains,
are meant to enlighten and soothe troubled mankind, and God
himself finds pleasure in song, as the example of the prophet
David and his harp testifies. Similarly, Orpheus gained the
freedom of Eurydice from Hell with his music. The *Prologue*
ends with this wish:

>   Now I pray that God may grant me the favor
>   Of creating works which will please women
>   Well; for by Saint Nichaise,
>   Whatever I find the power to say
>   I will do for their honor.
>   And truly I would commit a grave error
>   If ever I failed to do this for them.

(V, lines 176-182)

The *Prologue* invites a number of readings, and this richness
reflects its function as offering both narrative fiction and
an explanation for the real Guillaume's creative avocation
(see Lukitsch 1983 for a thorough discussion which differs at
several points from the brief account offered here). Within
the fiction itself, Guillaume represents his creative persona
in strictly conventional terms, that is, as a subject activated
by the call from heavenly higher authority, empowered by traditional skills and ideas, situated within a context of writing
(i.e. service for two patrons), and charged with a duty carefully defined by the hierarchies of creation in its multiform
senses. The two dialogues, of course, are also conventional
to the degree that they consciously align themselves with both
religious and literary figures. Receiving the commandments
of both Nature and Love, Guillaume finds himself constituted
in the very way medieval Christianity maintained that every
individual soul was constituted: as created but also creating,
as effected but also responsible. The scene is resonant, however, not only with religious values, but also with reminiscences of the many similar scenes from traditional love poetry
where the archetypal lover is situated by allegorical characters, those representatives of the principles of human experience and the universals of psychology. Traditionally,
their functioning is associated, as here, with the "forming"
that releases the lover to act.

Viewed autobiographically, as an explanation, that is, for
Guillaume's historical situation, the two dialogues invite
another kind of reading. The different gifts of Nature and
Love, as well as the fact that the two heavenly donors make
separate appearances to the potential poet, anticipate the
distinction between talent and social opportunity which defines

the position of the Machaut poetic *persona*. For Machaut, *clergie* (learning, the intellectual functions of the educated)
always contrasts, sometimes conflicts with *fin'amors* (the "re-
fined" experience of love normally available only to those
born into nobleness). As we will see, the fact that Guillaume
as character in *The Judgment of the King of Navarre* belongs
more to the world of *clergie* than that of *fin'amors* is an important element of the poem's meaning. For there his troubles
with the heavenly lady Good Fortune arise not from his failure
as a lover, but from the anger provoked by the doctrinal conclusions reached in his earlier judgment poem. In short, as
the *Prologue* suggests, Guillaume is a writer first (because
of talent and education) and a lover second (Love sends her
three children to him only because she has overheard Nature's
command that he make poetry and music). To be a poet, however,
means that he must have access not only to Nature's gifts (a
kind of artistic trivium), but also to the kind of emotional
experience ordinarily denied him by his class. Thus Love gives
him an understanding of emotional idealism as it is manifested
in the three principal states that control it; these are not
qualities or skills, but rather the modes of being through
which lovers pass on their way to eventual happiness. Love
explicitly states that her gifts are meant to help him in the
task assigned by Nature, to assist him in completing poetry
with love themes (see III, lines 1-10). And Guillaume responds
that her children and Love herself have "greatly clarified
for me the themes I have to treat" (IV, lines 13-4). Yet the
appearance of Love to Guillaume in the traditional manner and
his subsequent promise to be better than all other lovers in
serving her suggest the ambiguity of this relationship to love.
As a poet, he is both without and within the world of *fin'amors*;
his last work, the aptly titled *Voir Dit (True Story)*, treats
the poet's own love affair with a young admirer of his work,
and this development is hardly surprising.

Nature and Love, of course, also constitute ways of viewing
literary tradition--not, of course, as we normally and perhaps
distortingly do as a series of texts, but rather as those rhetorical and thematic structurings which are the grounds of
love poetry as a genre. Receiving those gifts, Machaut simul-
taneously accepts the regulation of both narrative and theme
made explicit by Love in her instructions. Thus literary tradition dictates to the poet, demanding not the re-presentation
of experience, but rather the continued production of texts.
These are to be judged, Love states, only by their conformity
to accepted rhetoric and the "truths" of love doctrine, not
by originality or realism in the modern senses. We might also
understand Love and Nature as the patrons of Machaut's artistic
production, as the donors--both figures offer gifts and expect

service in return--who commission and authorize the kind of
work which pleases them, even to making available its themes
and meaning (see Kelly 1987 for an illuminating discussion of
the important role of the patron in this kind of poetry).
And yet the fiction of the *Prologue* hardly tells the whole
truth, for it constructs an imaginative world in which Guillaume de Machaut is only the perfect servant, the clerk who
with all humility and good will dedicates himself to the call
he receives from life itself, as it were, and from those particular noble individuals who engage his services. Rhetorically, the document serves quite a different purpose, one whose
audacity is suggested by the prediction of renown and acclaim
which Machaut the poet puts in the mouth of Nature, his creature. For the collected edition of his works, and the *Prologue*
written especially to introduce it, were produced not for any
single patron (as far as we know) but rather to boost Machaut's
reputation and standing. In this way the *Prologue* advertises
Machaut's greatness more than his subservience, testifies to
the career marked out for him by powers beyond his control
who have picked him, perhaps because of his innate abilities.
These abilities must have included, even at an early age, a
certain facility at self-promotion; for the young Champenois
to have secured an important position for himself with the
famous John of Bohemia must have been no inconsiderable feat.
The *Voir Dit* likewise suggests that Guillaume became unsatis-
fied with the role established here for him by Nature and Love;
in that work he becomes the central character of a love drama,
not the spokesperson for a noble experience denied him by his
low birth.

To understand the artistry and complexity of *The Judgment
of the King of Navarre* it is vital to consider the tensions
which the *Prologue* manifests between what it literally says
and what, rhetorically speaking, it signifies. For the second
judgment poem dramatizes an imagined conflict between the poet
Guillaume de Machaut, proud author of many different works,
and Good Fortune, who represents not only those forces responsible for what we would now term career success but also the
court and the tradition of love poetry toward which the poet's
works are oriented. Here Guillaume is accused of violating,
in the earlier *Judgment of the King of Bohemia*, the injunction
not to slander women which is spelled out so carefully to him
by Love in the *Prologue* and which he himself explicitly promises to keep. The *Navarre*, in other words, though it makes
use of the allegorical disputation popularized by the *Romance
of the Rose*, is much more a poem about the writing of poetry;
it is, in effect, a complex and humorous treatment of the same
themes treated in the *Prologue* (which, we must remember, was
written later even if Machaut intended his readers to see it

first). In the *Prologue* the poet's mission is clearly spelled
out and humbly accepted by the grateful figure who receives
the call to earthly achievement. In the *Navarre*, however,
the poet's accomplishments are called into question, and his
fictional counterpart expends every effort in refuting the
charges made against him, eventually losing his control and
evidencing the very antifeminism he had maintained he was innocent of at the outset.

Because the *Navarre* is also unusual in taking one of the
poet's earlier works as a pre-text, we must first consider
The Judgment of the King of Bohemia in some detail (see Palmer
1984, pp. xvi-xxxvii, for a fuller account, the essentials of
which I will reproduce here).

The poem opens with the narrator's reminiscences about a
late April morning, the time appointed by Nature and God for
love. Love, he says, is an emotional experience that affects
many men and women, bringing them joy and pain. This narrator,
we learn, is an experienced and successful lover and therefore
can give himself over quite contentedly to the enjoyment of
the beautiful sunshine and a reawakening nature. He wanders
out into the warm and clear air, taking pleasure in the bird-
song he hears. Following a nightingale, he enters a lonely
glade, there to contemplate in solitude the indescribable
beauty of the natural music. We expect that, like his counterpart in the *Romance of the Rose*, this unnamed lover will fall
asleep and provide the arena for a psychological allegory
treating various aspects of the love experience (Machaut's
first narrative poem, the *Story of the Garden*, follows this
traditional pattern). Instead, the narrator suddenly witnesses
a drama that unfolds nearby. He sees a lady and a serving
girl approach down a lonely path; the lady appears troubled.
At the same moment, from the other direction, he sees a solitary knight coming closer. The two noble personages cross
paths and, although the knight salutes the lady with proper
courtesy, she ignores him. Puzzled, he takes the hem of her
robe and asks the reason for her rudeness. The lady then confesses to being lost in thought because of the troubles that
oppress her. Like a true gentleman, the knight offers his
assistance, but is refused since, as the lady declares, her
troubles are so severe that no one, save God, could alleviate
them or the pain they cause. The knight responds that he too
is suffering and undoubtedly more intensely, more than any
human being ever has or could. This disagreement then leads,
somewhat surprisingly, to a joint undertaking; the lady and
knight will each confess their troubles in full so that it
can be determined which one bears the greater burden of grief.
Their debate, finally inconclusive, occupies the greater part
of the poem's first half.

From the viewpoint of the *Prologue*, this opening is both remarkable and revealing. At first the narrator's solitude indexes both the importance of his subjectivity (potential and authorized source of a meditation on the love experience) and his openness to instruction or enlightenment, which conventionally comes in the dream that attends this character's falling asleep in the springtime setting. The dramatic interchange between the lady and knight, however, means that his solitude comes to indicate his sudden displacement from the narrative, his conversion into an unseen and eavesdropping witness. In effect, the narrator becomes a more recognizable figure; no longer the anonymous consciousness in which the story of love unfolds, he is now the very image of Guillaume the court poet, observing the noble personages, actions, and thoughts which he, making use of his clerkly powers, will convert into poetry. Kevin Brownlee has interestingly suggested that one of the cardinal features of Machaut's conception of himself as author is a collapsing of the distance between the subjective-I (direct source of the love experience) and the compositional-I (the shaping consciousness which, with appropriate *clergie*, guides the making of the poem). And, indeed, it is true that, at least in general, "for Machaut, love service and poetic service are conflated in such a way as to present the poète's fundamental 'lyric' experience as the activity of poetic composition" (Brownlee 1984, p. 15). Or, following the emphases of the *Prologue*, we should perhaps say that assuming the responsibilities and reaping the rewards of the writer's role mean that the poet must immerse himself in, suffer the emotional turbulence of the lover's lyric experience. In any case, the conflation Brownlee points to, like so much of the Machaldian *oeuvre*, is fundamentally unstable. Here in the *Judgment of the King of Bohemia* Machaut plays with and deconstructs his assigned position, collapsing it into its two somewhat irreconcilable halves (because the clerkly poet writing for the socially distant members of the noble court is by definition separate from the emotional experiences of the class he writes about).

The unexpected narrative twist in this first judgment poem emphasizes the poet's function as servant. Listening to the debate, the narrator watches helplessly as the knight and lady come to an impasse. The two agree to find a judge to settle their dispute, but are unable to decide on the proper authority. At this moment, the lady's dog discovers the narrator in the bushes where he has been hiding, and this gives him the opportunity to offer himself as a guide to the nearby castle of Durbuy where, he avers, the famous King of Bohemia will willingly decide their case. The disputatious pair gratefully accept his offer, and the narrator guides them to the

king (with whom he is on friendly terms). After hearing the
case, John turns it over to his courtiers (all of whom are
allegorical personages in the tradition of the *Romance of the
Rose*) for a proper decision. The poem ends with their judgment
that the man suffers more because his beloved lady, with no
justification, has proved faithless to him. The lady, who
mourns her lover's death, is advised that this sorrow will
pass in time and that, eventually, she may find another lover.

In *The Judgment of the King of Bohemia* the conflation of
roles assigned by Nature and Love to Guillaume the poet is
effectively deconstructed. The narrator's own experiences
with love are put into question at the very beginning, but
are then permanently displaced in favor of those of the class
he serves. The narrator's function is related to but ultimately distinct from the experiences of noble hearts. One
way to read the poem is to see it as an exploration--and perhaps a somewhat humorous one--of Machaut's uncertainties about
or dissatisfaction with the ambiguous position of the clerkly
author who, assigned the lyric "I" by literary tradition, is
prevented from unproblematically assuming emotional subjectivity by the social necessities of his role as servant to
the nobility. Granted access to the direct experience of ex-
alted feelings, he discovers that the goal of that access is
to write for his patrons, whose emotional vicissitudes must
matter more than his own. Listening from his hiding place to
the debate, the narrator displays no further inclination to
attend to his own emotional transport, to fall asleep and experience that vision which would be his alone. But he is not
completely displaced from the drama of love (conceived here,
in somewhat clerkly fashion, as an issue to be debated con-
clusively). Not only does the narrator witness the event; he
plays an important, yet finally subservient role in its resolution. If his experience of love is denied the privilege of
narrative focus, the narrator's clerkly duties cannot be laid
aside so lightly: he guides the knight and lady to the court
where they may resolve their differences and find comfort for
their sorrows.

William Calin has stated that "the greatest gift Machaut
offers Chaucer is the notion of a poet writing poetry about
the writing of poetry by a poet" (Calin 1987, p. 14). Calin
is surely correct that the most original aspect of Machaut's
works is that they are, for the most part, intensely self-
reflexive; nothing in the *Romance of the Rose*, or the similar
love vision poems that follow it, prepares us for the ways in
which Machaut offers us both a traditional poetic fiction and
a meditation, within the fiction, on the discontents, liabil-
ities, and joys of the poet's role. I have argued elsewhere
(Palmer 1987) that Machaut's literary practice closely resem-

bles that of many modern/postmodern authors who produce what
is now commonly termed metafiction. As Patricia Waugh defines
it, metafiction is multilevelled, offering both a created world
with which the reader is meant to engage as a second or imitative reality and a commentary/interpretation/comic undermining
of that world which calls attention to its status as an artistic production, as a text (see Waugh 1984 for a full account
of this literary practice). Most contemporary metafiction
criticizes--even as it continues--the practices of realism.
Machaut's poetry is metafictional in a different sense; it
displays and plays with its fictionality in order to call attention to the poet's role in its making and to the literary
tradition within which it belongs. Thus in *The Judgment of
the King of Bohemia* the device of the little dog apparently
derives directly from the popular romance *La Châtelaine de
Vergy*. Furthermore, in Machaut's poem characters twice refer
to dramatically presented speeches as being "written" in the
"text above" (lines 1592-6; 1780-4). Similarly, the mixture
of "real" and fictional elements in the depiction of John's
court incongruously joins a continuation of the allegorical
disputation made popular by the *Romance of the Rose* to a representation of the contemporary reality so pointedly excluded
by that literary tradition. As a result, the poem locates a
conventional idealism in the world of individual, historical
experience, testifying to the power of its author to remake
the courtly setting to which the poem is itself addressed and
within which it was consumed. Thus, the way in which the narrator's changing function reflects the ambiguous role of Machaut the court poet is merely one element of the work's meta-
fictionality. The insistent breaking of the fictional illusion
means that the reader readily perceives the doubleness of the
judgment rendered therein; it belongs to King John as a character, but more to the existential Guillaume. The tension between the fictional and real Guillaumes evoked by *The Judgment
of the King of Bohemia* is the same tension we observed in the
Prologue between the obedient servant of Nature and Love (Guillaume as character) and the poet eager for acceptance and renown (Guillaume as implied author).

The Judgment of the King of Bohemia displays its indebtedness to the *Romance of the Rose* in order to mediate its reception as one of both sameness and difference; here the concern
with a love question leads not only to a debate between allegorical characters (most prominently *Reason*, one of the most
important characters in the earlier allegory); it also leads
to a representation of the central contradiction which defines
the clerkly poet's role (a subject never raised by the two
authors of the *Rose*). Similarly, *The Judgment of the King of
Navarre*, though composed as much as a decade later and for a

different patron, mediates its reception through a series of
references to the *Rose*, though these are not, as was the case
before, to the first part of that poem written by Guillaume
de Lorris, but rather to Jean de Meun's continuation of Guillaume's narrative. Like the second part of the *Rose*, the *Navarre* offers a lively, occasionally raucous debate about male
and female experiences with love, a debate that raises the
issue of antifeminism. Furthermore, the debaters frequently
use exempla of different kinds to make their points, though
these *exempla* are not as fully developed as the similar ones
in Jean's *Rose*. In addition, there is an important structural
resemblance between the two works. The *Navarre* is the only
work in the Machaut corpus which explicitly takes a previous
poem as its subject matter or pre-text; in fact the work's
full title in MS A is *Le Jugement dou Roy de Navarre contre
le Jugement dou Roy de Behaingne* (*The Judgment of the King of
Navarre against the Judgment of the King of Bohemia*). The
intertextual link between the two works is thus established
from the outset, and it is characterized by a desire for correction or emendation, something similar to Jean's motives
(or those of his narrator, at least) in continuing Guillaume's
unfinished poem.

What prompted Machaut to write a sequel to one of his most
popular works which suggested that the earlier poem was somehow
deficient or faulty? Scholars have usually suggested that
Guillaume had personal reasons for writing the *Navarre*. *The
Judgment of the King of Bohemia*, it is inferred, must have
been criticized for its unusual "doctrine" in noble circles;
Guillaume's second judgment poem, then, would be an answer to
those charges, an answer that, in William Calin's formulation,
is a retraction of the earlier judgment that cunningly does
not refute it (Calin 1974). The fact is, however, that we
know nothing about the reception of *The Judgment of the King
of Bohemia* beyond an evident popularity attested to by the
large number of surviving manuscripts (see "Editorial Policy
for this Text and Translation" later in the introduction for
further details). We therefore have no good reason to think
that the second judgment poem was motivated by anything other
than what the *Prologue* tells us about Machaut's literary production; these "new" poems about love come into existence because Guillaume has undertaken to spend his intellectual career
creating them. *Story of the Lovers' Fountain* and *Comfort for
a Friend*, it is true, are both motivated by extraliterary
events: the departure of Jean de Berry for temporary exile as
a hostage and Charles of Navarre's imprisonment by the king
of France, respectively. These events, however, are very
clearly established as extraliterary motivations within the
texts themselves (i.e. Charles is addressed by name and the

anonymous nobleman in *Story of the Lovers' Fountain* is revealed
to be Jean in a closing anagram). In contrast, the allegorical
character Good Fortune in *The Judgment of the King of Navarre*,
whose dissatisfaction triggers Guillaume's bungling defense
of his earlier poem, cannot plausibly be identified as a real
figure in Guillaume's life. The poem contains references to
real events; its opening section treats the narrator's melancholic reaction to the plague and other disasters of the years
1349-50. But these real events do not include any mention of
attacks on Guillaume's reputation. It seems best, therefore,
to conclude that *The Judgment of the King of Navarre* constructs
the problems of Guillaume the protagonist for the purpose of
generating a playful and entertaining text.

By making his previous poem the issue of a contentious debate, Guillaume, moreover, was able to focus on a character
other than the experiencing-I which he inherited from Guillaume de Lorris and which figures, as we have seen, in the
opening of *The Judgment of the King of Bohemia*). In its place,
the counter-judgment can offer a fictionalized version of the
real Guillaume, a clerk protective of his literary reputation
even as he is concerned about--must be concerned about--the
reaction of the nobility to his representation of their experience. Thus, Guillaume discovers in this poem a new way
of understanding the "I" bequeathed him by tradition. *The
Judgment of the King of Navarre* constructs the complexities
and ironies of the producing-I, the self whose experiences
with writing texts become the material of other texts written
by the same self. This "modern" understanding of the poet's
role is not anticipated in the *Prologue*, which envisions textual production as motivated solely by technical resources,
on the one hand, and traditional subject matter, on the other.
To my knowledge, only Geoffrey Chaucer, in his *Legend of Good
Women*, offers the same kind of fictionalized self. But this
work is directly imitative of *The Judgment of the King of Navarre*, and it avoids the most audacious element of Machaut's
poem: the fact that Machaut the writer is the main character
and struggles, however vainly, to assert his importance in
the face of disapproval from his patrons.

Machaut's focus on his own experiences (even when these
are only "imagined" for the purpose of generating the text)
is obvious from the beginning 540 lines of the poem, which
treat, with accurate historical detail, the disturbing events
of 1349-50 and the clerk's reactions to them. This section
starts with an evocation of fall, the season of death and loss
which suits historical calamity, and ends with the joyful coming of spring, when the passing of the epidemic allows the
poet to resume solitary enjoyments--especially hare-hunting--
and be open to the love experience, which here assumes a very

untraditional shape. The movement from fall to spring and
the attendant transformation of the historical subject into a
character more suited to the love themes of courtly poetry
have both encouraged some critics to view the opening part of
the poem as a tedious irrelevance (see Muscatine 1957 especially). Others more sympathetic to Machaut's architechtonic
skill have sought thematic links of various kinds between the
opening and the more conventional poetic fiction that follows
(most successfully William Calin 1974 and David Lanoue 1981).
But the different parts of the poem become a difficulty only
if we believe that Machaut was attempting to write a traditional love allegory and, for some dim reason, included an
introduction which drew on tangential, historical material.
The love allegory section itself, however, is hardly traditional, in fact makes use of inherited structures in order to
explore very different themes and issues. Both parts of the
Navarre in fact make it clear that the subject here is the
poet himself, first viewed, with great seriousness, as a historical person caught up in a tumult of events beyond his control, and then examined, rather humorously, as a bumbling ver-
sifier who slanders ladies even as he defends his attempts to
exalt them. One important connection between the two parts
of the poem is the poet's melancholy: the state of the world
saddens him and then, with the disappearance of the disease,
allows him pleasure again. Soon after, his hare-hunting is
interrupted by the "call" from Good Fortune, who sinks him back
into a melancholy from which he is somewhat rescued by the
lightheartedness of the debate's conclusion. Unlike the *welt-
schmerz* that so affects him at the work's beginning, this melancholy can be (and is) overcome by Guillaume's gracious acceptance of the judgment against him and his cheerful agreement
to do appropriate penance (which is the composition of three
lyrical pieces in fixed forms with, this time, the "correct"
doctrine).

   If the true subject of the poem is the "real" Guillaume,
then the historical references and analysis in the opening
make good artistic sense: they ground the fiction which follows
in the truth of the poet's experience. After referring to
the cold north wind which has destroyed the greenery of summer
(lines 34-6), the narrator describes how in the contemporary
world there is no justice or truth, only a rapacious avarice
which destroys social and familial trust; the result is a constant warfare which has brought down a heavenly vengeance in
the form of destructive weather (lines 37-108). This description is a conventional, apocalyptic one (the topos is usually
called *mundus senescit* or "the world grows old"), but it is
followed by a return to the narrator's state of mind. The
fall season had made him sad, and reflecting on the decay of

the world sinks him into melancholy, which he tries to resist,
following the wisdom of Ecclesiastes (lines 109-142). But,
leaving behind the thoughts of social decay, the narrator considers those present ills which make him even more melancholic.
These include (lines 152-166) ominous heavenly signs (particularly the lunar eclipse of January 17, 1348, the various
astrological configurations of that year widely interpreted
as predicting the subsequent epidemic, and the appearance of
a fiery comet). Guillaume also makes reference to the great
earthquake which devastated parts of Eastern Europe and Italy
(January 25, 1348); see lines 167-180, a passage that mentions
a heavenly rain of blood that boded ill. God revealed the
meaning of these signs quickly by permitting a great outbreak
of wars and killing, another apocalyptic reference with some
basis in contemporary reality (e.g. the continuing hostilities
of the Hundred Years' War, in which Machaut himself took some
minor part). This long passage (lines 181-228) mentions as
well the outbreak of anti-Semitism which accompanied the first
appearances of the plague in northern Europe; like many at
the time, Machaut believed that the Jews had poisoned wells
and thus deserved the murderous fury of the persecutions which
followed the spreading of these rumors (lines 229-240). Guillaume connects the phenomenon of wandering companies of flagel-
lants to the disastrous events predicted by the heavens, even
though this bizarre form of religious piety had come into existence during the previous century, and continued to be active
in Bohemia during the 1340s (lines 241-256). Because men were
so intent on destroying themselves, Guillaume suggests, Nature
decided to assist in this destruction by sending terrible
storms to the earth, in expectation that the world would soon
end; such weather had the end result of giving rise to terrible, corrupting mists, the cause of the epidemic which immediately followed (lines 271-346).
  Throughout this part of the poem, Guillaume gives the distinct impression that he is following one of the numerous Latin
chronicles of the period, though no specific source can be
identified. His selection of events (and their explanation
as well) both resemble closely what contemporary historians
have to say about the outbreak of the epidemic. In any case,
it is interesting that Guillaume here assumes the voice and
manner of the historian (a narrative posture which can depend
on personal experience). The last part of his account is by
far the most dramatic. God sees from his house that the world
is everywhere corrupted, and so he sets Death loose on suffering humanity; Death is a beast so greedy and insatiable that
he must consume heaps of corpses every day. The towns and
villages are soon emptied of people; ditches must be dug in
churchyards to bury the unnumbered dead (in lines 393-399 Guil-

laume says that no one will be able to count how many have
died or *will* die, an important indication that this part of
the poem was indeed written during the epidemic); pasture and
field go untended because there are none to work or guard them
(lines 347-430). At this point the narrator returns to his
own reactions. Horrified by an imminent death, he confesses
his sins thoroughly and resigns himself to the inevitable,
closing up his doors and staying inside the whole winter (a
precaution that probably saved his life). In this way he suffered less melancholy than he would have—for many of his
friends died and were buried, a fact of which he remained ig-
norant. Finally, the end of the epidemic is signaled by a
merrymaking throughout the town which Guillaume hears in his
house. Asking one of his friends what is happening, Guillaume
learns that the survivors are celebrating. He decides that
he will do the same and goes to his horse and dogs, proceeding
to some hare-hunting in the springtime fields. This is an
activity which he defends with great seriousness, saying that
its practice so absorbed him he would not have recognized anyone had they ridden up to him and spoken (lines 431-540).

     At this point Machaut begins to reprise and adapt the struc-
ture of his earlier judgment poem. In *The Judgment of the
King of Bohemia* the sorrowing lady, lost in gloomy thoughts,
ignores the knight's greeting; this prompts their conversation
and leads to the debate. Similarly, Guillaume's enthusiasm
for hare-hunting here blinds him to the arrival in the fields
of a "lady of great nobility," who, alerted to the poet's identity by her squire, sends him a message to appear before her.
Indeed, she is the very lady whom Guillaume serves, although
it is only later that he learns her name. This inconsistency
conceals a hidden meaning, namely that Guillaume is unthink-
ingly aware he owes service to Good Fortune without knowing
who she truly is or the power she wields over him. Like the
traditional instructress figures of love allegory or the mys-
terious, supernatural ladies of Arthurian romance, Good Fortune
appears to correct and enlighten her male subject. As it turns
out, what she has to offer is advice about Guillaume's career;
her judgment involves a renewal of the poet's contract to write
about ladies and love in the appropriate fashion. As their
debate develops, however, what is most significant is the fact
that in this poem Guillaume takes the place of the knight as
the male member of the debating pair. This change signals
the most important difference of *The Judgment of the King of
Navarre*. In the earlier poem, the narrator/clerk is displaced
from the poem as the debate begins; here the narrator/clerk,
no longer an anonymous and traditional figure but a fictional
version of Guillaume himself, becomes the accused who must
defend himself against the charges of Good Fortune. In *The*

Judgment of the King of Bohemia the levels of traditional love
allegory/debate and commentary on the poet's role in its making
are kept distinct; the twist in the conventional structure of
the poem calls attention to itself, focussing the reader on
the narrator's role (and its reflection of the author's historical predicament as court poet/lyric voice). In the later
judgment poem, on the contrary, the fiction itself becomes an
examination of the poet's performance as poet.

Instead of a response to a conventional *demande d'amors*
(question of love), the debate here is more like a law suit
in which the plaintiff makes a complaint whose rightness or
wrongness is to be determined by an impartial judge. Unlike
the interlocutors in the earlier poem, Guillaume is literally
put on trial for an alleged crime: the promulgation of the
"incorrect" view that the man whose beloved has betrayed him
suffers more than the lady who has experienced the death of
her lover. Good Fortune begins by faulting Guillaume for not
noticing her arrival on the scene, a charge against which he
defends himself successfully (lines 760-801). Then she accuses
him of having sinned against ladies, but does not tell him
how or when. Frustrated, Guillaume pleads for more specific
information which, apparently impressed by the persuasiveness
of his argument, she finally furnishes him, making reference
to the conclusion reached in *The Judgment of the King of Bohemia* (lines 801-1038). Though she advises that Guillaume
admit his fault immediately and correct his error by promul-
gating the opposite opinion (lines 1031-38), Guillaume refuses
to do so because the original judgment is his published view.
He resolves to win the debate if he can even though this means
opposing himself to a grand and noble person whom he ought to,
perhaps, unquestioningly obey. Guillaume's attitude here contrasts sharply with that of the character Guillaume in the
Prologue; the latter is appropriately obedient, humble, self-
effacing, and eager to please, agreeing wholeheartedly with
everything Nature and Love ask. In fact, in the light of the
circumstances of literary production set out in the *Prologue*,
the reaction of Guillaume to Good Fortune's charges is most
surprising. Nature gives the poet Meaning, Rhetoric, and Music
so that "in writing poetry you cannot fail at all" (I, line
17); the three natural children of artistic technique and content will make sure that his works will never "contain anything
which will cause you to be blamed" (I, line 20). This command
hardly makes room for error, and that is because it does not
grant Guillaume any control over what his works will contain.
Certainly it does not authorize his willful disagreement with
anything a figure of authority--especially a heavenly lady--
might offer by way of correction.

The Judgment of the King of Bohemia metafictionally explores

xxxiv   Introduction

the contradictions of the poet's artistic/social position,
representing his eager endorsement of them. *The Judgment of
the King of Navarre*, in contrast, concerns itself with the
poet's paradoxical subservience to but command of the love
experience, marking out, in ironic fashion, the limits of the
author's creative freedom (for the confrontation offered here
is manifestly "fictional"). The poet is brought to heel for
his obstreperousness, but only so that he can be authorized
to produce even more texts in a scene which recalls his encounter with Nature in the *Prologue*.

Agreeing to debate the issue of his "error," Guillaume and
the lady decide that the young King of Navarre, a man with
amorous interests, shall be their judge. The pair ride on,
accompanied by the lady's entourage, to a handsome manor house
where she holds court (described as a state of absolute repose
and enjoyment, this manor house is a more realistic version
of the traditional *locus amoenus* where love allegory is often
set). There the poet is introduced to the twelve damsels who
comprise the lady's court: these include psychological per-
sonifications like Discretion and Recognition as well as traditional virtues such as Prudence, Temperance, and Charity (for
an intelligent discussion of the tradition behind Machaut's
allegory here see Ehrhart 1979). The narrator relates that
the lady is served well by her court, who insure that she does
only what's right and avoids all evil. It should be added at
this point that the scheme adopted here is a fluid one; an
important allegorical personage, Moderation, appears later
but is not introduced at this point. This long passage of
description (lines 1155-1328) is the poem's most impressive
set piece. The appearance of the lady and her court dazzles
the impressionable Guillaume, who for a moment is tempted to
give up his defense; his strength, however, is restored by
Reason (lines 1329-1356). The lady then wishes to rehearse
her complaint to the assembled court and, despite Guillaume's
wish that they wait for the arrival of their judge, she does
so impressively. As she finishes, the King of Navarre arrives
by chance and immediately agrees to judge the dispute, picking
appropriate members of Good Fortune's court to advise him
(lines 1443-1628). The debate finally begins with a long presentation of the case by the lady, who uses examples drawn
from the bestiary tradition--the turtledove and the swan (lines
1629-1702)--to argue that Guillaume is wrong.

Though he refuses Good Fortune's request to change his mind,
Guillaume answers with extreme politeness, asking the judge's
permission to speak, and simply restating his contention that
the pain which a man feels because of his beloved's infidelity
is more severe than any other (lines 1703-68). Guillaume ends
by asking for the judgment on his behalf, and this arrogance

angers Temperance, who chastises him for wanting to circumvent
proper legal procedure and for deliberately misinterpreting
one of the lady's points. Temperance suggests that the man,
even though betrayed, can find relief in many ways, while the
woman, seeing her lover dead, will suffer unending sorrow.
And, to illustrate her point, Temperance introduces the debate's first *exemplum*, the story of a young girl who, upon
learning her lover had been killed, soon dies despite the efforts of a host of doctors (lines 1769-2024). Guillaume agrees
that the story is interesting, but finds in it a point for
his side, namely that the lady died quickly and did not suffer
long, while the cuckolded man finds no end to his misery (lines
2025-2076). Reminding the court of something he had maintained
in his earlier work (see *JRB*, lines 1110-21; 1716-23), Guillaume states that the dead are soon forgotten, making the heart
recover from grief. Once again, he asks for the decision on
his behalf.

This time Peace objects to his impertinence, declaring that
he has not made enough argument to win the judgment. Intending
to give Guillaume more to think about, she relates the death
of Dido, who, betrayed by Aeneas, committed suicide. This
exemplum diverts the course of the debate in an interesting
way, because Dido did not suffer the death of her lover, but
rather his faithlessness. Such a divergence is anticipated
in the original judgment poem where the debate between John's
courtiers about the issue of who suffers more soon turns to
the question of whether Reason or Youth should command the
lover. Peace seems to be implying here that women have a
greater capacity to suffer, whatever the cause. In any case,
she also reproves Guillaume for stating that Nature overrides
the commands of Love, allowing the grief-stricken beloved to
forget her loss. Love, Peace suggests, always rules lovers
and does not heed the wishes of Nature in any way (lines 2077-
2206). Guillaume, still polite, begs to disagree, relating
the story of a clerk from Orleans whose distant lover proves
unfaithful to him, marrying another man. Learning of her betrayal in a letter, the clerk goes mad and for the next twenty
years lives in the wild like an animal, speaking to no one.
Such a man, Guillaume avers, suffered a hundred times more
pain than any woman who lost her lover (lines 2207-2314).
Faith takes exception to Guillaume's *exemplum*, noting that he
has not proved that the letter which caused the man to go mad
actually was written by his beloved; her angry tone distresses
Guillaume, and he asks her to stop threatening him (lines 2315-
80). At this Faith confers with Charity, and the latter is
chosen to relate another *exemplum*, one which surely will prove
Guillaume wrong. Charity tells the story of a rich man who,
planting a sapling in his garden, goes to see it one day and

finds it a full-grown tree. The story, as Charity explains
it, signifies the behavior of the proper lover who, seeing
his beloved grow into marriage with a powerful man, rejoices
at her new-found station and happiness (lines 2381-2532).
Guillaume then challenges his opponents to prove only that no
lady has ever suffered so much as to offer herself to death
(has he forgotten the story of Dido, just related to him by
Peace?). Honesty doesn't address this point, but attacks his
story about the clerk of Orleans, maintaining that, once mad,
the man did not suffer at all. Guillaume's response is typi-
cally clerkly, a short disquisition on the distinction between
primary and secondary causes which he thinks supports his view
about the clerk's continued ordeal (its relevance seems problematic at best).

At this point the debate turns completely toward the issue
broached earlier by Peace, the supposed greater capacity of
women to suffer. In a long speech (lines 2699-2822), Generosity offers *exempla* from Classical literature, the stories of
Ariadne and Medea, which, she believes, illustrate the point
that women are made to suffer by men but emerge victorious in
the end. Guillaume rudely attacks this argument, saying that
he could easily find a host of examples to prove the opposite,
namely that men have a greater capacity for suffering than
women. He then relates one of the strangest *exempla* of the
debate. A woman has given her lover a ring on the condition
that he never remove it unless she do it for him. One day
her husband notices that the ring is missing and demands to
see it. She sends a message to him asking for its return,
and he sends it to her along with his finger in order not to
break his word. Though he recognizes that extremes in loving
are to be condemned, Guillaume suggests that the man surpassed
all women in loyalty and suffering (lines 2823-2924). Prudence
does not agree, and she launches a long refutation of Guillaume's contention, which the poet ignores, preferring to return to the issue raised by Generosity. Though he recognizes
that the debate has broadened to include an issue not mentioned
in the beginning, Guillaume offers his opinion that men are
far superior to women in love because there's nothing stable
or firm about a woman's emotions or beliefs. These anti-
feminist statements, he affirms, are endorsed by everyone,
and that is why he advanced them in his poem (lines 2009-3070).

These views give rise to an outburst which must eventually
be settled by the judge (Guillaume admits to some satisfaction
and pleasure in seeing the assemblage of ladies so discomfited,
lines 3157-3162). Fear tells the story of Pyramus and Thisbé
and Sufficiency the tale of Hero and Leander as proof of wom-
en's capacity to endure. But Guillaume counters with the observation that in the latter case Leander suffered more since

he suffered first (once again a somewhat dubious point).
Thinking that the debate has continued long enough, the lady
now asks the judge to go in private to deliberate. The judge
and his advisors then leave, but Guillaume is informed of their
proceedings by an attendant at court. Reviewing the aspects
of proper judgment, the advisors condemn Guillaume unanimously.
Moderation rebukes Guillaume for daring to debate such a noble
and respected personage, for advancing a mistaken opinion,
and for offering insufficient and dubious evidence in support
of his position. Reason agrees, and when the court has reas-
sembled with the accused, condemns him on these three counts
(lines 3767-3832). Seeing Guillaume saddened by the outcome,
Reason reveals to him the identity of the lady and describes
her immense powers; in the tradition of Boethius's *Fortuna*,
Good Fortune distributes talents and wisdom to those she fa-
vors. Reason's long description particularly emphasizes the
different gifts she accords to *clergie* and *chevalerie* (lines
3839-4006). More reconciled to his fate, Guillaume asks to
be sentenced, and the judge signifies to him that he owes three
amends for his three different faults. Reason and the judge
confer about the specifics of the sentence, a meeting which,
Guillaume perceives, is somewhat lighthearted. Meanwhile Discretion recounts the allegorical meanings of the different
parts of Good Fortune's dress (lines 4075-4170). The judge
then returns to Guillaume and tells him he must compose three
lyric poems, of different types, as penance. The poem closes
with Guillaume's confession that he has made this poem in order
to recognize his fault better and intends to present it to
the lady along with his promise of continued service. Guillaume then expresses his desire to complete his penance quickly
by composing a lay concerned with love.

In MSS B, E, and M the *Lai de Plour* (*The Lay of Weeping*)
follows the end of the judgment immediately; in the later MSS,
especially F-G and A, the lay either is missing entirely or
is found among the other lyric poems. It seems that Machaut
initially thought it should follow the narrative poem which
is its pre-text but later changed his mind. I have followed
the practice of the earlier MSS in including it as a continuation of *The Judgment of the King of Navarre*. The reader may
judge for himself whether Machaut's original plan is artistically successful or not (I happen to think it is, of which
more below).

In assessing the artistic achievement of *The Judgment of
the King of Navarre*, we must, I think, read the poem metafictionally, in the same way the original audience likely did.
For we must, as did they, distinguish between the seriousness
of Guillaume the character, who resents the accusations of
Good Fortune and loses his composure as the trial begins to

slip away from him, eventually mouthing, somewhat gleefully,
the very anti-feminist statements he declared himself innocent
of at the beginning; and the seriousness of Guillaume de Machaut the poet, who with remarkable *sprezzatura* puts his own
poetry on trial in a work whose sophistication and finesse
equally testify to his commanding, confident talent. The poem
playfully treats the relationship of the poet to his *métier*
and to his patrons, problematizing the very traditional poetics
of the *Prologue* by turning the poet's individual control over
the content of his works (and the reputation they make or do
not make for him) into an issue to be debated. Within the
fiction, Guillaume's temerity is roundly condemned, as much,
if not more than, the antifeminism he proves himself guilty
of. But the poem itself testifies to the ways in which Guillaume, as creative source of his works, can forge something
entirely new from the givens of tradition, including a different sense in which "poetic identity" can be represented.
Focussing on the producing-I, *The Judgment of the King of Navarre* traces the ways in which authorial intertext, rather
than traditional techniques and subject matter, "creates" poetry. *The Judgment of the King of Bohemia* generates *The Judgment of the King of Navarre* which in turn generates the *Lai
de Plour*. The audacity here is that Guillaume produces poetry
which is intensely self-reflexive, thematizing the discontents
of an author controlled by the reader, who consumes his work,
even as this poetry asserts the power of the poet to exceed
or controvert the position assigned him by tradition (i.e.
here Guillaume the *writer* not the *lover* is the main character).
For this reason I believe the poet's original plan to have
the *Lai de Plour* follow the end of the judgment poem was most
effective artistically.
   The Judgment of the King of Navarre is unlike all other
medieval works in its complex exploration of the poetics of
authorship, in its meditations on and comic reduction of the
difficulties posed by a literary tradition and its underlying
ideology to the creative author. What model can we suggest
for such a novel and innovative text? One way of understanding
Machaut's accomplishment is to see the poem as part of that
slow and complex movement toward the modern novel. Mikhail
Bakhtin has suggested that as a literary tradition begins to
assert less authority over those who write within it the pres-
entness of the writer's situation calls more insistently for
its own representation (Bakhtin 1981). At the same time, the
process of writing becomes more problematic, for the certain-
ties of conventional subject matter and sanctioned methods or
attitudes for the writer fall away. The self-reflexive and
"personal" elements of this text could well have been motivated
by the breakdown and loosening of the literary tradition of

allegorical love poetry, even as this tradition insistently
calls for its own space within the poem. For Machaut, the
final result of the artistic development we witness here is
the paradoxical work *The True Story*, which offers not only
the abstractions and idealizations sanctioned by long literary
tradition but the vagaries and inconclusiveness of individual,
authorial experience. The early stages of this development
can be traced in the two judgment poems. In *The Judgment of
the King of Bohemia* the poet's situation calls for representation within the traditional debating and allegorical structures
of the poem. Here is a poetic presence still willing to efface
its own demands for centrality, to be eliminated from narrative
focus and, in the process, assume the burden of supporting
the emotional life of the class above (i.e. the poet's role
as guide). In *The Judgment of the King of Navarre* the poet
becomes his own subject even as conventional elements of debate
poetry are now marshalled not to examine some point of love
doctrine so much as to scrutinize the success or failure of
literary creation itself.

SOURCES AND INFLUENCES

Like many of Machaut's *dits*, *The Judgment of the King of Navarre* finds its most immediate and important source in the
Romance of the Rose, especially the second part for which Jean
de Meun was responsible. As I have already suggested, it seems
likely that Machaut was inspired by Jean's continuation of
Guillaume de Lorris's love allegory to do much the same with
the most popular of his early poems. The emphasis on rancorous
debate, the use of a number of *exempla*, including several drawn
from Classical literature, and the prominence of antifeminism
as an issue all suggest a close connection with Jean's poem.
But *The Judgment of the King of Navarre* is hardly a simple
imitation or unimaginative recycling of that earlier text;
Jean's *Rose* is a complex and unwieldy dialogue treating a number of issues associated with love, while Machaut's poem uses
the conventional debate structure to probe themes connected
with authorship and the production/consumption of courtly
poems. There are no models for this important aspect of *The
Judgment of the King of Navarre*; but it is characteristic of
late medieval French narrative poetry to be self-reflexive,
if not to this extent (see Dembowski 1987 for a convincing
demonstration that one of Jean Froissart's earliest works is
similarly self-reflexive; Kelly 1987 discusses the ways in
which the patron system figures within texts by Machaut and

other authors of the period). *The Judgment of the King of
Bohemia* functions as the pre-text for the later judgment poem;
its "doctrine" becomes a subject for debate (and is ultimately
corrected), while its basic structures (including the male/
female debating pair, the use of allegorical personages in
the debate, and the fictional presence of the patron) are repeated. The later poem, however, is a much different work,
for it abandons the conventional idealism of *The Judgment of
the King of Bohemia* (especially the nameless narrator, knight,
and lady) in order to represent, albeit in somewhat humorously
altered form, the poet's "real" self.

Machaut, we might say, asks us to read *The Judgment of the
King of Navarre* through the *Romance of the Rose* and his own
Judgment of the King of Bohemia. These intertextual connections mediate the poem's reception, alerting the courtly audience to important innovations and changes of emphasis; such
contrasts establish the "poetic identity" implied by the work,
the creative presence who must be held responsible for what
is contained therein. The poem, however, has other antecedents
which Machaut, likely, was only dimly aware of (if at all)
and which would not have functioned as points of literary reference for his readers. These poems never achieved the same
popularity as either the *Romance of the Rose* or his own first
judgment poem, belonging, in any case, to a much earlier age.
Debate poetry in the vernacular languages derives from a long-
established, learned Latin tradition. Virgil's third, so-
called "contention" eclogue inspired a host of late Latin imitations; the genre achieved particular popularity during the
Carolingian revival (for a full account see Walther 1920).
Of more interest than these rather dry arguments between roses
and lilies or water and wine over relative merits, however,
is the *Council of Remiremont*, a Latin work probably written
during the early years of the twelfth century. It features a
lively and rather irreverent debate over the merits of clerks
and knights as lovers; the debate takes place in the abbey of
Remiremont, and the disputants are all nuns of the establish-
ment. The humorous and occasionally disorderly disputation
of *The Judgment of the King of Navarre* can certainly be traced
through the *Romance of the Rose* back to this much earlier work,
which achieved a good deal of popularity, to judge by the large
number of French imitations it spawned (the complex inter-
relationships of these are discussed by Jung 1971 and Langlois
1890; for texts see Oulmont 1911). The vernacular French ver-
sions all feature the same subject of debate, but alter the
setting of the Latin poem and reduce the debaters to two women,
one of whom loves a clerk and the other a knight.

Our interest in these early texts, which are all relatively
unaccomplished and simple, is what they reveal, by contrast,

about Machaut's sophisticated handling of the debate framework.
In none of these poems, or, for that matter, in either part
of the *Romance of the Rose*, do we find a narrator who is an
active participant in the debate; in none of these texts does
the author himself figure as the main character. Furthermore,
The Judgment of the King of Navarre is also exceptional in
altering, at least in part, the subject of the debate. In
Machaut's poem two somewhat traditional questions are raised:
who suffers more, the betrayed knight or the bereaved lady;
and who loves more faithfully and intensely, men or women?
The slippage from the first to the second issue is also somewhat conventional; *The Judgment of the King of Bohemia* and
the second part of the *Romance of the Rose* feature similar
shifts (several important ones, as a matter of fact, in the
latter text). The embedding of the two questions within the
larger issue of the poet's (in)correct performance, however,
is unique to this text and reveals the subtle manner in which
Machaut is able to turn traditional fictional elements to pur-
poses for which they were originally unintended. The debate
genre, especially Jean's part of the *Rose*, is essentially
clerkly and intellectual, affording as it does the opportunity
to reproduce not only the *sic et non* of academic disputation
but the complexities of a logical and dialogical approach to
certain questions. As Machaut transforms it, the debate becomes the arena for problematizing (and also glorifying) the
career of the poet; Machaut's Good Fortune, unlike the Boethian
figure she is modeled on, concludes by endorsing the author's
continued production of works (a continuation that is ratified,
extratextually, by the presence of the *Lay of Weeping* in the
early MS tradition).

Machaut's poem, however, is also traditional in another
way. Part of the obsessive literariness and intellectuality
of Jean's *Rose* (as opposed to Guillaume's) is exemplified by
its many stories, which are generated by the different stages
of the argument; these *exempla*, as texts called into being by
the text of the poem, function as a *mise-en-abyme*, that is,
as a representation of the work's own structure, which is itself a text that responds to another text.(See Gunn 1952 for
an interesting account of the *Rose*'s structure). *The Judgment
of the King of Navarre* is self-reflexive in a very similar
way; here the characters generate new texts in order to make
argumentative points, and this dialogism reflects the intertextual origins of the poem itself. These *exempla* are derived
from a number of different sources (for full details see
Hoepffner, *Oeuvres*, I, pp. lxxiii-lxxxvii, on whose specula-
tions this brief account is largely based; for a discussion
of the *mise-en-abyme* as a device in Chaucer and Machaut see
Calin 1987).

The death of Dido (lines 2095-2130) derives ultimately from
the account of Virgil in *Aeneid IV*; this Latin poem, in somewhat altered form, had been translated during the 12th century
as the *Roman d'Énéas*, and the story had likewise been told,
in the following century, by Jean de Meun in his part of the
Romance of the Rose. Machaut's account reproduces the essential details of the story found in these two vernacular accounts, but what we know of his education makes it likely that
he knew Virgil's text directly. Machaut, however, does add a
detail unknown to earlier French authors and Virgil as well:
the fact that Dido, being pregnant by Aeneas, kills two with
her suicide. This detail figures in Ovid's *Heroides*, but it
may have been added by Machaut independently for dramatic effect (i.e. it parallels significantly Medea's murder of her
two children by Jason, and thus fits slyly into the anti-
feminist subtext of this poem).

No particular source can be identified for Machaut's story
of Theseus and Ariadne (lines 2707-69; 2805-8); though it often
figures in Latin compendia of mythological and legendary material, texts common enough in the later Middle Ages, the story
had not been reproduced in the vernacular before Machaut.
The text he followed may well have been a rather abridged one,
for Machaut, while giving the essentials of the legend, leaves
out some important details (e.g. the precise nature of Ariadne's aid to Theseus, the motif of the white/black sail, the
tribute of seven young people rather than just one, and the
voluntary sacrifice of Theseus).

The story of Jason and Medea (lines 2770-2804) had been
told in French before Machaut by both Benoît de Sainte-More-
(in the *Roman de Troie*) and Jean in his part of the *Rose*.
This may explain why Machaut's account is more allusive than
detailed, leaving unglossed such unusual features as the golden
fleece and the army of the dead. Neither French author, however, treats in any detail the treason of Jason, the part of
the story which most interests Machaut; this means that he
likely had read the two accounts by Ovid (in the *Heroides* and
Metamorphoses), which offer a much more unflattering account
of the hero. The same source likely furnished Machaut with
all the essential details of his brief account of Pyramus and
Thisbé (lines 3171-9); he may have also known the vernacular
version of the *Ovide moralisé* (*Ovid Moralized*). Machaut was
the first in Northern France to offer a vernacular version of
the story of Hero and Leander (lines 3221-98), also derived
from Ovid's *Heroides* (or parts of this compilation thought in
the Middle Ages to be by Ovid), perhaps from *Ovid Moralized*
as well.

The *exempla* which do not treat figures from Classical my-
thology or literature have varied sources. The narrator's

tale of the lover who cuts off his finger with his beloved's
ring still on it was likely invented by the poet himself; his
story about the clerk from Orleans probably issues from the
same source (see Picherit 1982 for an illuminating discussion
of the narrator's use of inferior *exempla*, of which these two
untraditional ones are the most interesting). Temperance's
tale of the young woman struck down by a grief that quickly
kills her was also likely invented for the occasion, but it
serves the lady's cause somewhat better (proving that, if accepted, women can indeed die from grief when they lose their
lovers, a point also attested to by the story of Dido). The
lady's reference to the habits of the turtledove and swan derives from the bestiary tradition of the Middle Ages (though
the particular habits of the swan noted here are not generally
acknowledged and likely came to Machaut from his reading of
Watriquet de Couvin's *Dit de la Cigogne*, or *Story of the Swan*,
written twenty-five years or so before Machaut's second judgment poem). Other brief references, to Tristan and Lancelot
and the popular poem *Chastelaine de Vergy*, indicate that Machaut intended his work for a fairly sophisticated and well-
read audience, who undoubtedly appreciated the Classical stories as well.

Probably because of its innovative treatment of the love
allegory and debate genres, *The Judgment of the King of Navarre*
had limited influence on other writers; Machaut's earlier judgment poem, which offers a more traditional type of poetic fiction, certainly enjoyed greater popularity and inspired two
notable imitations (Christine de Pizan's *Dit de Poissy* and
much of Chaucer's *Book of the Duchess*). Interestingly, there
are indications that Machaut himself changed his mind about
the nexus of intertextual relations he set up between *The Judgment of the King of Bohemia* (the pre-text of the second judgment poem) and *The Lay of Weeping* (the lyric penance which
uses that second judgment poem itself as a pre-text). In MS
A *The Lay of Weeping* is placed in the section of that compen-
dium devoted to lyric poetry (though the two judgment poems
are still juxtaposed here as well, violating the chronological
order which is followed for the other narrative works). In
any case, *The Judgment of the King of Navarre* exerted the most
influence on Geoffrey Chaucer, whose experimentation with self-
reflexivity and narrational modes of address comes to seem less
original as his great indebtedness to Machaut is correctly
re-assessed (a key text in this process of re-assessment is
Calin 1987, who argues for Machaldian influence not only on
Chaucer's early works but also on several of his later ones).
Traditionally, *The Book of the Duchess* has been seen as a re-
working of motifs derived from Machaut's *Story of the Lovers'
Fountain* and *Judgment of the King of Bohemia*; in fact, it can

be maintained that Chaucer largely re-writes the early debate poem in the rhetorical form of the later love vision (see Wimsatt 1968 for a most useful summary of source and influence work on Chaucer's first poem).

The influence of *The Judgment of the King of Navarre* has been considered marginal, confined largely to the imitation or reminiscence of certain lines. I would argue, however, that the opening movement of Chaucer's poem, a self-portrait of the melancholic narrator who searches for the kind of reading which might afford him the relief of sleep, is most likely derived from both the opening section of *The Judgment of the King of Navarre* and the narrator's encounter with literary tradition as embodied both in the figure of Good Fortune and in the *exempla* of the subsequent debate. I note here the following significant areas of similarity: 1. a focus in both works on the narrator's personal experience: particularly his melancholic reclusiveness and analysis of his own feelings; 2. a concern in both works with traditional texts or Classical *exempla* and their interpretation: *The Book of the Duchess* treats the narrator's encounter with the story of Ceyx and Alcyone and his desire to probe its truth value or relevance to his own life, a hermeneutic activity similar to that which goes on during the debate in Machaut's poem; 3. a movement away from reflection to a debate or discussion that follows an encounter (during a dream in Chaucer's poem) with a hunting party: the debate involves the narrator and a noble personage; 4. in both works the debate ends with the narrator's apparent release from melancholy; 5. in the dream vision section of Chaucer's poem the narrator is wakened by the sound of trumpets and other instruments; then he proceeds to go out into the springtime air, soon coming upon a noble hunting party, a sequence of events which very much recalls the Machaldian narrator's learning of the end of the epidemic, his decision to enjoy the spring weather, and his subsequent meeting with the lady and her party.

Though they have hardly been recognized by most Chaucerians, these similarities seem striking. They suggest that Machaut's poem may well have been more of a deliberate model for *The Book of the Duchess* than has been hitherto realized. At the same time, however, the differences between the two works are instructive. If Chaucer's narrator is a version of the author, he is an image of the author as reader (not writer) and as a consciousness preoccupied with important issues relating to love and loss. More so than Chaucer's unnamed narrator, Machaut's is an obvious mask of the poet himself, seen not so much as reader and sympathetic heart, but as a writer involved with the difficulties of composing for a noble audience who is mindful of the tradition which should shape the content

and form of his poetry. Chaucer's poem, in short, is not about
the "producing-I"; thus in his first work, he does not adapt,
in any way, the most striking innovation he must have recognized in his reading of Machaut's second judgment poem. The
Book of the Duchess, instead, utilizes the more traditional
structure of *The Judgment of the King of Bohemia*. In both
these works, the initial focus on the narrator's state of mind
and activity makes way for a central concern which subsumes,
and to some degree subverts that focus. The amorous clerk
walking in the woods happens upon the debating noble pair, to
whom he listens attentively, helping them when the moment is
right. The melancholic and sleepless bookworm, puzzled yet
soothed by his reading, has a vision in which, making the acquaintance of a sorrowing nobleman, he becomes the narratee
for the knight's sad tale of bereavement. First addressed by
his book and then, within the theater of his own unconscious-
ness, by a grieving lord, the narrator can never attend to
any experiences that might properly be his own, only to the
hermeneutic quest to understand what others have written and
felt.

Though *The Book of the Duchess* draws on both the judgment
poems as sources, it is thus most like the earlier one in its
metafictional treatment of the court poet's role; in their
different ways, the narrators of the two works embody a self-
hood that is ultimately defined by service, not self-examina-
tion. A change of mind, perhaps induced by some further meditation on the intriguing relationship between Machaut's two
judgment poems, apparently led Chaucer, somewhat later, to
compose a poem which is much more obviously indebted to *The
Judgment of the King of Navarre: The Legend of Good Women.*
Like the *Romance of the Rose* and *The Judgment of the King of
Bohemia*, among traditional love allegories, the prologue to
The Legend of Good Women offers the narrator's wandering
through a springtime setting, his contemplation of beautiful
flowers (especially the daisy), and his eventual falling asleep
in the warm air. Dreaming, he experiences a vision of a noble
company who come upon him; this company, consisting of a multitude of women, is led by two noble figures, Alceste and the
God of Love. Discovering the narrator contemplating his flowers, the God of Love proceeds to denounce him in an angry and
dismissive way for the antifeminist sentiments of a number of
works (including *Troilus and Criseyde*). Alceste defends the
narrator, who ultimately agrees to do appropriate penance by
writing (or, more properly, translating) a number of well-known
stories by dealing with virtuous women, the "legends" that
follow. It is a mark of the neglect which Machaut's poems
have been subjected to by most Chaucerians that the influence
of *The Judgment of the King of Navarre* on the prologue has

been scarcely appreciated (see Frank 1972 and Kiser 1983 for
critical and historical analyses of the work that, otherwise
excellent and perceptive, are hardly conscious of Machaldian
influence; Wimsatt 1970 offers texts and discussion of Machaut's Marguerite poetry, an important influence, along with
key works of Froissart and Deschamps as well, on the myth of
the daisy developed in the prologue). In fact, Machaut furnishes Chaucer with all his principal motifs, with the exception of the myth of the daisy (derived largely from other Machaldian texts) and the dream vision framework, a conventional
structure. These motifs include: 1. the development of the
narrator as a fictionalized version of the author, seen not
only as a reader of old texts (as in *The Book of the Duchess*)
but also as the producer of new ones, which are mentioned specifically; 2. the complaint levelled against the narrator by
an allegorical figure for his purported failure to avoid the
antifeminism to which the clerkly, educated mind was then li-
able; 3. the presence of two noble figures to judge the narrator's alleged transgression, one a historical character and
the other an allegorical personification; 4. a debate over
the supposed sin of the author; 5. the ultimate resolution
that the narrator/writer is to produce other texts, this time
with the "correct" viewpoint; 6. the intertextual connection
of the work with the literary penance it generates. As we
have seen, the uniqueness of *The Judgment of the King of Navarre* within the tradition of courtly literature prior to
Chaucer is the way in which it thematizes the discontents of
authorship, problematizing the court poet's dependence on (yet
independence from) the patrons he serves. The similar concerns
of the prologue to *The Legend of Good Women* therefore must be
traced to their source in Machaut's poem.
    Once again, however, Chaucer's handling of this inherited
material is more conservative, less audacious. In *The Judgment
of the King of Navarre*, Guillaume eagerly accepts the burden
of his own defense, manifesting a temerity for which he is
ultimately condemned. In the prologue, however, the narrator
witnesses the argument between Alceste and the God of Love
over his authorial merits; acquiescing in the judgment they
arrive at, he obediently produces more texts, and it is these
texts which are the principal focus of the work that follows.
In other words, the prologue is properly a pre-text that generates an anthology of stories; for Machaut, however, *The Judgment of the King of Navarre* only generates *exempla* insofar as
these condemn or exonerate Guillaume from Good Fortune's
charges. The focus for Machaut is the poet's difficulties with
his readers; the focus for Chaucer is the continued activity
of the poet as translator/adapter. Chaucer does not, in the
manner of his French counterpart, make his problematic situation as creative artist the center of his text.

EDITORIAL POLICY FOR THIS TEXT AND TRANSLATION

The Judgment of the King of Navarre is found in seven manuscripts, all of which are devoted exclusively to the works of
Machaut; these are manuscripts A, B, D, E, F, M, and V according to the sigla assigned to them by Ernest Hoepffner, one of
Machaut's early editors. In contrast, the companion piece
Judgment of the King of Bohemia appears in these manuscripts
and also in CKJ, the remaining "collections" that survive devoted exclusively to the works of Machaut; it also is contained
in manuscripts PR, which contain works by other authors. The
fact that *The Judgment of the King of Navarre* assumes the existence (and perhaps the popularity) of the other judgment poem
means that it was composed later. This accords well with what
we know from other sources about Machaut's relationships with
the two monarchs; evidence suggests that *The Judgment of the
King of Bohemia*, in any event, was written prior to 1342, while
the *terminus ab quo*, that is, the earliest possible date, for
The Judgment of the King of Navarre must be November 9, 1349,
the date named by the narrator at the very beginning of the
work. Though the two poems were written some years apart (perhaps as many as fifteen or more), Machaut wished them to be
read sequentially. Wherever it occurs, *The Judgment of the
King of Navarre* immediately follows the earlier judgment poem
even though there is good reason to assume that both *Fortune's
Remedy* and the *Dit dou Lion* (*The Story of the Lion*) were written after the composition of the first judgment poem and before
the completion of the second. Otherwise, the narrative *dits*
are presented in what is to all appearances the order of their
composition.
     In the *Voir Dit* (*The True Story*), the poet/protagonist men-
tions a manuscript that contains "all that I have written."
Assuming that this statement described Machaut's actual practice, Hoepffner concluded that "this manuscript was only constituted bit by bit, as the poet finished his poems and in-
serted them into the collection of his works" (Hoepffner, *Oeuvres*, I, xlix). During the last decade or so this conclusion
has been challenged from a number of quarters (see Keitel 1982;
Günther 1982; Manley Williams 1969; and Wimsatt/Kibler 1987
for detailed discussion of the various issues involved).
Hoepffner's thesis, in any event, means that the later MSS of
Machaut's works (or, more precisely in some cases, those MSS
deriving from later original MSS of his works) are generally
to be accorded priority in establishing the texts of individual
poems. Considering Machaut more like a modern than a medieval
author, Hoepffner thought that the poet would be attentive to
the textual details of his collected *oeuvre* and concerned about

its proper and correct distribution (see Brownlee 1984 and
Manley Williams 1978 for further argument on this point).
Recently, it has been convincingly demonstrated that, at least
in the case of *The Judgment of the King of Bohemia*, the later
MSS are hardly superior to certain earlier ones (this argument
is made in Wimsatt/Kibler 1987). To my mind, however, such a
discovery does not cancel out the authority granted to the
later MSS for the text of *The Judgment of the King of Navarre*.
There is good reason, in particular, to regard MS A (Biblio-
thèque National 1584) as one prepared under the direct supervision of the poet; such supervision may well have included,
for the text of *The Judgment of the King of Navarre*, editorial
revisions of one kind or another.

Along with F-G (a two volume manuscript), only MS A contains
a full version of the *Prologue*, an introduction to his collected works that Machaut apparently composed toward the end
of his life. In addition, MS A bears a cachet over its index
which reads "Here follows the word of the works which G. de
Machaut wishes his book to have" (Vesci l'ordenance que G. de
Machaut vuet quil ait en son livre). A recent study of the
illuminated MSS containing the works of Machaut provides even
more interesting evidence about this particular codex. François Avril observes that MS A consists of two parts, one containing the prologue and index which, on the evidence of its
technique of illumination, was composed at Paris during the
last years of the poet's life. The rest of the manuscript is
illuminated in a quite different manner: "Its somewhat provin-
cial style, while strongly influenced by the Parisian illu-
minators of this period, manifests more spontaneity and freedom
of invention, while presenting several points of contact with
certain workshops located in the east and north of the kingdom." This, and the other evidence I have mentioned, leads
Avril to conclude that "MS A could have been copied and illuminated at Rheims itself, under the supervision of the poet,
a fact which confers upon it a value without equal, as editors
of Machaut have otherwise long felt" (Avril 1982, pp. 127-8).

For this edition I have therefore adopted MS A as my base
text. Because Machaut probably oversaw its production (and
may well have edited the text of *The Judgment of the King of
Navarre*, though there is no internal evidence to support this
claim), I have adopted a conservative editorial policy, following the readings of A whenever they give reasonable sense and
ignoring the principle of common error. As I see it, the editor's judgment must be limited to distinguishing between errors
and variant readings (since both these categories can be determined by comparison with the other MSS). I have corrected
A's readings only in those instances when, for various reasons,
Machaut's intervention in the text could be reasonably ruled

out. I have found it occasionally difficult to discriminate
between spelling variation and truly different forms; in those
cases I have tried to give indications of what the other principal MSS offer, letting the reader judge for himself. MS A
contains a fair number of common scribal errors, but this text
of the poem is very similar to that of other MSS. In short,
editorial decisions are hardly particularly crucial in establishing a fairly authentic text. The spellings of A have been
retained, while manuscript numerals have not been expanded to
words.

As far as the translation is concerned, my intention has
been to provide an easy check for those reading the original
as well as a version simple to follow for those with no French.
This means that I have tried to offer a translation that is
literal but also readable. Occasionally Machaut's idiom or
the complexity of his syntax make it impossible to achieve
this double effect. In those cases I have always attempted
to produce readable English true to the spirit of the original.
The translator of a Machaldian *dit amoreux* is faced with a
related problem as well: in English there is no stylistic reg-
ister corresponding to the love discourse which constitutes
Machaut's largely traditional style. The syntax of late Old
French, however, is in most cases quite similar to that of
Modern English. These two facts mean that the translator of
Machaut can produce syntactic forms very much like those of
the original; but he can discover semantic equivalents only
for individual words or expressions, not for the complex para-
digmatic relationships and semantic fields in the original
discourse. The result is an English text that resembles the
original closely in form and content but inevitably fails to
reproduce its full meaning.

ACKNOWLEDGEMENTS

This book could not have been written without the support and
assistance of my colleagues in the College of Arts and Sciences, Georgia State University, especially Dean Clyde Faulkner
and Dr. Virginia Spencer Carr, head of the English department,
who provided needed released time and financial help. If the
translation possesses any virtues, these are due largely to
General Editor James Wilhelm and the anonymous reviewer for
Garland, who prevented me from falling into numerous infelic-
ities of expression and outright errors. My wife Carla inspired this labor with her unending respect for and support
of my research; the final version of the text, in fact, was

prepared in the office of the Day Care Center she manages under
her watchful and benevolent eye and amidst the joyful noise
of playing children (an atmosphere which suited well the gentle
ironies and light-hearted humor of Machaut's poem). My mother
Cele provided me with food and shelter during the year I spent,
in part, first engrossed in the intricate and demanding task
of translating the subtleties of Machaldian verse. I could
hardly have written this book without her continuing interest
and enthusiasm. My son Colin has tolerated cheerfully Daddy's
preoccupation with books and typed sheets of paper. I hope
that he will grow up to appreciate and, perhaps, enjoy the
rigors of intellectual labor.

SELECT BIBLIOGRAPHY

I. EDITIONS OF GUILLAUME DE MACHAUT'S POETRY

Chichmaref, V. *Guillaume de Machaut: Poésies lyriques.* 2
vols. Paris: Champion, 1909. Reliable edition of Machaut's
large corpus of lyric poetry. Introduction contains some
useful discussion of Machaut's life and the MS tradition
but also contains a number of errors and must be used with
caution.

Hoepffner, Ernest. *Oeuvres de Guillaume de Machaut.* Société
des Anciens Textes Français. 3 vols. Paris: Firmin-Didot,
1908-21. A most impressive but unfortunately never completed edition of the narrative poetry. Includes *Prologue,*
Jugement dou Roy de Behaingne, Jugement dou Roy de Navarre,
Le Lay de Plour (Volume 1); *Remede de Fortune, Le Dit dou*
Lyon, Le Dit de l'Alerion (Volume II); and *Le Confort d'Ami,*
La Fonteinne Amoureuse (Volume III). Valuable introductory
material. Useful short biography of the poet.

Mas Latrie, L. de. *La Prise d'Alexandrie ou Chronique du roi*
Pierre 1er. Genève: Flick, 1877.

Palmer, R. Barton. *Guillaume de Machaut: The Judgment of the*
King of Bohemia. Volume 9. Series A. Garland Library of
Medieval Literature. New York: Garland Publishing, 1984.
Edition, translation, and commentary.

Paris, Paulin. *Le Livre du Voir-Dit de Guillaume de Machaut.*
Paris: Société des Bibliophiles François, 1875. Inadequate
edition according to modern standards. Numerous passages
from MSS deleted without comment. A new edition of this
poem is currently being compiled by Paul Imbs.

Wilkens, Nigel. *La Louange des Dames.* Edinburgh: Scottish
Academic Press, 1972. Useful edition of the lyric poetry.

Wimsatt, James I. *The Marguerite Poetry of Guillaume de Machaut.* Chapel Hill: University of North Carolina, 1970. Excellent edition of some minor poems. Helpful commentary and discussion.

Wimsatt, James I., and Kibler, William W. *Guillaume de Machaut: Le Jugement du roy de Behaigne and Remede de Fortune.* Athens: University of Georgia Press, 1987. Careful, revisionist edition of two important Machaut *dits.* Useful commentary.

II. CRITICISM AND STUDY GUIDES

Amon, Nicole. "Le Vert: Guillaume de Machaut, poète de l'affirmation et de la joie." *Revue du Pacifique,* 2 (1976), 3-11. Discusses color symbolism in the *Voir Dit.*

Avril, Francois. "Les manuscrits enluminés de Guillaume de Machaut." In Chailley 1982, 117-133. The most authoritative study of the illuminated manuscripts of Machaut's works.

Beer, Jeanette M.A. "The Ambiguity of Guillaume de Machaut." *Paregon,* 27 (1980), 27-31.

Bossuat, Robert. *Le Moyen Âge: Histoire de la littérature française,* I. Paris: Del Duca, 1931. Contains a well-written and brief discussion of Machaut in the context of fourteenth-century literature.

Brownlee, Kevin. *Poetic Identity in Guillaume de Machaut.* Madison: University of Wisconsin Press, 1984. Important study of narrative technique and authorial presence in certain of the narrative *dits.*

————. "The Poetic *Oeuvre* of Guillaume de Machaut: The Identity of Discourse and the Discourse of Identity." In Cosman and Chandler, 219-33. Important discussion of Machaut's conception of himself as poet. Useful analysis of the *Prologue.*

————. "Transformations of the lyric 'Je': The Example of Guillaume de Machaut." *L'Esprit Créateur,* 18 (1978), 5-18. Interesting analysis of Machaut's career and the relationship between his lyric and narrative poetry.

Burke, Mary Ann. "A Medieval Experiment in Adaptation: Typology and Courtly Love Poetry in the Second Rhetoric." *Res Publica Litterarum* 3 (1980), 165-175.

Calin, William C. *A Muse for Heroes: Nine Centuries of the Epic in France.* Toronto: Toronto University Press, 1983. One of the few histories of French literature to pay adequate attention to Machaut's prominence and significance.

————. "A Reading of Machaut's *Jugement dou Roy de Navarre.*" *Modern Language Review,* 66 (1971), 294-97.

————. *A Poet at the Fountain: Essays on the Narrative Verse of Guillaume de Machaut.* Lexington: Kentucky, 1974. The only full-length critical treatment of Machaut's narrative poetry. Full of useful information and interesting interpretations, but from an ahistorical approach. Bibliography.

————. "Le *Moi* chez Guillaume de Machaut." In Chailley 1982, 241-252. Interesting analysis of the representation of poetic subjectivity and its role in narrative structure.

————. "The Poet at the Fountain: Machaut as Narrative Poet." In Cosman and Chandler, 177-87.

————. "Machaut's Legacy: The Chaucerian Inheritance Reconsidered." In Palmer 1987, 9-22.

————. "Problèmes de technique narrative au moyen-âge: Le *Roman de la Rose* et Guillaume de Machaut." In *Mélanges de langue et littérature françaises du moyen-âge offerts à Pierre Jonin.* Paris: Champion, 1979, 125-38. Treats relationship of Machaut's narrative poetry to the *Romance of the Rose.*

Cerquiglini, Jacqueline. *"Un Engin si soutil:" Guillaume de Machaut et l'écriture au xive siècle.* Geneva: Slatkine, 1985.

Chailley, Jacques. "Du cheval de Guillaume de Machaut à Charles II de Navarre." *Romania,* 94 (1973), 251-57.

Chailley, Jacques *et al.,* eds. *Guillaume de Machaut: colloque, table ronde organisé par l'Université de Reims.* Paris: Éditions Klincksieck, 1982. Important collection of articles by leading Machaudistes.

Cosman, Madeleine Pelner, and Bruce Chandler, edd. *Machaut's World: Science and Art in the Fourteenth Century.* Annals of the New York Academy of Sciences, 314. New York: Academy of Sciences, 1978. Indispensable collection of useful and appreciative analyses of the various aspects of Machaut's career.

De Looze, Laurence. "Guillaume de Machaut and the Writerly Process." *French Forum* 9 no. 2 (May 1984), 145–161.

Dembowski, Peter F. "Tradition, Dream Literature, and Poetic Craft in *Le Paradis d'amour* of Jean Froissart." In Palmer 1987, 99–109.

Ehrhart, Margaret J. "Guillaume de Machaut's *Jugement dou Roy de Navarre* and Medieval Treatments of the Virtues." *Annuale Mediaevale,* 19 (1979), 46–67.

————. "Guillaume de Machaut's *Jugement dou Roy de Navarre* and the Book of Ecclesiastes." *Neuphilologische Mitteilungen,* 81 (1980), 318–25.

————. "Machaut's *Dit de la fonteinne amoureuse,* the Choice of Paris, and the Duties of Rulers." *Philological Quarterly* 59 no. 2 (Spring 1980), 119–137.

————. "The 'Esprueve de Fines Amours' in Guillaume de Machaut's *Dit dou lyon* and Medieval Interpretations of Circe and Her Island." *Neophilologus,* 64 (1980), 38–41.

Faral, Edmond. *Recherches sur les sources latines des contes et romans courtois du moyen âge.* Paris: Champion, 1913. Important discussion of the relationship between Latin literature and vernacular love poetry.

Gauvard, Claude. "Portrait du prince d'apres l'oeuvre de Guillaume de Machaut: etude sur les idees politiques du poete." In Chailley 1982, 23–39.

Gunn, Allan F. *The Mirror of Love: A Re-Interpretation of "The Romance of the Rose."* Lubbock: Texas Tech Press, 1952. Useful discussion of backgrounds of the love-vision genre.

Guthrie, Steven R. "Machaut and the Octosyllabe." In Palmer 1987, 55–75. Important and persuasive study of Machaut's metrical practice considered as part of the tradition of Old French poetry.

Gybbon-Monypenny, G.B. "Guillaume de Machaut's Erotic 'Auto-biography': Precedents for the Form of the *Voir-Dit*." In *Studies in Medieval Literature and Language in Memory of Frederick Whitehead*, edited by W. Rothwell *et al.* Manchester: Manchester University Press, 1973, 133-152.

Haidu, Peter. "Making it (New) in the Middle Ages: Towards a Problematics of Alterity." *Diacritics*, 4 (1974), 2-11. Important discussion of poetic originality and the criteria for its analysis and judgment in medieval French poetry.

Hieatt, Constance. *"Une Autre Forme*: Guillaume de Machaut and the Dream Vision Form." *Chaucer Review*, 14 (1979), 97-115.

Hoepffner, Ernest. "Anagramme und Rätselgedichte bei Guillaume de Machaut." *Zeitschrift für romanische Philologie*, 30 (1906), 401-13. Discusses the anagrams which close a number of Machaut poems, including *The Judgment of the King of Bohemia*.

Johnson, L.W. "'Nouviaus dis amoureux plaisans': Variation as Innovation in Guillaume de Machaut." *Le Moyen Francais*, 5 (1979), 11-28.

Jung, Marc-René. *Études sur le poème allégorique en France au moyen âge*. *Romanica Helvetica*, 82. Berne: Francke, 1971. Studies allegorical poetry of the High Middle Ages. Useful analysis of love-debate genre.

Keitel, Elisabeth. "La Tradition manuscrite de Guillaume de Machaut." In Chailley 1982, 75-94.

Kelly, Douglas. "Courtly Love in Perspective: The Hierarchy of Love in Andreas Capellanus." *Traditio* 24 (1968), 119-147.

————. *Medieval Imagination: Rhetoric and the Poetry of Courtly Love*. Madison: Wisconsin, 1978. A full chapter on Machaut's narrative poetry. Intriguing discussion of the narrative poems in relationship to the *Romance of the Rose*. Traces Boethian influence. Full bibliography.

————. "The Genius of the Patron: The Prince, the Poet, and Fourteenth Century Invention." In Palmer 1987, 77-97.

————. "Translatio Studii: Translation, Adaptation, and Allegory in Medieval French Literature." *Philological Quarterly* 57 (1978), 287-310.

Kittredge, George L. *Chaucer and His Poetry.* Cambridge: Harvard, 1915. Important early document in the scholarly dismissal of Machaut.

Klapp, O., ed. *Bibliographie der französischen Literaturwissenschaft/Bibliographie d'histoire littéraire.*

Langlois, Ernest. *Origines et sources du "Roman de la rose."* Paris: Champion, 1890. Discusses sources of the *Romance of the Rose*, including the love-debate poems.

Lanoue, D.G. "History as Apocalypse: the Prologue of Machaut's *Jugement dou Roy de Navarre.*" *Philological Quarterly*, 60 (1981), 1-12.

Lukitsch, Shirley, "The Poetics of the *Prologue*: Machaut's Conception of the Purpose of His Art." *Medium Aevum* 52 no. 2 (1983), 258-271.

Machabey, Armand. *Guillaume de Machaut, 130?-1377: La Vie et l'oeuvre musicale.* 2 vols. Paris: Richard-Masse, 1955. The fullest biography of Machaut.

Manley Williams, Sarah Jane. "An Author's Role in Fourteenth-Century Book Production: Guillaume de Machaut's 'livre où je met toutes mes choses.'" *Romania*, 90 (1969), 433-54. This and the following article are concerned with Machaut's poetic career.

————. "Machaut's Self-Awareness as Author and Producer." In Cosman and Chandler, 189-97.

Nelson, Jan A. "Guillaume de Machaut as Job: Access to the Poet as Individual Through His Source." *Romance Notes* 23 no. 2 (Winter 1982), 185-190.

Oulmont, Charles. *Les Débats du clerc et du chevalier dans la littérature poétique du moyen-âge.* Paris: Champion, 1911. Somewhat unreliable edition of love-debate texts. Some discussion of the genre's background.

Palmer, R. Barton, editor. "Chaucer's French Contemporaries: The Poetry/Poetics of Self and Tradition." *Studies in the Literary Imagination* 20 no. 1 (Spring 1987).

————. "The Metafictional Machaut: Self-Reflexivity and Self-Mediation in the Two Judgment Poems." In Palmer 1987, 23-39.

————. "Vision and Experience in Machaut's *Fonteinne Amoureuse*." *Journal of the Rocky Mountain Medieval and Renaissance Association*, 2 (1981), 79-86.

Picherit, Jean-Louis. "Les *Exemples* dans le *Jugement dou Roy de Navarre* de Guillaume de Machaut." *Les Lettres Romanes* 36 no. 2 (May 1982), 103-116.

Poirion, Daniel. *Le Moyen Age. Littérature Francaise*, 2. Paris: B. Arthaud, 1971. Contains an excellent general discussion of Machaut's career in the context of late medieval French poetry.

————. *Le Poète et le prince: l'évolution du lyrisme courtois de Guillaume de Machaut à Charles d'Orléans*. Paris: Presses Universitaires de France, 1965. Although Poirion's main concern is the lyric poetry, this study is invaluable for its treatment of Machaut's narrative works as well. Important discussion of social context. Useful bibliography.

————. "The Imaginary Universe of Guillaume de Machaut." In Cosman and Chandler, 199-206. Interesting discussion of the implied world of Machaut's poetry, stressing the Boethian influence.

Prioult, A. "Un Poète Voyageur: Guillaume de Machaut et la *Reise* de Jean L'Aveugle, roi de Bohème, en 1328-9." *Lettres Romanes*, 4 (1950), 3-29. Discusses Machaut's relationship with John of Bohemia.

Roy, Maurice. *Oeuvres Poètiques de Christine de Pisan*. Vol. II. Paris: Firmin-didot, 1891. Contains an edition of her *Le Livre du dit de Poissy*.

Rychner, Jean. "La flèche et l'anneau (sur les dits narratifs)." *Revue des Sciences Humaines*, 183 (1981), 55-69. Relates the narrative poetry to the *Romance of the Rose*. Dismisses *The Judgment of the King of Bohemia* as didactic, having no concern with "the real."

Taylor, Stephen M. "Portraits of Pestilence: The Plague in the Work of Machaut and Boccaccio." *Allegorica* 5 no. 1 (Summer 1981), 105-118.

Uitti, Karl D. "From *Clerc* to *Poète*: The Relevance of the
    Romance of the Rose to Machaut's World." In Cosman and
    Chandler, 209-16. Guillaume de Lorris and Jean de Meun
    established the vernacular poet as an author in the classi-
    cal sense. Machaut continued in this tradition.

————. "Remarks on Old French Narrative: Courtly Love and
    Poetic Form (I)." *Romance Philology* 26 (1972-3), 77-93.

————. "Remarks on Old French Narrative: Courtly Love and
    Poetic Form (II)." *Romance Philology* 28 (1974-5), 190-199.

————. "The Clerkly Narrator Figure in Old French Hagiography
    and Romance." *Medioevo Romanzo* 2 (1975), 394-408.

Waugh, Patricia. *Metafiction: The Theory and Practice of Self-
    Conscious Fiction.* New York: Methuen, 1984.

Walther, H. *Das Streitgedicht in der lateinischen Literatur
    des Mittelalters.* Quellen und Untersuchungen zur latein-
    ischen Philologie des Mitelalters, 5. Part Two. München:
    C.H. Beck'sche, 1920. Discussion of debate genre.

Wimsatt, James, and Kibler, William. "Machaut's Text and the
    Question of His Personal Supervision." In Palmer 1987,
    41-53. Very important revision of traditional theories
    concerning the Machaut MS tradition.

III. COMPARATIVE STUDIES OF CHAUCER AND MACHAUT

Bakhtin, M.M. *The Dialogic Imagination.* Translated by Caryl
    Emerson and Michael Holquist. Austin: University of Texas
    Press, 1981.

Brewer, Derek S. "The Relationship of Chaucer to the English
    and European Traditions." In *Chaucer and Chaucerians: Crit-
    ical Studies in Middle English Literature.* Tuscaloosa:
    Alabama, 1966, 1038. A good general introduction to
    Chaucer's connections to medieval French poetry.

Clemen, Wolfgang. *Chaucer's Early Poetry.* London: Methuen
    and Co., 1963. Notable for its inaccurate and distorted
    appraisal of Machaut. Continues traditional view of Chaucer
    as "creative" and Machaut as "conventional."

Frank, Robert Worth Jr. *Chaucer and "The Legend of Good Women."* Cambridge: Harvard University Press, 1972.

Harrison, Benjamin S. "Medieval Rhetoric in the *Book of the Duchesse.*" *Publications of the Modern Language Association,* 49 (1934), 428-42.

Kiser, Lisa J. *Telling Classical Tales: Chaucer and "The Legend of Good Women."* Ithaca: Cornell University Press, 1983.

Kittredge, George L. "Chauceriana. I. *The Book of the Duchess* and Guillaume de Machaut." *Modern Philology,* 7 (1909-10), 465-71. In this and the following three articles Kittredge pinpointed the dependence of Chaucer on Machaut noted in general terms by earlier scholars such as Sandras and Ten Brink.

————. "Chauceriana. II. 'Make the metres of hem as thee leste.'" *Modern Philology,* 7 (1909-10), 471-74.

————. "Chaucer's *Troilus* and Guillaume de Machaut." *Modern Language Notes,* 30 (1915), 69.

————. "Guillaume de Machaut and *The Book of the Duchess.*" *Publications of the Modern Language Association,* 30 (1915), 1-24.

Lowes, John L. "Chaucer and the *Ovide Moralisé.*" *Publications of the Modern Language Association,* 33 (1918), 302-25.

Meech, Sanford Brown. "Chaucer and the *Ovide Moralisé*: A Further Study." *Publications of the Modern Language Association,* 46 (1931), 182-204.

Muscatine, Charles. *Chaucer and the French Tradition: A Study in Style and Meaning.* Berkeley: California, 1957. Argues for the appreciation of Chaucer's conventionalness, but depreciates the influence of Machaut.

Palmer, R. Barton. "*The Book of the Duchess* and *Fonteinne Amoureuse*: Chaucer and Machaut Reconsidered." *Canadian Review of Comparative Literature,* 7 (1980), 380-93. Discusses Chaucer's exploration of the meaning of the love experience that is the subject of Machaut's poetry, especially *Fonteinne Amoureuse.*

Pelen, Marc M. "Machaut's Court of Love Narratives and
    Chaucer's *Book of the Duchess*." *Chaucer Review*, 11 (1976),
    128-55. Suggests that the Court of Love is a modernization
    of the "heavenly Neo-Platonic adjudicating epithalamic coun-
    cils of Martianus Capella" and other late Latin poets.
    Chaucer alters its meaning as he found it in Machaut. Much
    useful detail and information.

Robbins, Rossell Hope. "Geoffroi Chaucier, poète français,
    Father of English Poetry." *Chaucer Review*, 13 (1978), 93-
    115.

Robertson, D.W., Jr. *A Preface to Chaucer: Studies in Medieval
    Perspectives*. Princeton: University Press, 1962. Important
    and still controversial study of the context of Chaucer's
    poetry.

Robinson, F.N., ed. *The Complete Works of Geoffrey Chaucer*.
    2nd ed. Cambridge: Harvard, 1957.

Schilperoort, Johanna Catharina. *Guillaume de Machaut et
    Christine de Pisan (étude comparative)*. The Hague: Mouton,
    1936. General discussion of Machaut's influence on other
    poets, especially Pizan.

Severs, J. Burke. "The Sources of *The Book of the Duchess*."
    Mediaeval Studies, 25 (1963), 355-62.

Wimsatt, James I. "The Apotheosis of Blanche in *The Book of
    the Duchess*." *Journal of English and Germanic Philology*,
    66 (1967), 26-44.

————. "Chaucer and French Poetry." In Derek Brewer, ed.
    Geoffrey Chaucer. Athens: Ohio University, 1975, 109-36.
    An important early document in the current re-evaluation
    of Machaut's poetry.

————. *Chaucer and the French Love Poets: The Literary Back-
    ground of the Book of the Duchess*. University of North
    Carolina Studies in Comparative Literature, 43. Chapel
    Hill, North Carolina: University of North Carolina Press,
    1968. A thorough study, including plot summaries, of the
    dits amoreux tradition. Full chart of sources of the *Book
    of the Duchess*.

————. "Guillaume de Machaut and Chaucer's *Troilus and Cri-
    seyde*." *Medium Aevum*, 45 (1976), 277-93. Rejects the views
    of both Muscatine and Kittredge that Chaucer "outgrew" his

dependence on Machaut. Suggests that all of the important features of the *Troilus* find their analogues in Machaut's poetry.

————. "The Sources of Chaucer's 'Seys and Alcyone.'" *Medium Aevum*, 36 (1967), 231-41.

The Judgment of the King of Navarre

Au departir dou bel esté
Qui a gais et jolis esté,
De fleurs, de fueilles faillolez,
Et d'arbrissiaus emmaillolez,
Arousez de douce rousée,   5
Sechiez par chaleur ordenée
Que le soleil li amenistre,
Et qu'oisillons ont leur chapitre
Tenu de sons et de hoquès,
Par plains, par aunois, par bosquès,   10
Pour li servir et honnourer,
Que tout ce couvient demourer
Pour le temps qui, de sa nature,
Mue sa chaleur en froidure
Un po après le temps d'autonne,   15
Que chascuns vandange et entonne
Qui a vingnes a vandangier,
Et qu'on a a petit dangier
Pesches, moust, poires, et roisins,
Dont on present a ses voisins,   20
Que li blez en la terre germe
Et que la fueille chiet dou cherme,
Par nature, ou dou vent qui vente,
L'an mil .ccc. nuef quarente,
Le .iꝗ. jour de novembre,   25
M'en aloie par mi ma chambre.
Et se li airs fust clers et purs,
Je fusse ailleurs; mais si obscurs
Estoit, que montaingnes et plains
Estoient de bruines pleins.   30
Pour ce me tenoie a couvert;
Quar ce qu'estre soloit tout vert
Estoit mué en autre teint,
Car bise l'avoit tout desteint,
Qui mainte fleur a decopée   35
Par la froidure de s'espée.

Si que la merencolioie
Tous seuls en ma chambre et pensoie
Comment par conseil de taverne
Li mondes par tout se gouverne;   40
Comment justice et verité
Sont mortes par l'iniquité
D'Advarice qui en maint regne
Com dame souvereinne regne,
Com maistresse, comme roÿne--   45
Qu'Avarice engenre haïne,

29. A pleins--32. Other mss Car

2

At the passing of a beautiful summer
Which had been pleasant and joyful,
Ornamented with flowers, with leaves,
Adorned with shrubbery,
Drenched with sweet dew,   5
Dried by seasonable heat
Which the sun provided it,
A summer in which the birds
Have held their assemblies with songs and lyrics
Through meadows, arbors, and glades,   10
To serve and honor the season
So that all this should linger
For the sake of the weather which, by its nature,
Changes the warmth into cold
A little after fall comes,   15
When everyone who has vines to pick
Does his harvest and puts it in casks,
When, with little difficulty, one has
Peaches, must, pears, and grapes
That he shares with his neighbors,   20
When the wheat sprouts in the ground,
And when the leaf falls from the tree,
By nature, or by the wind that blows,
In the year thirteen hundred forty-nine,
On the ninth day of November,   25
I was walking around in my room.
And if the air had been clear and pure,
I'd have been elsewhere; but it was
So dark that the mountains and plains
Were filled with haze.   30
And so I stayed inside;
For that which ordinarily was all green
Had been changed into another hue,
For the north wind had discolored everything
And had cut down many a flower   35
With the coldness of his sword.

So there I suffered sadness
All alone in my room and gave thought to
How the world in all things
Was ruled by the drunkard's wisdom;   40
How justice and truth
Had been murdered by the iniquity
Of Greed which in many realms
Rules as sovereign lady,
As mistress, as queen——   45
And Greed spawns hatred,

3

Et largesse donne et rent gloire,
Vraiement, c'est parole voire,
Qu'on le scet et voit clerement
Par vray et juste experiment--   50
Comment nuls ne fait son devoir,
Comment chascuns quiert decevoir
Son proisme; car je ne voy pere,
Fil, ne fille, ne suer, ne frere,
Mere, marrastre, ne cousine,   55
Tante, oncle, voisin, ne voisine,
Mari, mouillier, amy, n'amie
Que li uns l'autre ne cunchie;
Et s'un en y a qui s'en garde,
Chascuns de travers le regarde   60
Et dist on qu'il est ypocrites,
Et fust sains Jehans li Ermites;
Come li signeur leur subges pillent,
Roubent, raembent, et essilent,
Et mettent a destruction   65
Sans pitié ne compation,
Si que grans meschiés (ce me samble)
Est de vice et pooir ensamble.
Et on le voit assez de fait,
Ne riens tant cuer felon ne fait   70
Com grant pooir qui mal en use.
Or voy que chascuns en abuse,   xxiiiR
Car je ne voy homme puissant
Qui n'ait puis .x., puis .xx., puis .c.
Tours, manieres, engiens, ou ars   75
Pour pillier hardis et couars.
Car couvoitise les atrape,
Si que nuls de leurs mains n'eschape,
S'il n'est dont tels qu'il n'ait que perdre.
A tels ne s'ont cure d'aërdre: 80
Car qui riens n'a, riens ne li chiet;
De tels gens riens ne leur eschiet.
Mais couvoiteus ont tel defaut
Que quant plus ont, plus leur deffaut,
Et quant plus sont puissamment riche,   85
Tant sont li plus aver et chiche;
Qu'avarice ardant qui d'euls vist,
Com plus vivent, plus rajonnist.
Et de ce la vient la tempeste
Qui destruit le monde et tempeste,   90
Les merveilles et les fortunes
Qui au jour d'ui sont si communes
Qu'on n'oit de nulle part nouvelle

53. A peire--82. A non written in margin--85. A puissant et
riche--92. A de hui

While generosity gives, bestows glory.
Truly that's an irrefutable notion,
Which is proved and clearly seen
Through just and certain experiment--   50
How no one does his duty,
How everyone seeks to deceive
His neighbor; for I see no father,
Son, no daughter, no sister, no brother,
Mother, relative, or cousin   55
Aunt, uncle, or neighbor,
Husband, wife, lover or beloved
Such that the one doesn't deceive the other;
And if anyone keeps to himself,
Everyone looks askance at him,   60
And it's said that he's a hypocrite,
Even if he is St. John the Hermit;
How the lords pillage their subjects,
Rob, despoil, and exile them,
Murdering all   65
Without pity or compassion,
So that it's a great misfortune (so it seems to me)
For vice and power to be united.
And one indeed often witnesses
That nothing makes a heart so criminal   70
As great power in whoever uses it for evil.
Now I see that everyone abuses it,
Because I see no powerful man
Who hasn't ten, now twenty, now a hundred
Towers, armies, engines, or bows   75
To despoil brave men and cowards.
For avarice draws them on
So that no one escapes their grasp
Unless he's someone who has nothing to lose.
They have no desire to rob such a man,   80
For whoever has nothing, nothing bothers him.
Such men are never troubled,
But the greedy have a failing, which is that
The more they have, the more they lack,
And when they are more powerfully rich,   85
They are that much more greedy and miserly;
And burning avarice which feeds on them
Grows younger the longer they live.
And from this comes the tempest
Which destroys the world and rages on,   90
The strange events and evil luck
Which today are so commonplace
That no one hears news from anywhere

Qui soit aggreable ne belle;
Car il a plus grant difference   95
Dou temps que je vi en m'enfance
A cestui qui trop est divers
Qu'il n'ait des estez aus yvers.
Mais la chose qui plus me grieve
A souffrir, et qui plus m'est grieve   100
C'est rendre a Dieu po reverence
Et ce qu'en riens n'a ordenance,
Et qu'au jour d'ui chascuns se pere
De ce qu'on claimme vitupere.
Pour ce en moy, plus que dire n'ose,   105
Estoit merencolie enclose.
Car qui le sceüst a demi
Asses meins en tenist de mi.

Et pour ce que merencolie
Esteint toute pensée lie,   110
Et aussi que je bien vëoie
Que mettre conseil n'i povoie,
Et que, s'on sceüst mon muser,
On ne s'en feïst que ruser,
Laissay le merencolier   115
Et pris ailleurs a colier,
En pensant que s'a Dieu plaisoit
Qui pour le milleur le faisoit.
Si cheï en autre pensée,
Pour ce que folie esprouvée   120
Est en tout homme qui se duet
De chose qu'amender ne puet;
Et me pensai que, se li temps
Estoit encore pires .x. temps,
Voire cent fois, voire cent mil,   125
N'i a il conseil si soutil
Comme de tout laissier ester,
Puis qu'on ne le puet contrester,
Et de faire selonc le sage
Qui dit et demoustre en sa page   130
Que, quant il a tout conceü,
Tout ymaginé, tout veü,
Esprouvé, serchié, viseté
Le monde, c'est tout vanité,
Et qu'il n'i a autre salaire   135
Fors d'estre liez et de bien faire.
Et tout einsi com je cuidoie
Laissier le penser ou j'estoie,
Il me sourvint une pensée

99. FG m'est grieve--100. FG me grieve--105. FG c'en
112. FG pooie

6

Which might be agreeable or pleasant;
For there's a very great difference   95
Between the weather I witnessed in my youth
And that which now is more different
Than winter from summer.
But what grieves me more
To suffer, and what is sadder to me,   100
Is that God's accorded little reverence,
There's no order to anything,
And today everyone ruins himself
With what's called vituperation.
Therefore, more than I dare say,   105
Melancholy was in my heart.
And whoever knew the half of it
Would think much less of me.

And because melancholy
Had extinguished every happy thought,   110
And also because I saw well
That I could do nothing about the situation,
And because, if anyone knew my mind,
He'd only have made fun of it,
I let my melancholy go   115
And sought otherwise to concern myself,
Thinking that he would please God
Who would make the best of things.
Thus I fell into another thought,
Because it is proven folly   120
For any man to be saddened
By something he cannot better;
And I thought that, if the weather
Were ten times worse,
Indeed a hundred times, even a hundred thousand   125
There'd be no counsel wiser
Than to let all this be
Because it cannot be resisted,
And instead to act like the wise man
Who says and demonstrates in his writing   130
That, when he had conceived everything,
Imagined everything, seen everything,
Tested, examined, observed
The world, that it's all vanity,
And that there's no other course   135
But to be happy and do good.
And just as I was intending to
Let go the reverie I was in,
A thought came to me,

Plus diverse, plus effreée,   140
Plus enuieuse la moitie
Et de plus grant merencolie.

Ce fu des orribles merveilles,
Seur toutes autres despareilles,
Dont homme puet avoir memoire   145
Car je ne truis pas en histoire
Lisant nulles si mervilleuses,
Si dures, ne si perilleuses
De .iiii. pars, non de .x. temps,
Comme elles ont esté de mon temps.   150
Car ce fu chose assez commune   xxiiiV
Qu'on vit le soleil et la lune,
Les estoiles, le ciel, la terre,
En signefiance de guerre,
De doleurs, et de pestilences,   155
Faire signes et demoustrances.
Car chascuns pot vĕoir a l'ueil
De lune esclipce et de soleil,
Plus grant et plus obscur assez
Qu'esté n'avoit mains ans passez,   160
Et perdre en signe de doleur
Longuement clarté et couleur.
Aussi fu l'estoile coumée,
En samblance de feu couée,
Qui de feu et d'occision   165
Faisoit prenostication.
Li ciel, qui de leur haut vĕoient
Les meschiés qu'a venir estoient
Au monde, en pluseurs lieus plourerent
De pitié sanc et degouterent,   170
Si que de leur mervilleus plour
La terre trambla de paour
(Ce dient pluseurs qui ce virent)
Dont villes et citez fondirent
En Alemaingne, en Quarenteinne,   175
Assez plus d'une quarenteinne,
Dont je n'en say mie la somme.
Mais on le scet moult bien a Romme,
Car il y a une abeÿe
De Saint Pol qui en fu perie.   180

Mais li sires qui tout a fait
Par experience de fait,
Com sires souvereins et dignes
Seur tous, de ces mervilleus signes

140. A et plus--168. A li

8

One much more bizarre, more frightening,   140
More troubling by half,
And filled with much greater melancholy.

This was of horrible, uncanny things,
Unlike all others
That a man might remember,   145
For in reading history I have not
Discovered any other happenings so strange,
So hard to bear, nor so dangerous
By a fourth or even a tenth part,
As these of my own time have been.   150
Since it's been a rather common thing
For the sun and the moon, the stars,
The sky, and earth to be seen
Displaying the signs of war,
Misery, and pestilence,   155
To be offering tokens and manifestations.
Indeed everyone could see with his own eyes
The eclipse of the moon and sun,
Greater and much darker
Than there had been for many years past,   160
And as a sign of misery these two lost
For a long time their color and light.
Furthermore that star had tresses
Like fire with a tail,
The one which predicted   165
Murder and conflagration.
The heavens, which from their heights bore witness to
The evil fortune to come
Into the world, cried tears in many places,
Poured out drops of blood from pity,   170
And because of their strange rain
The earth trembled with fear
(So said many who saw this),
And as a result villages and cities were destroyed
In Germany and Carinthia--   175
So many more than forty
That I cannot tell the number.
But the event is well known at Rome,
For an abbey there
Of St. Paul's was destroyed by it.   180

But the Lord who made everything
Through his direct intervention,
Like a sovereign gracious lord
Over all things, showed us the meaning

9

Nous moustra la signefiance,   185
Et nous en mist hors de doubtance
Si a point et si proprement
Que chascuns le vit clerement.
Car les batailles et les guerres
Furent si grans par toutes terres   190
Qu'on ne savoit en tout le monde,
Tant comme il tient a la rëonde,
Païs, regne, ne region,
Qu'il n'i heüst discention;
Dont .v͡c mil hommes et femmes   195
Perdirent les corps et les ames,
Se cils qui a tous biens s'acorde
Ne les prent a misericorde;
Et maint païs destruit en furent,
Dont encor les traces en durent;   200
Et des prises et des outrages
Et des occisions sauvages
De barons et de chevaliers,
De clers, de bourgois, d'escuiers,
Et de la povre gent menue   205
Qui morte y fu et confondue,
De rois, de duz, de bers, de contes
Seroit lons a faire li contes.
Car tant en y ot de perdus
Qu'on en estoit tous esperdus,   210
L'un par feu, l'autre par bataille.
Après ce, vint une merdaille
Fausse, traïtre et renoïe:
Ce fu Judée la honnie,
La mauvaise, la desloyal,   215
Qui het bien et aimme tout mal,
Qui tant donna d'or et d'argent
Et promist a crestienne gent,
Que puis, rivieres, et fonteinnes
Qui estoient cleres et seinnes   220
En pluseurs lieus empoisonnerent,
Dont pluseurs leurs vies finerent;
Car trestuit cil qui en usoient
Asses soudeinnement mouroient
Dont, certes, par .x. fois cent mille   225
En morurent, qu'a champ, qu'a ville,
Einsois que fust aperceüe
Ceste mortel descouvenue.

Mais cils qui haut siet et long voit,
Qui tout gouverne et tout pourvoit,   230

208. Other mss dire--209. AM desperdus--216. Other mss bien
het

10

Of these marvelous tokens,   185
And brought us beyond the point of doubt
So directly and so properly
That everyone saw it clearly.
For battles and wars
Were so great throughout every land   190
That no one knew in all the world,
As much as it encompasses,
A country, kingdom, or region
Where there was no dissension;
From this five hundred thousand men and women   195
Would have lost their bodies and their souls,
If He who is in harmony with all good
Did not take pity upon them;
And many countries were destroyed by this,
And the results endure still;   200
The story would be long to tell
About captures and outrages
And savage killings
Of noblemen and knights,
Of clerks, of townspeople, of squires,   205
And of the poor people of little note
Who died as a result or were destroyed,
Of the kings, the dukes, the lords, the counts.
For so many of them thus were lost
That everyone was completely confounded by it,   210
Some by fire, others in war.
After this, a group of scoundrels appeared
Who were false, traitorous, and heretical:
This was shameful Judea,
The evil, the disloyal,   215
Who hate good and love all evil doing,
Who gave and promised much
Gold and silver to the Christian people,
And then, in many places,
They poisoned the wells, streams, and fountains   220
Which had been clear and healthy,
And thus many lost their lives;
For all of those who used them
Very suddenly died.
As a result, it's certain, ten times a hundred thousand   225
Died in the country and in town
Before this mortal affliction
Was taken notice of.

But He who sits on high and sees far,
Who governs all and provides all things,   230

11

Ceste traïson plus celer
Ne volt, eins la fist reveler
Et si generaument savoir   xxivR
Qu'il perdirent corps et avoir.
Car tuit Juïf furent destruit,   235
Li uns pendus, li autres cuit,
L'autre noié, l'autre ot copée
La teste de hache ou d'espée.
Et meint crestien ensement
En morurent honteusement.   240

En ce temps vint une maisnie
De par leur dame Ypocrisie
Qui de courgies se batoient
Et adens se crucefioient,
En chantant de la lopinelle   245
Ne say quelle chanson nouvelle,
Et valoient miex, par leurs dis,
Que sains qui soit en paradis.
Mais l'Eglise les entendi
Qui le batre leur deffendi,   250
Et si condempna leur chanson
Que chantoient li enfançon,
Et tous les escommenia
Dou pooir que Diex donné li a,
Pour itant que leur baterie   255
Et leur chans estoit herisie.

Et quant Nature vit ce fait
Que son oeuvre einsi se desfait,
Et que li homme se tuoient
Et les yaues empoisonnoient   260
Pour destruire humeinne lignie
Par couvoitise et par envie,
Moult en desplut la belle et gente,
Moult se coursa, moult fu dolente.
Lors s'en ala sans atargier   265
A Jupiter et fist forgier
Foudres, tonnoirres, et tempestes
Par jours ouvrables et par festes.
Car ceste ouevre tant li tardoit
Que jour ne feste n'i gardoit.   270

Après Nature commanda
Aus .iiii. vens qu'elle manda
Que chascuns fust aparillies
Pour tost courir, et abillies,

235. A furent furent--236. A li un pendu li autre cuit

12

Did not wish that this treason
Be hidden any longer; instead He revealed it
And made it known so widely
That they lost their lives and possessions.
For all the Jews were destroyed--   235
Some hung, others burned alive,
One drowned, another beheaded
By the axe's blade or sword.
And many Christians in turn
Died shamefully as a result.   240

At this time a company arose
At the urging of Hypocrisy, their lady,
Who beat themselves with whips
And crucified themselves flat on the ground,
While singing to an instrument   245
Some new song or other,
And according to them, they were worth more
Than any saint in Paradise.
But the Church attended to them,
Forbidding them to beat themselves,   250
And likewise condemned their song,
Which little children were singing,
And excommunicated all of them
By the power God had granted it,
Because their self-abuse   255
And their song were heresy.

And when Nature saw what was happening,
Namely that her work was destroying itself in this way
And that men were killing each other
And had poisoned the waters   260
In order to destroy the human race
Through greed and envy,
That beautiful and noble creature was much displeased,
Quite vexed, greatly sorrowed.
So she went without delay   265
To Jupiter, and had forged
Lightning, thunder, and storms
On working days and feasts,
For she began this task so late
That she didn't reckon either weekday or holiday in this. 270

Afterward Nature ordered
The four winds over which she had command,
That each should make ready
And prepare to race off,

13

Et qu'il issent de leurs cavernes   275
Et facent leurs mervilleus cernes,
Si qu'il n'i ait resne tenue,
En ciel, en terre, er mer, n'en nue,
Qu'il ne soient a l' ir contraire
Et facent pis qu'il porront faire.   280
Car quant ses ouevr s voit derompre,
Elle vuet aussi l'air corrumpre.
Et quant li vent orent congié,
Et Jupiter ot tout forgié,
Foudres, tempestes, et espars,   285
Qui lors veïst de toutes pars
Espartir mervilleusement
Et tonner trés horriblement,
Vanter, gresler, et fort plouvoir,
Les nues, la mer esmouvoir,   290
Bois tambler, rivieres courir,
Et, pour doubtance de morir,
Tout ce qui a vie seur terre
Recept pour li garentir querre,
C'estoit chose trop mervilleuse,   295
Trop doubtable et trop perilleuse!
Car les pierres dou ciel chëoient
Pour tuer quanqu'elles ataingnoient,
Les hommes, les bestes, les fames;
Et en pluseurs lieus a grans flames   300
Cheïrent li tempès et la foudre
Qui mainte ville mist en poudre;
N'au monde n'avoit si hardi
Qui n'eüst cuer acouardi;
Car il sambloit que decliner   305
Vosist li mondes et finer.

Mais nuls endurer ne peüst,
S'auques durer cils temps deüst.
Si que ces tempestes cesserent,
Mais tels bruïnes engendrerent,   310
Tels ordures et tels fumées
Qui ne furent gaires amées;
Car l'air qui estoit nès et purs   xxivV
Fu ors et vils, noirs et obscurs,
Lais et puans, troubles et pus,   315
Si qu'il devint tous corrompus;
Si que da sa corruption
Eurent les gens opinion
Que corrumpu en devenoient
Et que leur couleur en perdoient.   320

279. All mss Qui--301. Other mss cheï

14

And that they should issue from their caverns   275
And make their raging whirlwinds,
So that there would be no king's realm
In heaven, on earth, on the sea, in the clouds
Where these would not struggle against the air
And do the worst that they could do.   280
For when she saw her works destroyed,
She wished the air corrupted as well.
And when the winds had taken their leave,
And Jupiter had forged everything,
Lightning, storms, and turbulence,   285
Who then watched them
Marvelously disperse in all directions
And thunder quite horribly,
Blow, hail, and rain in torrents,
Rouse up the clouds, the sea,   290
Shake the woods, make the rivers run fast,
And force everything
That lives on the earth to seek shelter
In fear of death so as to save itself,
That was an event too horrible,   295
Too fearful, and too filled with peril!
For stones fell from the sky
Killing whatever they touched,
Men, beasts, women;
And in many places lightning and storm   300
Fell down with great flames
Which turned many villages into dust;
Nor was there anyone in the world so brave
Who didn't then have a coward's heart;
For it appeared that the world   305
Intended to fall into ruin, and end.

But no one could have endured
If this weather had lasted long,
And so these storms came to an end,
But they gave rise to such haze,   310
Such filth, and such vapors
Which were hardly loved;
For the air which had been clear and pure
Was now vile, black, and hazy,
Horrible and fetid, putrefied and infected,   315
And so it became completely corrupted,
And concerning this corruption
Men held the opinion
That they in turn had become corrupted by it
And that they had thus lost their health;   320

Car tuit estoient mal traitié,
Desc ou0louré et deshaitié:
Boces avoient et grans clos
Dont on moroit, et a briés mos,
Po osoient a l'air aler,   325
Ne de près ensamble parler.
Car leurs corrumpues alainnes
Corrompoient les autres sainnes.
Et s'aucuns malades estoit,
S'uns siens amis le visetoit,   330
Il estoit en pareil peril;
Dont il en morut .vͨ mil;
Si que li fils failloit au pere,
La fille failloit a la mere,
La mere au fil et a la fille   335
Pour doubtance de la morille;
N'il n'estoit nuls si vrais amis,
Qui ne fust adont arrier mis
Et qui n'eüst petit d'aïe,
S'il fust cheüs en maladie.   340
Ne fusicien n'estoit, ne mire
Qui bien sceüst la cause dire
Dont ce venoit, ne que c'estoit
(Ne nuls remede n'i metoit)
Fors tant que c'estoit maladie   345
Qu'on appelloit epydimie.

Quant Dieus vit de sa mansion
Dou monde la corruption
Qui tout partout estoit si grans,
N'est merveilles s'il fu engrans   350
De penre crueuse vengence
De ceste grant desordenance;
Si que tantost, sans plus attendre,
Pour justice et vengence prendre,
Fist la mort issir de sa cage,   355
Pleinne de forsen et de rage,
Sans frein, sans bride, sans loien,
Sans foy, sans amour, sans moien,
Si trés fiere et si orguilleuse,
Si gloute et si familleuse   360
Que ne se pooit säouler
Pour riens que peüst engouler.
Et par tout le munde couroit,
Tout tuoit and tout acouroit,
Quanqu'il li venoit a l'encontre,   365
N'on ne pooit resister contre.

16

For everyone was badly affected,
Discolored and rendered ill;
They had buboes and large swellings
From which they died, and, to be brief,
Few dared to venture in the open air,   325
Or to speak together closely.
For their infected breath
Corrupted others who were healthy,
And if anyone was ill,
And one of his friends did visit him,   330
He fell into the same peril;
Five hundred thousand died as a result,
So that father lacked son,
Mother lacked daughter,
Son and daughter lacked mother   335
Because of fear for the Plague;
And no one was so true a friend
That he was not thereupon neglected
And received little help
If he fell ill with the disease.   340
Nor was there a physician or any healer
Who knew enough to name the cause
Of its coming, nor what it was,
(Nor applied any remedy to it)
Except that this was a disease   345
Which was called the Plague.

When God from his house saw
The corruption in the world
Which was everywhere so great,
It's no wonder that he was eager   350
To revenge himself cruelly
For this great disorder;
And so at once, without waiting longer,
In order to exact justice and vengeance,
He made death come forth from his cage,   355
Full of rage and anger,
Without check, without bridle, without rein,
Without faith, without love, without measure,
So very proud and arrogant,
So gluttonous and so famished   360
That he could not be satisfied
By anything that he could consume.
And he raced across the world;
He killed and destroyed one and all,
Whomever he came across,   365
Nor could he be withstood.

Et briefment tant en accoura,
Tant en occist et devoura,
Que tous les jours a grans monciaus
Trouvoit on dames, jouvenciaus,   370
Juenes, viels, et de toutes guises
Gisans mors parmi les eglises;
Et les gettoit on en grans fosses
Tous ensamble, et tous mors de boces,
Car on trouvoit les cimatieres   375
Si pleinnes de corps et de bieres
Qu'il couvint faire des nouvelles.
Ci a mervilleuses nouvelles.
Et si ot meinte bonne ville
Qu'on n'i vëoit, ne fil, ne fille,   380
Femme, n'homme venir n'aler,
N'on n'i trouvoit a qui parler,
Pour ce qu'il estoient tuit mort
De celles mervilleuse mort.
Et ne gisoient que .iii. jours   385
Ou meins; c'estoit petis sejours.
Et maint en y ot vraiement
Qui mouroient soudeinnement;
Car ceuls meïsmes qui les portoient
Au moustier, pas ne revenoient   390
(Souvent la vit on avenir),
Eins les couvenoit la morir.   xxvR
Et qui se vorroit entremettre
De savoir ou d'en escript mettre
Le nombre de ceuls qui moururent,   395
Tous ceuls qui sunt et ceuls qui furent
Et tous ceuls qui sont a venir
Jamais n'i porroient venir,
Tant s'en sceüssent encombrer;
Car nuls ne les porroit nombrer,   400
Ymaginer, penser, ne dire,
Figurer, moustrer, ne escrire.
Car pluseurs fois certeinnement
Oÿ dire et communement
Que, mil .ccc. .xlix.,   405
De cent n'en demoroit que neuf,
Dont on vit par deffaut de gent
Que maint bel heritage et gent
Demouroient a labourer.
Nuls ne faisoit les chans arer,   410
Les blez soier, ne vingnes faire.
Qui en donnast triple salaire,
Non, certes, pour .i. denier vint

380. Other mss except AB filz--386. A secours--391. Other mss
le

18

And in short he killed so many,
Struck down and devoured such a multitude
That every day could be found
Great heaps of women, youths,   370
Boys, old people, those of all stations,
Lying dead throughout the churches;
And these were thrown all together
In great trenches, all of them dead from the buboes,
For one found the cemeteries   375
So full of bodies and biers
That it was necessary to make new ones.
These were strange new tidings.
And so there was many a fine town
Where no boy, no girl, no man or woman   380
Was seen to come and go,
Nor was anyone to be found there to talk to,
For they were all dead
From this devastating attack.
And they did not languish more than three days,   385
Sometimes less; it was a short time.
And there were certainly many who
Died of it suddenly;
For those same men who carried them
To the church did not return;   390
(One often witnessed this there)
Instead they were to die right on the spot,
And whoever wished himself to undertake
To learn or to put down in writing
The number of those who died,   395
Those who are still here and those who were,
And all those who are to come,
Never would they be able to arrive at a figure.
A great many they'd amount to;
For no one could number them,   400
Imagine, conceive, nor tell,
Compute, make known, or record them.
For to be sure many times
I've heard it said, and openly,
That in thirteen hundred and forty nine,   405
From one hundred only nine remained.
And so one saw because of a lack of people
That many a fine, noble estate
Lay unworked.
No one had his fields plowed,   410
His grain sowed, or the vines tended,
Who would have given triple wages,
No, surely, not for twenty to one,

Tant estoient mort; et s'avint
Que par les champs les bestes mues   415
Gisoient toutes esperdues,
Es blez et es vingnes paissoient,
Tout partout ou elles voloient,
N'avoient signeur, ne pastour,
Ne home qui leur alast entour,   420
N'estoit nuls qui les reclamast,
Ne qui pour siennes les clamast.
Heritages y ot pluseurs
Qui demouroient sans signeurs;
Ne li vif n'osoient manoir   425
Nullement dedens le manoir
Ou li mort avoient esté,
Fust en yyer, fust en esté;
Et s'aucuns fust qui le feïst,
En peril de mort se méist.   430
Et quant je vi ces aventures
Si diverses et si obscures,
Je ne fui mie si hardis
Que moult ne fusse acouardis.
Car tuit li plus hardi trambloient   435
De päour de mort qu'il avoient.
Si que trés bien me confessai
De tous les pechiez que fais ay
Et me mis en estat de grace
Pour recevoir mort en la place,   440
S'il pleüst a Nostre Signeur.
Si qu'en doubtance et en cremeur
Dedens ma maison m'enfermay
Et en ma pensée fermay
Fermement que n'en partiroie   445
Jusques a tant que je saroie
A quel fin ce porroit venir;
Si lairoie Dieu couvenir.
Si que lonc temps, se Dieus me voie,
Fui einsi que petit savoie   450
De ce qu'on faisoit en la ville,
Et s'en morut plus de .xx. mille,
Cependant que je ne sceus mie,
Dont j'eus meins de merencolie;
Car riens n'en voloie savoir,   455
Pour meins de pensées avoir,
Comment qu'asses de mes amis
Fussent mors et en terre mis.

Si qu'einsi fui lonc temps en mue,

420. Other mss N'homme

20

So many had died; and so it happened
That the cattle roamed   415
Through the fields completely abandoned,
Grazing in the corn and among the grapes,
Anywhere at all that they wished,
Nor did they have a master, a cowherd,
Or any man to go among them;   420
Nor was there anyone to call them back,
None to claim them as his own.
There were many estates
Which remained without owners;
Nor did the living dare to remain   425
At all inside the houses
Where the dead had been,
Either in winter or in summer;
And if there was anyone who did this,
He put himself in peril of death.   430
And when I saw these events
So strange and so ominous,
I was not at all so brave
That I did not become very cowardly.
For all the bravest trembled   435
With the fear of death that came over them,
And so I confessed myself very thoroughly
Of all the sins I had committed,
And put myself into a state of grace
In order to accept death at that moment,   440
If it should please our Lord.
Therefore in doubt and fear
I closed myself up inside the house
And determined in my mind
Resolutely that I'd not leave it   445
Until that moment when I would know
What conclusion this might come to;
And I would leave it for God to decide.
And so for a long time, may God help me,
I remained there, knowing little   450
Of what was being done in the city,
And more than twenty thousand died,
Though I knew nothing of this,
And so I felt less melancholy;
For I did not wish to know anything   455
In order to have fewer worries,
Though many of my friends
Had died and had been put into the ground.

And so for a long time I remained there in hiding,

Si comme un esprevier qu'on mue,   460
Et tant qu'une fois entroÿ
(Dont moult forment me resjoÿ)
Cornemuses, trompes, naquaires,
Et d'instrumens plus de .vii. paires,
Lors me mis a une fenestre   465
Et enquis que ce pooit estre;
Si que tantost me respondi
Uns miens amis qui m'entendi
Que ceuls qui demouré estoient
Einsi com tuit se marioient   470
Et faisoient festes et noces;
Car la mortalité des boces
Qu'on appelloit epydemie   xxvV
Estoit de tous poins estanchie;
Et que les gens plus ne moroient.   475
Et quant je vi qu'il festioient
A bonne chiere et liement
Et tout aussi joliement
Com s'il n'eüssent riens perdu,
Je n'os mie cuer esperdu,   480
Eins repris tantost ma maniere
Et ouvri mes yeus et ma chiere
Devers l'air qui si dous estoit
Et si clers qu'il m'amonnestoit
Que lors ississe de prison   485
Ou j'avoie esté la saison.
Lors fui hors d'esmay et d'effroy,
Se montai seur mon palefroy
Grisart qui portoit l'ambleüre
Moult souëf et de sa nature   490
S'alay aus champs isnellement
Chevauchier par esbatement,
Pour moy jouer et soulacier
Et la douceur a moy lacier
Qui vient de pais et de deduit,   495
Ou cuers volentiers se deduit
Qui n'a cure de cusenson
Qui touche a noise, n'a tenson,
Mais bien vorroit cusensonner
Ad ce qui puet honneur donner.   500
En celle cusenson estoie
Pour honneur a quoi je tendoie.
Cusençon avoie et desir
Que je peüsse, a mon loisir,
Aucuns lievres a point sousprendre,   505
Par quoy je les peüsse prendre.

485. Other MSS hors--489. A portoie

22

Just like a hawk in moult,   460
Until finally one time I heard
(And for this I greatly rejoiced)
Horns, trumpets, drums,
And more than seven pairs of instruments.
Then I placed myself at a window   465
And inquired what this might be;
And at once one of my friends
Who heard me answered
That those who remained were acting
Just as if all were marrying   470
And having feasts and wedding celebrations,
For the deadly plague of the buboes
Which was called epidemic
Had completely ceased;
And that people were no longer dying.   475
And when I saw they were celebrating
Joyfully and with happy cheer,
And all just as merrily
As if they had lost nothing,
I no longer had a troubled heart,   480
But resumed at once my composure,
And my eyes and face brightened
In the air which was so sweet
And so clear that it encouraged me
Then to leave the prison   485
Where I had passed the season.
At that moment I was beyond grief and worry,
And I mounted on my palfrey
Grisart, who moved at a pace
Which was quite calm because of his nature.   490
And I went quickly through the fields
Riding for pleasure,
In order to entertain and solace myself
And to claim for my own the sweetness
That came from the country and from that enjoyment   495
In which the heart willingly delights
Which has no concern for the pain
That is a part of trouble or strife,
But would rather seek out
Whatever might bestow honor.   500
I was very excited about
The honorable thing I was bent on.
I had the desire and the urge
(If I could manage it, in my good time)
To surprise some hares just right   505
So that I could hunt them down.

Or porroit aucuns enquester
Se c'est honneur de levreter.
A ce point ci responderoie
Que c'est honneur, solas, et joie;   510
C'est uns fais que noblesse prise,
Qui est de gracïeuse emprise,
Et trés honneste a commencier,
Dont il s'en fait bel avencier;
S'est en faisant plaisans a faire,   515
Et li honneurs gist ou parfaire.
Dont en celle perfection
Avoie si m'entencion
Qu'a autre chose ne pensoie.
Et li bon levrier que j'avoie   520
Renforçoient si mon solas
Que je n'en peüsse estre las
Quant le les os mis en conroy,
Et je les vi de tel arroy
De courir a point sus les chans,   525
Et puis des oisillons les chans
Qui estoient melodïeus,
Et li airs dou temps gracïeus
Qui tout le corps m'adoucissoit.
On puet bien croire qu'einsi soit   530
Que, se pluseurs gens chevauchassent,
A fin que point ne m'araisnassent,
Et aucuns bien en congneüsse,
Que ja ne m'en aperceüsse,
Tant y avoie mis ma cure.   535
Se m'en avint une aventure
Qui me fu un petit doubteuse,
Mais briefment me fu gracïeuse,
Si comme tantost le diray
Ci après; point n'en mentiray.   540

Tandis que la m'esbanioie
Qui en moy oublié avoie
Toutes autres merencolies,
Tant les dolentes, com les lies,
Une dame de grant noblesse,   545
Bien acesmée de richesse,
Venoit a belle compaingnie.
Mais je ne les vëoie mie,
Car dou chemin estoie arriere,
Et, d'autre part, pour la maniere   550
De ce que j'estoie entendus
Et tous mes engins estendus

524. Other MSS bel--542. A Que; other MSS Qui

24

Now a person might ask
If hare-hunting is an honorable business;
To this question I would respond
That it is an honor, diversion, and joy;   510
It's an activity that the noble choose,
Something of gracious enterprise,
And quite advantageous to undertake
For it improves one nicely;
So the thing itself is pleasant enough to do,   515
And honor comes with its completion.
Now toward that end
I had so directed my attention
That I was thinking of nothing else.
And the good hares that I had come upon   520
So multiplied my enjoyment
That I could not have felt tired
After I flushed them out
And saw them in a group
Running just so across the fields,   525
And also the songs of the birds
Which were lovely to hear,
And the air of the temperate weather
Which soothed all my body.
A person might well believe that if perhaps   530
Some people rode up
Until they could speak to me,
Though I might somehow gain thereby,
I would not notice them,
So much had I given this my attention.   535
And then an adventure came my way
That frightened me somewhat,
But in the end was pleasant enough,
Just as I will now relate
Hereafter; I'll not lie about it at all.   540

While I was disporting myself there,
I who had forgotten all
Those former melancholic thoughts,
As much the sorrowful as the ones I found pleasant,
A lady of great nobility,   545
Nicely decked out with rich clothes,
Appeared with a beautiful company.
But I didn't see them at all,
For I was back from the road,
And, moreover, because of the way   550
I was attending to
And had concentrated all my attention

A ma queste tout seulement.
Mais la dame premierement
Me vit eins que nuls me veïst,   555
Ne que nuls samblant en feïst,
C'est assavoir d'ycelle gent
Qui conduisoient son corps gent.
Lors .i. escuier appella
Et li dist: "Vois tu celui la   560
Qui bel se deduit et deporte?
Va a lui, et si me raporte
Qui il est, et revien en l'eure
Sans la faire point de demeure."
Li escuiers n'en failli pas,   565
Eins vint a moy plus que le pas
Et hautement me salua.
Mes propos de riens n'en mua.
Si li dis: "Bien veingnies, biau sire."
S'il s'en retourna, sans plus dire,   570
Au plus tost qu'il pot a la dame:
"Dame," dist cils, "foi que doi m'ame,
C'est la Guillaumes de Machaut.
Et sachiez bien qu'il ne li chaut
De riens fors que de ce qu'il chace,   575
Tant est entendus a sa chace.
Bien croy qu'il n'entent a nelui
Fors qu'a ses levriers et a lui."
Quant la dame ces mos oÿ,
Samblant fist de cuer esjoÿ,   580
Nom pas samblant tant seulement,
Mais de fait enterinement,
De cuer joiant, a chiere lie,
Comme dame gaie et jolie.
Nom pourquant moy, ce ne di je point;   585
Eins y avoit .i. autre point,
Pour aucune cause certeïnne
Dont sa volenté estoit pleinne.
Si le me voloit prononcier
Pour li deduire et soulacier   590
Et moy mettre en merencolie.
A ce point ne failli je mie,
Car je fui de li galïes,
Ramposnes, et contralïez,
Aussi com se j'eüsse fait   595
Encontre li un grant meffait.

Quant li escuiers ot compté
De moy toute sa volenté,

570. Other MSS Cils--575. Other MSS rien--585. AFM pourquant
BDE pourquoy Other MSS pour

On my hunting alone,
But the lady saw me
First, before anyone else spied me,   555
Or before anyone made a sign of doing so,
This is to mean of that company
Which was conducting her noble person.
Then she summoned a squire
And said to him: "Do you see that man there   560
Who is nicely disporting and enjoying himself?
Go to him, and then report to me
Who he is, and return quickly
Without making any delay at all."
The squire did not fail at this,   565
But came to me in some haste
And loudly said hello.
My good sense did not desert me,
And I said to him: "You are welcome, fair sir."
He returned, without saying any more,   570
As fast as he could to the lady:
"Lady," he said, "by the faith I owe my soul,
That's Guillaume de Machaut there.
And know well that nothing concerns him
Except what he's pursuing,   575
He's so much involved with his hunting.
I believe firmly that he's concerned with no one
Except his hares and himself."
When the lady heard these words,
She seemed to rejoice at heart,   580
And this was no appearance alone,
But the absolute reality,
For her heart was joyful, her manner happy,
She was like a woman gay and merry.
Not for my sake, this I don't say at all;   585
But rather it was for another reason,
For the sake of a particular matter
She was quite excited about,
And she wished to bring it to my attention
In order to delight and entertain herself   590
And sink me into melancholy.
I did not fail to do so,
For I was mocked by her,
Reproached and contradicted,
Just as if I had sinned   595
Quite grievously against her.

When the squire had related
All he wished about me,

La dame dist tout hautement:
"Or vëons .i. petit, comment   600
Guillaumes est faitis et cointes.
Il m'est avis qu'il soit acointes
De trestoute jolieté
Apartenant a honnesté.
De nuit, en estudiant, veille,   605
Et puis de jours son corps traveille
En travail ou li bons s'atire
Qui a honneur traveille et tire.
Einsi va son corps deduisant
Toutes heures en bien faisant.   610
Si fais estas donne couleur
De maintenir homme en valeur.
Mais je li osterai briefment
Grant part de son esbatement;
Car je li donrai a ruser,   615
Pour li bonne piece muser.
Lonc temps a que je le desir:
S'en acomplirai mon desir.

Or t'en reva a li tantost,
Car je me merveil qui li tost   620
A ci venir. Si li diras
Par plus briés mos que tu porras
Qu'il veingne ci apertement.
Et se li di hardiement
Que ce soit sans querir essoingnes,   625
Non contrestant toutes besongnes,
Et que c'est a mon mandement."
"Dame, a vostre commandement,"
Dist li escuiers, "sans nul 'si,'
Je li vois dire tout einsi   630
Com vous dites, ou au plus près
Que je porrai; j'en sui tous près."
Lors li escuiers chevaucha   xxviV
Devers moy, tant qu'il m'aprocha.
Et quant il me vint aprochant,   635
Il m'appella en chevauchant,
En galopant d'uns pas menus,
Tant qu'il fu près de moy venus.
Et si tost com j'oÿ sa vois,
Erraument devers lui m'en vois,   640
Car de lonc temps le congnoissoie.
Et il, en signe de grant joie,
Me salua de Dieu le pere
Et de sa douce chiere mere;

606. Other MSS except D jour

28

The lady said in a loud voice:
"Now let's see just how   600
Agreeable and wise Guillaume is.
To all appearances he's knowledgeable
About those sorts of merriment
Which accord with morality.
By night, studying, he stays awake,   605
And then by day, he occupies himself
With the labor the good man seeks out,
He who aims at and strives after honor,
And so he goes about amusing himself
At all times with doing what's proper.   610
Such activities do give a man the well-being
To maintain himself in worthiness.
But shortly I will take away from him
The greater part of his enjoyment
Because I'll have some fun with him   615
That will keep him wondering a good while.
I've been eager to do so a long time now:
And thus in this way I'll fulfill my desire.

Now go back to him as fast as possible,
For I am quite anxious for him   620
To be drawn over here. So tell him
In as few words as you can
To come here directly
And be firm with him that
This should be without his looking for excuses,   625
In spite of any business,
And that it's at my order."
"Lady, at your command,"
Said the squire; "Without any 'but'
I will go tell him just what   630
You've said, or as close to it as
I can; I'm quite willing to do so."
Then the squire rode off
In my direction, until he neared me,
And when he did approach,   635
He called out to me as he rode,
Galloping at a quick pace,
Until he came fairly close,
And as soon as I heard his voice,
I went toward him quickly,   640
For I had known him a long time.
And he, in token of his great joy,
Saluted me by God the father
And by his sweet dear mother;

Et je li respondi briefment   645
En saluant courtoisement.
Puis li demanday quels nouvelles
Pour moy seront bonnes et belles,
Se ma dame est preus et haitie,
En pais, sans estre courrecie.   650
"Guillaume, de riens n'en doubtez;
Car ma dame est de tous costez
En pais, preus, et haitie, et seinne;
Et que ce soit chose certeinne,
Assez tost savoir le porrez,   655
Selonc ce que dire m'orrez.
Il est bien voirs qu'elle vous mande,
Nom pas qu'elle le vous commande,
Mais d'un mandement par tel guise
Qu'il vaut auques près commandise;   660
Non prier et non commander,
Einsi li plaist il a mander,
Entre le vert et le meür.
Mais tenez ceci pour seür,
Que c'est bien de s'entencion   665
Que, sans point d'excusation,
Venrez a li moult liement;
Elle le croit fiablement.
Dont, s'il vous plaist, vous y venrez,
Ou vo plaisir responderez."   670

Après ces mos li respondi:
"Trés chiers amis, ytant yous di
Qu'a ma dame, ne quars, ne tiers
Ne sui, mais mes pooirs entiers
Est tous siens, sans riens retenir.   675
Se ne me porroie tenir
D'aler a li, ne ne vorroie,
Pour tant que de vray sentiroie
Que ma dame le penseroit;
Dont, quant elle me manderoit,   680
Ce seroit bien folie a croire
Que point en vosisse recroire.
Mais un po vous vueil demander,
Afin qu'il ni'i ait qu'amender,
Combien ma dame est loin de ci?   685
"Guillaume, je respon einsi,
Qu'il n'i a pas bien trois journées.
Bel soient elles adjournées!"
Dis je: "Or alons sans sejour,
Si chevauchons et nuit et jour   690

660. ABDE Qui--664. Other MSS ce point--667. A verrez

30

And I responded at once   645
While saluting him courteously.
Then I inquired what news,
Good and pleasing, there was for me,
If my lady was hale and happy,
At peace, not annoyed in any way.   650
"Guillaume, don't worry at all,
For my lady is in every way
At peace, hale, happy, and well;
And that this is certain,
You'll be able to find out rather quickly   655
From what you hear me say:
For it is quite true that she summons you,
Not that she really orders you to go to her,
But rather that she requests this in such a fashion
That it counts the same as an order;   660
Neither begging not ordering,
Rather it pleases her to request,
Somewhere between the 'green' and the 'ripe.'
But mark this point for certain,
Namely that it is her intention   665
For you to come to her willingly
Without making any excuses;
She trusts that you'll do so,
And thus, if you please, come on,
Or tell me what you want."   670

After these words I answered him:
"My very dear friend, this much I'll tell you,
Namely that not a fourth or a third
Of what I am, but my entire being
Is wholly hers, with nothing held back.   675
And I could not hold myself back
From going to her, nor would wish to,
Or keep from anything I truly feel
That my lady wishes.
And so when she sends for me,   680
It would surely be madness to believe
That I would ever refuse.
But I do wish to ask you a small point,
Just so there'll be nothing to remedy,
Namely how far is my lady from here?"   685
"Guillaume, here is my answer,
That it's not really even three days travel.
And may those days dawn brightly!"
I said: "Now let us go on without any rest,
Riding by night and day   690

Pour les bons ma damme accomplir.
Je ne me puis mieus räemplir
De joie que son plaisir faire;
Se n'useray point dou contraire."
"Guillaume, j'ay bien entendu   695
Ce que vous avez respondu.
Je vous vueil un po apaisier
D'autre chose que de baisier.
Resgardez en celle grant pleinne
Un po dela celle versainne: 700
C'est ma dame a grant chevauchie
Qui pour vous s'est la adressie.
La vous atent, soiez certeins
Or ne soit point vostres cuers teins
De päour pour trop loing aler;   705
Car la porrez a li parler."
A ces mos ma chiere dressay,
Et puis mon regart adressay
D'icelle part ou cils disoit.
Et quant je vi qu'einsi gisoit,   710
Que mes chemins yert acourciez,
Je n'en fui mie courreciez,
Eins en fui liez; s'en pris a rire,   xxviiR
Et puis a celui pris a dire:
"Biaus amis, par merencolie   715
M'avez tenté de moquerie,
De bourde, et de parole voire,
Quant vous me donnastes a croire
Ma dame long par bel mentir.
Yl me plut moult bien a sentir   720
Le vray de ce que vous mentistes,
En ce qu'après le voir deïstes,
Que ma dame estoit assez près.
Je m'en vois; or venez après,
Ou vous demourrez, s'il vous plaist."   725
"Guillaume, bien heure de plait
Est encor; ne vous hastez point.
Vous y venrez assez a point
Se ma dame y puet adrecier.
Se vous savies un po tencier,   730
Bon seroit et pour certein cas
Ou vous devenez advocas;
Car on vous porra bien sousprendre
Se vous ne vous savez deffendre."
De si fais mos nous debatiens,   735
Par gieu si nous en esbatiens;
Dont tout en parlant chevauchames

693. Other MSS quen--721. A mentites--722. A deites--725. A
plait--737. AFD tout; other MSS tant

32

In order to fulfill my lady's good wishes.
I cannot better supply myself
With joy than by doing her pleasure.
And so I'll offer no opposition at all."
"Guillaume, I have listened attentively   695
To what you've said in response.
And I wish to appease you a little
With something other than a kiss.
Look toward the broad clearing
A bit below that fallow field: 700
That's my lady with a great troop,
And she's drawn herself up there for your sake.
At that very spot she attends you, this you may be certain.
Now let your heart be troubled not at all
With the fear of travelling too far;   705
For there you can speak to her."
At these words my face brightened,
And I turned my glance toward
The place he was speaking of.
And when I saw that she was waiting there,   710
That my journey was shortened,
I was scarcely annoyed,
Instead I was very pleased; and I began to laugh,
And then started to speak to him:
"Good friend, you've nearly made me   715
Melancholy with your jokes,
And with your deceptions, and with your true words,
Insofar as you made me believe
Through a clever lie that my lady was far away;
It has pleased me much to realize   720
The truth of what you lied about,
Because afterward you spoke the truth,
Namely that my lady was rather close by.
I'm on my way to her; now come along,
Or stay here, as you please."   725
"Guillaume, there's still time
For talking; no need to hurry.
You'll get there soon enough
If my lady can arrange it.
And if you know a little something about debating,   730
It'll be good for you in this situation,
For you'll play the lawyer's role;
And you could be badly shocked
If you prove unable to defend yourself."
We bandied about these words,   735
And with such game amused ourselves;
Thus absorbed in talk we rode on

Que la gent la dame aprochames.
Lors m'avansai, et quant je vi
Son gentil corps amanevi   740
D'onneur, de grace, et de science,
En signe de grant reverence
Vos jus de mon cheval descendre;
Mais tantost le me va deffendre.
En disant debonnairement: 745
"Hola, Guillaume, nullement,
Pour certein, n'i descenderez.
A cheval a moy parlerez."
Quant je l'oÿ, je m'en souffri,
Et si bel salu li offri,   750
Comme je pooie et savoie,
Et comme faire le devoie,
Einsi comme j'avoie apris
A honnourer gens de tel pris.
Et elle aussi, sans contrefaire,   755
Sceut moult bien le seurplus parfaire,
En respondant par amisté,
Gardant honneur et honnesté.
Puis me dist moult rassisement:

                        LA DAME

"Guillaume, mervilleusement   760
Estes estranges devenus.
Vous ne fussiez pas ça venus,
Se ce ne fust par mes messages,
Je croy que vous estes trop sages
Devenuz, ou trop alentis,   765
Mausoingneus, et mautalentis,
De vos deduis apetisiez,
Ou trop po les dames prisiez.
Quant je fui la dessus montée
En celle plus haute montée   770
Mon chemin tenoie sus destre,
Et je regardai vers senestre,
Tout de plain vous vi chevauchier,
Vos levriers siffler et huchier.
Tels ouevres faire vous öoie   775
Tout aussi bien com je vëoie
Vous et vostre contenement.
Dont je croy bien certeinnement,
Guillaume, que vous nous veites.
Et pour quoy dont, quant vous oites   780
Nos chevaus passer et hennir,
Et se ne daignies venir,

756. FMBDE faire--757. A amite--762. A sa--779. Other MSS
veistes--780. Other MSS oistes--782. Other MSS si...deingnastes

                        34

Until we neared the lady's company.
Then I went on ahead, and when I saw
Her noble person replete   740
With honor, grace, and learning,
As a sign of great reverence
I made to get off my horse;
But at once she started to forbid it,
Saying quite politely: 745
"O no, Guillaume, this won't do.
You must not dismount;
Speak to me from your horse."
And when I heard this, I was embarrassed,
And gave her as fine a greeting   750
As I could and knew how to,
Just as I should do,
Since I had learned
To honor people of such rank.
And she in turn, without dissembling,   755
Knew how to accomplish everything else,
Responding in friendship,
Keeping her honor and integrity.
Then she spoke to me quite deliberately:

THE LADY

"Guillaume, you have acted   760
Too much the stranger.
You would not have come here
Had it not been for my messenger;
I think you've become
Too wise, or too backward,   765
Inattentive and disagreeable,
Eager for your sport,
Or else you value ladies too little.
When I climbed the ground over there
On that rather steep rise,   770
I took the path on the right,
And looked toward the left;
Quite plainly I saw you riding,
Whistling up and calling after your hares.
I heard you so engaged,   775
And likewise I saw
You and your goings-on.
I believe quite surely,
Guillaume, that you must have seen us.
And why then, when you heard   780
Our horses pass by and whinny,
Did you not deign come forward

Jusqu'a tant que je vous manday
Einsi com je le commanday?
Dont je vous merci tellement   785
Come je doy, et non autrement."

                    GUILLAUME

Lors li dis je: "Pour Dieu merci,
Ma dame, ne dites ceci.
Je respon, sauve vostre honneur,
Car foy que doy Nostre Signeur,   790
Je ne vi riens, ne riens n'oÿ,   xxiiV
Tant avoie cuer esjoÿ
De ma chace a quoy je pensoie,
Pour la fin a quoy je tendoie;
S'estoie einsi comme ravis   795
Ma dame, je feroie envis
Riens encontre vostre voloir.
Et que me porroient valoir
A faire tels menuz despis?
Bien say que j'en vaurroie pis,   800
Si m'en devez bien escuser."

                    LA DAME

"Guillaume, plus n'en vueil ruser.
Puis qu'einsi va, mes cuers vous croit.
Mais d'une autre partie croit
Moult durement une autre chose   805
Encontre vous qui porte glose.
Se vous donray assez a faire,
Et se vous ferai maint contraire,
Se pour confus ne vous rendez.
Guillaume, oëz et entendez: 810
Vers le dames estes forfais,
S'en avez enchargié tel fais
Que soustenir ne le porrez,
Ne mettre jus quant vous vorrez."
Avec ces paroles diverses,   815
En leurs diversetez perverses,
Me moustra elle une maniere
Aspre, crueuse, male, et fiere,
En signe de grant mautalent,
Pour moy faire le cuer dolent   820
Et mettre ma pensée toute
En effroy, en song, et en doubte.
De ce se mettoit en grant peinne,
Qu'ele se tenoit pour certeinne
Que de tant bien la priseroie   825

790. A Signour

                        36

Until I asked you,
Just as if I had made it an order?
So I thank you just as much for this   785
As I must and no more."

                    GUILLAUME

Then I said to her: "For God's sake,
My lady, don't say such things;
I'll give you an answer, saving your honor,
But by the faith I owe Our Lord   790
I saw nothing, nor did I hear a thing,
So much was my heart excited
By the hunting I was intent on,
By the goal I wanted to attain;
And so I was spellbound.   795
My lady, I would do reluctantly
Anything against your will.
And how would it profit me
To commit such petty spiteful acts?
I know well that I'd be the less worthy for it.   800
And so you ought well excuse me."

                    THE LADY

"Guillaume, I don't want to fool with this further.
Since it's come to this, my heart believes you.
But on the other hand another matter
Has mounted up--and seriously--   805
To your discredit, one that needs explanation.
And I will give you much to do and think about,
Offering much argument against you
If you don't admit your error.
Guillaume, listen and pay attention: 810
You have sinned against women,
And thus you've taken on a burden
That you'll not be able to bear up under,
Nor put down when you'd like to."
With these strange words,   815
Perverse in their obscurity,
She showed me a manner
Bitter, cruel, hurtful, and haughty,
As a sign of her great anger,
In order to render my heart sad   820
And make fearful, careful, and doubting
My every thought.
She took great pains in doing so,
For she was convinced
That because I valued her highly   825

                        37

Que son courrous moult doubteroie.
Et si fis je; je le doubtay,
Quant ces paroles escoutay,
Nom pas pour cause de meffait
Qu'endroit de moy heüsse fait,   830
Mais je doubtay pour mesdisans
Qui sont aucunes fois nuisans
Par fausseté et par envie
Aus bons qui mainnent bonne vie.
Si doubtay si faite aventure;   835
Mais seürs fui qu'enforfaiture
N'avoie fait en ma vie onques
Envers nulles dames quelsquonques.
Se li respondi par avis.

                    GUILLAUME

"Dame, fait avez .i. devis   840
Ou ma grant deshonneur moustrez,
Mais li procès n'est pas outrez,
Ne mis en fourme justement.
Pour faire certein jugement,
Vous me deüssiez dire en quoy   845
J'ay forfait, et tout le pourquoy
Amener a conclusion.
Or est en vostre entention
Secretement mis en enclos.
S'il ne m'est autrement desclos,   850
Je n'en saveroie respondre.
Or vueilliez, s'il vous plaist, espondre
Le fait de quoy vous vous dolez;
Et s'einsi faire le volez
Vous ensieurez la droite voie   855
De droit, ou je ne saveroie
Le fait congnoistre ne niër.
Se non, vous devez ottriër
Que je m'en voise frans et quittes
De ce forfait que vous me dites;   860
J'en atenderoie bien droit."

                    LA DAME

"Guillaume, sachies, orendroit
N'en arez plus de ma partie.
Car la chose est einsi partie:
Se je le say, vous le savez,   865
Car le fait devers vous avez
En l'un de vos livres escript,
Bien devisié et bien descript: xxviiiR

855. Other MSS juste voie--858. A ce

                    38

I would fear her anger greatly.
And so I did; I feared her
When I heard these words,
Not for the sake of any misdeed
That I had committed myself,   830
But rather because I feared the gossip-mongers
Who are at all times harmful,
Through falseness and envy,
To the good people who lead decent lives.
And so I dreaded such a turn of events.   835
But I was certain that I had done
No harm in my entire life
To any lady whomsoever,
And I answered her with this in mind:

GUILLAUME

"Lady, you have brought up something   840
That would manifest my great dishonor,
But the trial is not yet set,
Nor begun in proper form
For a certain judgment to be made.
You ought to tell me how   845
I have erred, and explain completely
All the facts of the matter.
At the present what you intend here
Remains secret and hidden from me.
And if it is not made known to me,   850
I'll not be able to respond.
Now please, if you will, expound upon
The matter that troubles you;
And if you agree to this,
You'll be following the correct path   855
Of the law, for otherwise I'll not be able
To know what the issue is or dispute it.
If not, you ought to grant
That I should be acquitted
Of the allegation you've made against me;   860
I do expect fair play here."

THE LADY

"Guillaume, know right away
That you'll get nothing more from me;
Rather the matter stands thus:
If I know about it, you know too,   865
Because the case against you is something
You've written in one of your books,
Something well laid out and described therein;

39

Si resgardes dedens vos livres.
Bien say que vous n'estes pas ivres   870
Quant vos fais amoureus ditez.
Dont bien savez de vos dittez,
Quant vous les faites et parfaites,
Se vous faites bien ou forfaites,
Dès qu'il sont fait de sanc assis   875
Autant a un mot comme a sis.
S'il vous plaist, vous y garderez,
Qu'autre chose n'en porterez
De moy, quant a l'eure presente.
Soiez certeins que c'est m'entente."   880

                    GUILLAUME

"Dame, qu'est ce que dit avez?
Selonc le bien que vous savez,
Trop mieus savez que vous ne dites:
J'ay bien de besongnes escriptes
Devers moy, de pluseurs manieres,   885
De moult de diverses matieres,
Dont l'une l'autre ne ressamble.
Consideré toutes ensamble,
Et chascune bien mise a point,
D'ordre en ordre et de point en point,   890
Dès le premier commancement
Jusques au darrein finement,
Se tout voloie regarder
--Dont je me vorrai bien garder--
Trop longuement y metteroie;   895
Et d'autre part, je ne porroie
Trouver ce que vous demandez
S'a vos paroles n'amendez.
Pour tel chose ne quier ja lire,
Dame, nom pas pour vous desdire,   900
Mais ce n'est pas chose sensible
Que vostre pensée invisible
Peüst venir a ma congnoissance,
Fors que par la clef d'ordenance
Dont vostres cuers soit deffermies,   905
Et que si en soie enfourmes
Que vostre bouche le me die.
Lorsqu'a respondre contredie,
Quant de bouche le m'arez dit,
J'en vueil moult bien, a vostre dit,   910
Estre blasmez et corrigiez.
Dame, s'il vous plait, or jugiez
Selonc la vostre opinion,

874. A parfaites--878. Other MSS emporterez--895. A repeats
lines 893 and 894--899. A ni--902. FMB nuisible--903. Other
MSS Puist

                        40

So look within your works.
I know well that you're not drunk   870
When you compose your love poems.
And so you know well your own poetry,
Since you composed it and saw it to completion;
You know if you did good therein or wrong,
Since you put your heart into them   875
As much in one word as in six.
If you please, look there for your wrongdoing,
For you'll have nothing more
From me, as far as the present is concerned.
You can be sure that this is what I mean."   880

GUILLAUME

"Madam, what have you said?
As you are quite aware,
You know much more than you've told.
I've many written works
In front of me, of various kinds,   885
Concerning quite different matters,
Each of which is unlike the other.
Considering all these together,
And each one rather thoroughly,
Section by section and sentence by sentence,   890
From the beginning of the first
To the very end of the last,
That is if I wished to look through all of them
(Something I'd indeed like to avoid)
I would spend too long in so doing;   895
And, in addition, I might not
Come across what you're taking issue with
If you don't tell me more.
For I'd never seek out such a thing to read,
Madam, except to contradict you.   900
But it's hardly to be expected
That I'd be able
To decipher your hidden thought,
Except through the controlling key
By which your heart might be unlocked,   905
And thus I then would be informed,
In that your mouth would speak the words.
If I refuse to respond,
After you yourself have told me,
I'd wish very much to be blamed   910
And corrected by your own word.
Madam, if you please, now decide
In your own mind

41

Se j'ay tort a m'entention."

"Guillaume, puis qu'il est einsi,   915
Je m'acort bien a ce point ci.
Orendroit me rens je vaincue;
Mais de vostre descouvenue,
Qui est contre dames si grande,
Afferroit bien crueuse amende,   920
S'il estoit qui la vosist prendre.
Or vueilles dès or mais entendre
Ad ce que je diray de bouche;
Car moult forment au cuer me touche.
Et quant dit le vous averay,   925
En tel lieu le reprocheray
Que vous en serez moult blasmez
Et vers les dames diffamez.

Une question fu jadis
Mise en termes par moult biaus dis,   930
Belle et courtoisement baillie,
Mais après fu trop mal taillie:
Premierement fu supposé,
Et en supposant proposé,
Qu'une dame de grant vaillance   935
Par trés amiable fiance
Ameroit .i. loial amant,
Si que toudis, en bien amant,
Seroit de cuer loial amie;
Se il, en gardant courtoisie,   940
Toudis de bon cuer l'ameroit
Et son pooir estenderoit
En li chierir et honnourer;
Et pour li miex enamourer   xxviiiV
Il meintenroit toute noblesse,   945
Honneur, courtoisie, et largesse.
Biaus homs seroit, a grant devis,
De membres, de corps, et de vis
Renommez, de grace parfais,
Et si bien espouvez par fais   950
D'armes, comme nuls homs puet estre
Qui a mis sa vie et son estre
En sieuir joustes et tournois
Et tous amoureus esbanois.
Cependant qu'einsi s'ameront   955
Et toudis bien se garderont
Les courtois poins de loiauté

940. Other MSS Et

42

If I have done wrong in insisting upon this."

"Guillaume, since things stand so,   915
I agree completely.
At the moment I admit myself defeated,
But concerning your false opinion,
Which is so seriously biased against women,
A severe penance is called for   920
If someone wishes to exact it.
Now in any case please attend from this point on
To what I'll speak with my mouth.
For the matter moves my heart greatly.
And when I shall have told it to you,   925
In a certain place I will reproach you with it
And you'll be much blamed,
Losing your reputation among ladies.

An issue was at one time
Advanced in a very pleasing poem,   930
Prettily and courteously embellished,
But afterward was very badly developed.
At first it was supposed,
And, in supposing, proposed
That a lady of great worth   935
Through a very loving bond
Did love a loyal lover,
So that always, in loving well,
She was a loyal beloved in her heart;
And he, maintaining courtesy,   940
Always loved her with a good heart
And expended his energy
In cherishing and honoring her;
And in order to deepen her love,
He upheld everything noble--   945
Honor, courtesy, and generosity.
He was an exceptionally handsome man,
For his limbs, his body, and his face
Renowned, perfect in grace,
And as well proven in deeds of arms   950
As any man could be
Who had spent his life and his being
In following tournaments and jousts
And other pursuits pertaining to love.
Even though they loved each other in this way   955
And always kept well
The courtly principles of loyalty

43

En raison et en verité,
Leur avenroit tele aventure,
Par violence ou par nature,   960
Que li amans devieroit;
Et celle, quant le saveroit,
Demouroit lasse et esgarée,
Loyal amie non amée.
Car ses cuers demorroit espris,   965
Et li cuers de l'amant de pris
Seroit selonc nature esteins,
Dont li siens cuers seroit plus teins
Pour cause de la departie.
Plus n'en di de ceste partie: 970
Eins vorrai d'une autre compter
Pour a ceste ci adjouster,
En faisant ma comparison.
Guillaume, or entendez raison:

Uns autres amans debonnaires,   975
Aussi vaillans en ses affaires
Comme cils de qui j'ay compté
Tant en grace comme en bonté,
Et de toutes autres parties
En honneur a point departies,   980
Amera aussi une dame
Sans mal penser et sans diffame;
Et se li fera a savoir.
Et quant elle en sara le voir,
Volentiers le recevera   985
Et s'amour li ottriera
Liement, sans faire dangier.
Pas ne vueil ce ci prolongier;
Car cils l'amera loyaument
Et se la croira fermement   990
Sans erreur et sans nulle doubte,
Car il cuidera s'amour toute
Avoir acquis toute sa vie,
Sans jamais faire departie.
Mais il ira bien autrement;   995
Quant il sera plus liement
Conjoins a li et affermez
En la fiance d'estre amez,
Elle li jouera d'un tour
Outréement, sans nul retour,   1000
Ou il trouvera fausseté
Contre lui, et desloiauté,
Et se ne le porra niër.

976. FMBDE a ses

44

In reason and in truth,
Such an accident happened to them,
Whether by violence or through nature,   960
That the lover did pass away;
And she, when she knew it,
Lived on sorrowful and abandoned,
A loyal beloved no longer loved:
Because her heart was still aflame,   965
And the heart of the worthy lover
Had been extinguished by the force of nature,
Her heart was the more afflicted
By his passing.
I'll say no more about this.   970
Instead I'd like to speak of something else
In order to set it beside the other,
Making a comparison for myself.
Guillaume, listen now and learn.

Another lover of high degree,   975
As worthy in his doings
As that one I've already spoken of,
In grace as much as in goodness,
And in all other respects
Rightly and honorably endowed,   980
Also loved a lady
Without thought of evil or infamy;
And he made this known to her,
And when she did know the truth,
Willingly she received him   985
And granted him her love
Joyfully, without making difficulties.
I don't wish to draw this out;
But he loved her loyally
And trusted her firmly   990
Without wavering and without any doubt,
For he thought he had acquired
All her love for the rest of his life,
Without ever having to share it.
But things went quite differently for him;   995
When he was the most happily
Joined to her, and confident
In the promise of being loved,
She did him wrong,
Outrageously and without any excuse,   1000
And in this he discovered her falseness
To him, and her disloyalty,
And he could not explain it away.

Si doit bien celui anuiër,
Ce n'est mie moult grant merveille.   1005
Mais ce n'est pas chose pareille
Au fait d'amours qui me remort,
Qui se defenist par la mort.
Guillaume, s'entendu m'avez,
Asses legierement devez   1010
Vostre meffaçon recongnoistre.
Pour vostre deshonneur desccroistre.
Vous avez dit et devisié
Et jugié de fait avisié
Par diffinitif jugement   1015
Que cils a trop plus malement,
Grieté, tourment, mal, et souffraite
Qui trueve sa dame forfaite
Contre lui en fausse maniere,
Que la trés douce dame chiere   1020
Qui avera son dous amy
Conjoint a son cuer, sans demy,
Par amours, sans autre moien,
Puis le savera en loien   xxixR
De la mort ou il demourra,   1025
Si que jamais ne le verra.
Et comment l'osastes vous dire,
Ne dedens vos livres escrire?
Il est voirs qu'einsi l'avez fait,
Dont vous avez griefment meffait.   1030
Si vous lo que vous tant faciez
Que ce jugement effacies,
Et que briefment le rapellez.
Guillaume, se vous tant valez,
Vous le pouez bien einsi faire   1035
Par soustenir tout le contraire.
Car li contraires, c'est li drois
En tous bons amoureus endrois."
"Dame, foy que doi sainte Eglise,
En qui ma foy est toute assise,   1040
Pour nulle rien ne le feroie;
Eins iray tout outre la voie
Dou fait, puisque j'y suis entrez.
Dès que mes jugemens outrez
Est de moy, je le soustenray,   1045
Tant com soustenir le porray.
Mais qui vorroit avant venir
Pour le contraire soustenir,
Moult volentiers oubeïroie
A quanqu'oubeïr deveroie.   1050

1007. FMDE Aus fais--1023. A sas

46

If this should have given him pain,
It's hardly much of a surprise.   1005
But this is not the same thing
As the love affair that gives me sorrow
And was ended by death.
Guillaume, if you have listened to me,
You ought very readily   1010
Acknowledge your misdeed
In order to lessen your dishonor.
You have said and described,
And also decided, advised of these facts,
In a conclusive judgment   1015
That this man has much more ill fortune,
Grief, torment, unpleasantness, and suffering,
He who found his lady false
To him through her hypocrisy,
Than has the very gracious, dear lady   1020
Who had her sweet lover
Joined to her heart irrevocably
Through love, and not in any other way.
Then she learned he was in the power
Of death, and there will remain,   1025
So that she'll never see him again.
And how did you dare say this,
Or write it down in your book?
It is true that you have done so,
And thus you have grievously erred.   1030
Therefore I advise you to do what you can
To erase this judgment
And quickly recall it.
Guillaume, if you are indeed worthy enough,
You could rather easily accomplish this   1035
By affirming just the opposite.
For the opposite view, that's the correct one
Wherever proper loving is valued."
"Madam, by the faith that I owe holy Church,
In which my trust is wholly placed,   1040
I would do this for no reason;
Instead I'll pursue the matter all the way
To the end, since after all I am involved;
Because this judgment was made public
By me, I will uphold it   1045
As long as I can uphold it.
But whoever might come forward
To support the other side,
I would quite willingly submit
To whatever I must.   1050

Car je ne suis mie si fors,
Ne si grans n'est pas mes effors,
Ne de science mes escus,
Que je ne puisse estre veincus.
Mais se je puis, je veinqueray;   1055
Se je ne puis, je soufferay.
Or voit einsi, quon puet aler;
Je n'en quier autrement parler.
Et nompourquant, ma dame douce,
Que vostres cuers ne se courrouce   1060
A moy, nous ferons une chose
Ouvertement, nom pas enclose,
Ou vostre pais soit contenue,
Et m'onneur y soit soustenue.
Car ce seroit a ma grant honte,   1065
Selonc vostre meïsme conte,
S'endroit de moy contredisoie
Le fait que jugié averoie,
De mon bon droit, tel et si fait
Que tout par moy avroie fait.   1070
Nous penrons un juge puissant,
De renommée souffissant,
Qui soit sages homs et discrez.
Se li soit comptez li secrez
Entierement de la besongne   1075
Qui a vous et a moy besongne.
Or soit einsi fait par acort;
Mais vous en ferez le recort
Dou prendre tel que vous vorrez.
Contredire ne le m'orrez,   1080
Einsi y sui acordans dès ci
A vostre plaisir, sans nul si.
Mes cuers y est ja tous entiers,
Car ce sera uns biaus mestiers
D'oïr les raisons repeter   1085
Et les parties desputer
Soutilment, par biaus argumens,
Qui vaurront auques jugemens."

                        LA DAME

A ces moz prist la dame a rire
Et en riant tantost a dire: 1090
"Guillaume, bien suis acordans
Ad ce qu'estes ci recordans;
S'en parlerai, comment qu'il aille.
Et nompourquant, vaille que vaille,
Je nomme et pren celui qui rois   1095

1057. Other MSS com--1068. A qua--1070. Other MSS aroie
1078. A feirs--1086. F. despitter

                        48

For I am hardly so powerful,
Nor is my endurance so great,
Nor my storehouse of knowledge,
That I could not be overcome.
But if I can, I will prevail;   1055
If I prove unable, I will pay the price.
Now I'll look to getting on with this.
I don't wish to speak about it any more.
And yet, my sweet lady,
So that you will not be angry with me in your heart,   1060
We will proceed with this singular matter
Not secretively, but openly,
And thus your peace of mind will be preserved
And my honor upheld.
For it would be to my great shame,   1065
According to what you yourself have said,
If for my own part I should reverse myself about
The case I already passed judgment on,
As was my place, having done it in such a way
That I accomplished it all alone.   1070
We will agree on a powerful judge,
Someone sufficiently renowned,
A person who would be wise and discreet,
And he will be told from beginning to end
The private details of this affair   1075
Which involves you and me.
Now let it be done through this kind of agreement,
Namely that you will assume responsibility
For selecting such a man as you would like.
You will not hear me gainsay this,   1080
Instead I am in agreement from this point on
With your pleasure, without any 'but.'
My heart is truly in this,
For it will be a pleasant task
To hear the arguments rehearsed   1085
And the parties dispute
With subtlety, with pretty distinctions,
All of which will merit some kind of judgment."

                            THE LADY

At these words the lady began to laugh,
And while laughing began at once to say: 1090
"Guillaume, I am very much in agreement
With what you've just said;
And I'll go ahead and debate, however it might turn out.
And so, for whatever it's worth,
I nominate and choose the man called   1095

                              49

Est appellez des Navarrois.
C'est uns princes qui aimme honnour
Et qui het toute deshonnour,
Sages, loiaus, et veritables,
Et en tous ses fais raisonnables.   1100
Il scet tant et vaut, qu'a droit dire,
Nul milleur ne porroie eslire.
Li fais li sera savoureus,
Pour ce qu'il est moult amoureus,   xxixV
Sages, courtois, et bien apris.   1105
Il aimme l'onneur et le pris
Des armes, d'amours, et des dames.
C'est li rois par cui uns diffames
Ne seroit jamais soustenus;
De toute villenie est nus   1110
Et garnis de toute noblesse
Qui apartient a gentillesse.
Trop de biens dire n'en porroie,
S'ui mais tout adès en parloie."

Einsi fumes nous acordé,   1115
Comme devant est recordé.
Dont puis d'amors asses parlames,
Et en parlant tant chevauchames
Que nous entrames es drois las
De pais, de joie, et de solas,   1120
C'est a savoir en .i. dous estre
Ou il faisoit si trés bel estre
Qu'on ne porroit miex, a mon gré:
C'estoit en souverein degré,
A mon avis, de bon propos,   1125
De deduit, et de bon repos,
Ou uns cuers se puet reposer
Qui a point se vuet disposer.
La avoit il un bel manoir
Ou elle voloit remanoir.   1130

Asses fu qui la descendi
Et qui entour li entendi;
Et, sans atendre, fu menée
Dedens une chambre aournée
Si bien, si bel, si cointement   1135
Et de tout si trés richement,
Qu'onques mais, dont j'eus grant merveille,
N'avoie veü la pareille.
Et briefment tuit, grant et meneur,
Li faisoient feste et honeur.   1140

1121. Other MSS assavoir

The King of Navarre.
He's a prince who loves honor
And hates dishonor of any kind,
A man wise, loyal, and truthful,
And reasonable in all his doings.   1100
He knows so much and is so worthy that,
To speak the truth, I could choose none better.
The affair will appeal to him
Because he is quite romantically inclined,
Wise, courteous, and well taught.   1105
He loves the honor and the glory
Of arms, of love, and of ladies.
He's the king who would never
Support any infamy;
He's devoid of all uncouthness   1110
And graced with all the nobility
That pertains to high degree.
I could not say too much of his virtues
If I spoke now the whole day about them."

In this way we came to an agreement,   1115
Just as it is recorded above;
Then we spoke much about love,
And while speaking we rode on
Until we fell into the rightful snare
Of peace, of joy, and of solace,   1120
Which means into that sweet state
Whose conditions were so pleasant
That one could not do better, to my liking:
It was of the highest degree,
In my opinion, replete with good sense,   1125
With delight, with sweet rest,
Where a heart could repose itself
Which wishes such comfort.
There was a handsome manor at the spot
Where she wished to stop.   1130

Many there were who helped her down
And who attended to her;
And, without delay, she was led
Inside a room decorated
So well, so beautifully, so expertly,   1135
And in all things so very richly
That never before (and at this I greatly marvelled)
Had I seen the like.
And quickly everyone, high and low,
Made over and honored her.   1140

Mais bien sambloit estre maistresse,
Car elle fu par grant noblesse
Entre coussins de soie assise.
Mais moult estoit sage et rassise,
Et fu d'aäge si seür   1145
Qu'entre le vert et le meür
Estoit sa trés douce jouvente,
Plus qu'autre simple, aperte, et gente.
Moult bien estoit acompaingnie
De belle et bonne compaingnie.   1150
N'i fu Margot ne Agnesot,
Mais .xii. damoiselles ot
Qui jour et nuit la norrissoient,
Servoient, et endoctrinoient.

La premiere estoit Congnoissance   1155
Qui li moustroit la difference
D'entre les vertus et les vices
Et des biens fais aus malefices,
Par Avis qui la conduisoit
Jusqu'a .i. miroir qui luisoit,   1160
Si qu'onques plus cler mirëoir.
Ne pot on tenir ne vëoir.

Raisons le tenoit en sa destre,
Une balance en sa senestre,
Si que la dame s'i miroit   1165
Plus souvent qu'on ne vous diroit.
La vëoit elle clerement,
Sans obscurté n'empecchement,
Quanque Diex et Nature donne
A bonne eüreuse personne.   1170
C'est le mal laissier et bien faire,
Et non voloir autrui contraire;
Car fols est qui autrui pourchace
Chose qu'il ne vuet qu'on li face.
Et s'il heüst en son atour,   1175
En son gentil corps, fait a tour,
Et en son cuer tache ne vice
Ou pensée d'aucun malice,
Ja ne fust si fort reponnue
Qu'en miroir ne fust veüe.   1180
Et la vëoit elle, sans doubte,
La guise et la maniere toute,
Comment Raison justement regle
Par bele et bonne et loial regle;   xxxR
Si que la prenoit exemplaire   1185

1168. Other MSS empeschement

52

And she seemed very much to be the mistress,
For she in great nobility
Was seated between cushions of silk.
Yet she was very wise and self-contained,
And was of such a confident age   1145
That her very sweet youth
Was between greenness and ripeness;
She was--more than any other--sweet, friendly, and noble.
She was very well attended
By a good and handsome entourage.   1150
None was a farm girl;
Instead they were twelve damsels
Who sustained her by day and night,
Served and instructed her.

The first was Understanding,   1155
Who showed her the difference
Between the virtues and the vices,
And between good deeds and evil ones,
Through Discretion who conducted her
Up to a mirror that gleamed   1160
So much that one could never find
Or see a clearer reflecting glass.

Reason held it in her right hand,
A scale   in her left,
So that the lady examined herself there   1165
More often than one could say.
There she saw clearly
Without obscurity or impediment
Whatever God and Nature might bestow
On a truly fortunate person.   1170
That's to leave off evil and do good,
And not to wish to cross anyone;
For he's a fool who does something to
Another that he does not wish done to him.
And if there might be on her person,   1175
Or on her noble body, so beautifully shaped,
Or in her heart any fault or vice,
Or the thought of any malice,
It would never be so well hidden
That it could not be seen in the mirror.   1180
And there she gazed on, without doubt,
The way and manner of all things,
Namely how Reason justly rules
Through fair and good and loyal precept;
And so there she found the exemplar   1185

De tout ce qu'elle devoit faire.
Et aussi la juste balance
Li demoustroit signefiance
Qu'elle devoit en tous cas vivre
Aussi justement com la livre   1190
Ou on ne puet, par nulle voie,
Mettre n'oster, qu'on ne le voie.

La tierce avoit nom Attemprance
Qui .i. chapelet de souffrance
Avoit sus son chief par cointise;   1195
Et avec ce, dont miex la prise,
Estoit de maniere seüre
Et, en parlant, sage et meüre,
N'en fait, n'en port, n'en contenence
N'ot vice, ne desordenance.   1200

La quarte, se bien m'en recorde,
Estoit Pais qui tenoit Concorde
Par le doy amiablement,
Et li disoit moult doucement,
De cuer riant, a chiere lie: 1205
"Ma douce suer, ma chiere amie,
Se nous volons vivre en leësse,
En pais, et repos, en richesse,
De tout ce qu'on puet faire et dire,
N'en mettons a nos cuers point d'ire,   1210
Et ne nous chaille dou dangier
Qu'on appelle contrevangier,
Car tels cuide vangier sa honte
Qui l'accroist et qui plus s'ahonte.
Tenons les bons en amitié,   1215
Et des mauvais aions pitié,
Car onques homs ne fu parfais
Qui volt vangier tous ses tors fais."

La cincisme fu appellée
Foy, qui richement endestrée   1220
Estoit de Constance la ferme
Qui si l'affermoit et afferme
Que riens ne la branle n'esloche,
Eins estoit com chastiaus sus roche,
Fort et ferme et seürement,   1225
Sans variable mouvement.

La setisme fu Charité
Qui avoit si trés grant pité

1188. ABDE demoustrent--1192. FM Mestre--1214. A lahonte--1218.
A vost--1223. A bransle--1227. A sisieme

Of all she ought to do.
Moreover the just scales
Demonstrated to her this meaning,
That she should in every instance live
As justly as the scales   1190
Which one, in no way,
Can add to or take away from such that it's not seen.

The third was named Temperance,
Who wore a flower crown of endurance
On her head as an adornment;   1195
And with this (for which one valued her the more)
She was of confident manner
And, in her speech, wise and mature;
Not in deed, nor in her carriage, nor in her demeanor
Was there any vice or impropriety.   1200

The fourth, and well I remember her,
Was Peace who held Harmony
By the finger in friendship,
And spoke to her very sweetly
With a laughing heart, a happy face: 1205
"My sweet sister, my dear beloved,
If we wish to live in joy,
In peace, in repose, in richness,
In all that can be said and done,
Let us not put in our hearts any anger at all,   1210
And let us not be concerned with the capriciousness
Which is called revenge,
For the same one who thinks to avenge his shame
Makes it increase and disgraces himself further.
Let us hold to good people in friendship,   1215
And let us take pity on the evil,
For no man who is perfect
Has ever wished to avenge the wrongs done him."

The fifth was called
Faith, and was grandly escorted   1220
By firm Constancy,
Who so strengthened and strengthens her
That nothing disturbs or shakes her up;
Instead she was like a castle built on rock,
Strong and securely founded,   1225
Without unpredictable change.

The seventh was Charity,
Who has such very great pity

55

Des besoingneus qu'elle savoit
Que leur donnoit quanqu'elle avoit.   1230
Mais ja tant donner ne sceüst
Qu'assez plus a donner n'eüst.

Après, Honnestez doucement
Se sëoit moult honnestement,
Qui parée par grant noblesse   1235
Estoit d'un mantel de simplesse.
Mais nette estoit, sans nul reproche,
De cuer, de corps, de main, de bouche.

La .ixe. estoit Prudence;
En son cuer portoit Sapience,   1240
Et si fermement la gardoit
Qu'après li d'amours toute ardoit.
Bien savoit la cause des choses
Qui sont ou firmament encloses,
Pourquoy li solaus en ardure   1245
Se tient, et la lune en froidure,
Des estoiles et des planettes
Et des .xii. signes les mettes,
Pourquoy Diex par nature assamble
Humeur, sec, froit, et chaut ensamble,   1250
Et pourquoy li .iiii. element
Furent ordené tellement
Qu'adès se tient en bas la terre,
Et l'iaue près de li se serre,
Li feus se trait haut a toute heure,   1255
Et li airs en moien demeure.
Brief des ouevres celestiennes
Et aussi des choses terriennes
Savoit tant qu'elle estoit experte,
D'engin si vive et si aperte,   1260
Que nuls ne le porroit despondre;
Car a chascun savoit respondre
De quanqu'on voloit demander
Si qu'on n'i sceüst qu'amender.

Après Prudence se sëoit   xxxV   1265
Largesse qui riens ne vëoit,
Einsois donnoit a toutes mains,
A l'un plus et a l'autre mains,
Or, argent, destriers, oisiaus, terre,
Et quanqu'elle pooit acquerre,   1270
Contez, duchez, et baronnies,
A heritages et a vies.

1229. A. besongnes--1236. FM Cestoit--1265. A line repeated
twice--1266. A que

56

On the needy that she was able
To give them whatever she had. 1230
But she could never give them so much
That she did not have much more to share.

Afterward Honesty sweetly
Seated herself quite politely,
She who was adorned in great nobility 1235
With the mantle of simplicity.
For she was proper, beyond any reproach,
In her heart, her body, her hand, her mouth.

The ninth was Prudence:
In her heart she carried Wisdom, 1240
And so closely did she guard it
That she was all aflame with love.
She knew well the explanation for the heavenly bodies
Which are suspended within the firmament,
Why the sun endures 1245
In conflagration, and the moon in freezing,
All about the stars and the planets
And the limits of the twelve signs;
Why God through Nature should mix
Moist, dry, cold, and hot together 1250
And why the four elements
Were ordered in such a fashion
That the earth always stays below
And the water clings quite close to it,
The fire rises up high at all times, 1255
And the air remains in between.
In short, of celestial workings
And also of earthly matters
She knew so much that she was an expert,
So quick and so able in her skill 1260
That no one could explain it:
For she could answer everyone
About whatever he might wish to ask
So that no one could add a word to it.

Afterward Prudence seated herself 1265
Near Generosity, who sees nothing,
But rather gives with both her hands,
More to one and less to another,
Gold, silver, chargers, hunting birds, estates,
And whatever else she might acquire, 1270
Counties, duchies, and baronetcies,
In perpetuity and for life.

57

De tout ce riens ne retenoit,
Fors l'onneur. Ad ce se tenoit;
Noblesse li avoit apris.   1275
Et avec ce, dont miex la pris,
Elle reprenoit Advarice
Comme de tout le pieur vice.
L'autre, dont pas ne me vueil taire,
Estoit Doubtance de meffaire,   1280
Qui tant se doubtoit de mesprendre
Qu'a peinne pooit elle entendre
A riens, fors estre sus sa garde.
En tous ses fais estoit couarde;
Car Honte et Päour la gardoient,   1285
Qui en tous lieus l'acompaingnoient.

La dousieme estoit Souffissance
Qui de trés humble pacience
Estoit richement äournée
Et abondanment säoulée   1290
Et pleinne de tous biens terriens.
Elle n'avoit besong de riens,
Ne li failloit chose nesune;
Hors estoit des mains de Fortune
Et de son perilleus dangier.   1295
De po se paissoit au mengier,
Car plus refaite estoit d'un ouef
Que ne fust un autre d'un buef.
Tant par estoit bonne eüreuse
Et parfaitement vertueuse;   1300
Encor est et toudis sera,
Tant com li mondes durera;
Que c'est, a droit considerer,
Li biens qu'on doit plus desirer.

Mais aussi com pluseurs rivieres   1305
Arrousent, et pluseurs lumieres
Radient et leur clarté rendent
En tous lieus ou elles s'estendent,
Ces .xii. nobles damoiselles
Qui de tous biens furent ancelles,   1310
Chascune selonc sa nature,
En meurs, en maintieng, en figure,
Embelissoient ceste dame
De cuer, de corps, d'onneur, et d'ame.
Car tant estoit d'elles parée,   1315
Arrousée et enluminée,
Que chascune l'embelissoit

1287. Other MSS dousisme--1296. FMBDE passoit--1302. Other
MSS siecles--1307. A leurs

58

Of all this she retains nothing,
Except what honor there is. She keeps to this;
Nobility has taught her to do so.   1275
And even more, wherefore the greater her worth,
She accuses Avarice
Of being the worst vice of all.
The next, about whom I will not be silent,
Was Fear of misdoing,   1280
Who was so afraid of error
That she could scarcely attend
To any matter, except to be on her guard.
She was such a coward in all she did;
But Shame and Fear protected her,   1285
And they accompanied her wherever she went.

The twelfth was Sufficiency,
Who with rather humble patience
Was richly turned out,
And gorged to overflowing,   1290
And full of all earthly goods.
She needed nothing.
For there was no thing she lacked;
She was beyond the grasp of Fortune
And her most fearsome domination.   1295
She ate little at her meal,
For she was more filled by an egg
Than another might be by a cow.
She was as happy as could be
And perfect in her virtue;   1300
She still is and always will be,
As long as the world endures;
For this is, to judge rightly,
The good which one should desire most.

But just as many rivers   1305
Give water, and many lights
Glow and send out their brightness
To all the places they can reach,
These twelve noble damsels,
Who were the servants of all goods,   1310
Each one according to her nature,
In customs, in manner, in appearance,
Embellished this lady's
Heart, body, honor, and soul.
For she was so well provided for by them,   1315
So well nurtured and illumined,
Because each improved her

De quanque de li bel issoit,
Et chascune la repartoit
De la vertu qu'elle portoit.   1320
Et encor des biens de nature
Avoit la noble creature:
Gente maniere, loiauté,
Faitis port, debonnaireté,
Grace, douceur, et courtoisie,   1325
Dont elle estoit moult embellie.
Mais sa souvereinne bonté
De trop long passoit sa biauté.

Quant je la vi si hautement
Assise, et si trés noblement   1330
De grans richesses acesmée,
Et si servie et honnourée
Chierement de tous et de toutes,
Dedens mon cuer venirent doubtes
Qui y entrerent par folie   1335
Et par droite merencolie.
Car j'estoie trop esbahis
Et aussi com tous estahis
Et d'erreur telement temptes,
Que je cuiday estre enchantes.   1340
Mais en si fait amusement
Ne demourai pas longuement;
Car j'usai dou conseil d'Avis
Qui fist retourner mon avis
Justement par devers Raison,   xxxiR   1345
Qui est tout adès en saison
Des loiaus cuers remettre a point
Qui sont issu hors de leur point.
Adont Raison me resgarda
Si que depuis en sa garde a   1350
Mon cuer, mon sens, et mon penser,
Pour resister et pour tenser
Aus fausses cogitations
Et oster les temptations
Qui cuidoient avoir victoire   1355
A moy faire faussement croire.

Or fui hors de celle pensée.
Mais la dame bien apensée
Moult sagement m'araisonna,
Et en parlant scens me donna   1360
De respondre après son parler;
S'en sceus miex et plus biau parler.

1340. A two illegibile lettres between estre and enchantes--
1341. F annuisement--1362. AF Sen   Other MSS Se

60

With whatever good she had,
And each shared with her
That virtue which she bore.   1320
And the noble creature in addition
Possessed the endowments of nature,
A gentle way, loyalty,
A handsome carriage, good breeding,
Grace, sweetness, and courtesy,   1325
By which she was much improved.
But her sovereign goodness
Surpassed her beauty by a great deal.

When I saw her so highly
Enthroned, and so very nobly   1330
Adorned with great riches,
And served and honored
So affectionately by all men and women,
My heart was filled with doubts
Which made their way there through my foolishness   1335
And through genuine melancholy.
For I was much taken aback
And also struck completely dumb,
At the same time so tempted by error
That I believed I had been bewitched.   1340
But in this state of bemusement
I did not remain for very long,
For I made use of the counsel of Discretion,
Who made my attention return
In the proper way through Reason,   1345
Who is always ready at the proper moment
To bring true hearts back to themselves,
Those who have wandered off too far.
Just then Reason took charge of me
So that afterward in her keeping she had   1350
My heart, my senses, and my thoughts,
And thus they could resist
And struggle against false ideas,
And expel the temptations
Which thought to have the victory   1355
Of making me think falsely.

Finally I got beyond this state of mind.
And the lady, her thoughts well considered,
Quite wisely addressed me
And in her speech gave me the inspiration   1360
To respond after she had talked;
In this way I could speak better and more effectively.

61

Se me dist: "Guillaume, biau sire,
Au primes fust il temps de dire
Ce que sus les champs avons dit.   1365
S'en rafreschissons nostre dit,
Present ces .xii. damoiselles
Qui sont sages, bonnes, et belles,
Et pluseurs gens qui y seront:
Volentiers nous escouteront."   1370

GUILLAUME

Je ne fis pas longue demeure.
Einsois m'agenoillay en l'eure.
Et humblement li respondi:
"Ma chiere dame, tant vous di:
Pleüst a Dieu de paradis   1375
Que cils qui doit oïr nos dis
Fust ci endroit presentement,
Li bons rois qui si sagement
Saveroit oïr et entendre,
Faire a point, et puis raison rendre,   1380
Quant il averoit escouté
Ce qu'on li averoit compté;
Bien saveroit examiner
Et encor miex determiner.
Et si croy bien qu'il jugeroit   1385
Selonc les parlers qu'il orroit.
Et non pour quant, puisqu'il vous plait,
Bien en poez dire hors plait,
En supposant sans prejudice.
Et je qui point n'i pens malice   1390
Volentiers vous escouteray,
Et, se bon m'est, j'en parleray."

LA DAME

"Guillaume, moult bel respondez.
Mais .i. bien petit m'entendes.
Levez vous, car il plaist a nous   1395
Que plus ne parlez a genous
Et se plus ci après parlez,
Parlez einsi, com vous volez,
Ou en sëant, ou en estant,
Car il nous souffist bien a tant."   1400

GUILLAUME

Lors me levay hastivement
Pour faire son commandement,

1363. FMBDE dit--1364. Other MSS Or prime--1368. A belle--1372.
AB agelongnai--1395. A Levez vous yeus il

62

THE LADY

And she said to me, "Guillaume, fair sir,
In the beginning it was the time to discuss
What we did out in the country.   1365
But let's rehearse our argument
In the presence of these twelve damsels,
Who are wise, good, and beautiful,
And also for these many good people here:
They will listen to us willingly."   1370

GUILLAUME

I did not hesitate at all,
But straightaway kneeled down
And humbly answered her:
"My dear lady, I've already said enough to you.
May it please God in paradise   1375
That the man who should hear our deliberations
Might be here soon,
The good king who so wisely
Would know to listen and attend,
To do what's right, and then render an opinion,   1380
After he has heard
What will be related to him;
He will know well how to consider it all
And then even better to make a determination.
And so I believe strongly that he will judge   1385
According to the testimony he will hear.
Yet nevertheless, since it pleases you,
You can certainly say something outside the debate,
Making suppositions without any prejudice.
And I, who intend no malice in the matter,   1390
Will listen willingly to you,
And, if it strikes me as good, I'll reply in turn."

THE LADY

"Guillaume, you answer quite eloquently.
But listen to me just a little.
Get up now, for it pleases us   1395
That you not speak any more on your knees.
And if you have something else to say,
Speak whichever way you please,
Either seated or standing,
For this much is all we require."   1400

GUILLAUME

At this I got up quickly
To carry out her wish,

Quant elle ot sa parole dite;
Et puis tout droit a l'opposite
De li m'en alai assëoir,   1405
Pour li en la face vëoir.
Car qui voit personne en la face
Qui de parler doit avoir grace,
Le parler trop miex en entent
A quel fin sa parole tent.   1410
Lors prist la dame une maniere
Able, diligent, et maniere
De parler par si bel devis
Qu'il estoit a chascun avis
Qu'elle veïst tout en escript   1415
Ce qu'elle disoit et descript.
Dont miex diter nuls ne porroit.
Nès que ses parlers atiroit.
Elle ordena son parlement
Dès le premier commancement,   1420
Qu'elle m'avoit envoié querre,   xxxiV
Et puis secondement requerre,
Et comment j'alai devers li,
Et comment elle m'assailli
De parole cusensonneuse.   1425
Et comment elle fu crueuse
De moy rudement ramposner
Pour moy seulement agoner
Et en merencolie mettre,
Dont bel se savoit entremettre.   1430
Que vous iroie je comptant?
Elle y mist de biaus parlers tant
Qu'elle mena l'entention
Dou fait a declaration,
De point en point, de tire a tire.   1435
Si bien qu'il n'i ot que redire.
Par quoy les damoiselles toutes
Furent tantost, sans nulles doubtes,
Dou fait sages et avisées
Et entierement enfourmées   1440
De quanqu'on avoit recordé
Dessus les chams et acordé.

Après ces paroles moustrées,
Bien dites et bien ordenées,
Eus tantos le cuer esjoÿ,   1445
Car tant escoutay que j'oÿ
Chevaus venir et gens debatre;
Dont en l'eure se vint embatre

1410. A La--1416. AFD Et--1421. A mavoit written twice
1426. FM fust--1445. FBE Eus

64

Just as soon as she had spoken her mind;
And then straight to the opposite side
From her I went to sit,   1405
So that I could look her in the face.
For whoever looks a person in the face,
When that one's desirous of finding favor in his speech,
He'll hear much better what's said,
To whatever end the other's words are directed.   1410
Then the lady assumed a manner
Capable, attentive, also a way of
Speaking so pleasingly
It was everyone's view
That she was looking at in writing   1415
What she spoke and related,
For no one could speak better,
Even if he drew up his speech in advance.
She organized her discussion,
Starting from the very beginning   1420
When she had ,sent to have me searched out
And then, the second time, fetched,
And how I had gone to her, proceeding to
How she had attacked me
With angry words,   1425
And how she had been cruel,
Reproaching me roughly,
Only to make me squirm
And sink me into melancholy,
Which she knew quite handily how to do.   1430
Should I go on telling you about it?
She expended so much fine talk on this
That she brought out the facts
Of the matter fully,
Point by point, in orderly succession,   1435
So competently that there was no need to repeat them.
And thus all the damsels
Were quickly, and without any uncertainty,
Made knowledgeable and enlightened about the case,
Entirely informed   1440
About all that had been discussed
And agreed to below in the fields.

After these words had been made public,
Well spoken and organized,
My heart was suddenly made joyful   1445
Because while listening I heard
Horses come up and people talking;
At that very hour the good and worthy king

Devers nous cils bons rois de pris
Que nous aviens a juge pris.   1450
Et la dame qui resgardoit,
Devers l'uis et ne s'en gardoit,
Le vit et congnut a l'entrée;
Se s'est tantost en piez levée;
S'ala a l'encontre de lui,   1455
Et se n'i atendi nelui.
Quant il la vit, il s'avansa
Et .i. bien petit l'embrassa,
Et elle lui moult humblement,
En saluant courtoisement,   1460
Liement, et a bonne chiere.
Et il li dist: "Ma dame chiere,
Moult me poise quant sa venistes.
Pour quel cause ne vous tenistes
En vostre siege toute coie?"   1465
"Trés chiers sires, se Diex me voie,
Jamais ne l'eüsse einsi fait,
Car trop pensasse avoir meffait.
Car on dit--et c'est chose voire
Qu'il est assez legier a croire--   1470
Qu'entre les grans et les meneurs
A tous seigneurs toutes honneurs.
Mais laissons ces parlers ester;
Petit y devons arrester,
S'alons en cest siege sëoir.   1475
La me vorrai je pourvëoir
De vous compter une merveille,
D'autres merveilles nom pareille.
Alez devant; j'iray après.
De vous me tenray assez près."   1480
"Par Dieu, ma dame, no ferai.
Aussi tost com j'y monterai,
Tout d'encoste moy monterez.
Ja a ce point ne me menrez
Qu'embedeus n'en alons ensamble.   1485
Encor fais je trop, ce me samble."
De ce point si bien s'acorderent,
Si qu'ensamble tous .ii. monterent.
Et quant il furent haut monté,
Encor, par grant humilité,   1490
D'assëoir moult se debatirent.
Toutes voies il se seïrent.
Et quant il furent la assis,
La dame dist de sens rassis:
"Sire, entendez un bien petit.   1495

1450. F cui--1463. A venites--1479. A je iray; other MSS jiray
1493. A rassis

Had come--for pleasure--into our presence,
He whom we had chosen for a judge.   1450
And the lady who had been looking
Toward the door and hadn't stopped,
Saw and recognized him as he entered;
And then at once she got to her feet
And went toward him,   1455
Waiting for no one.
When he saw her, he moved forward
And embraced her lightly,
And she him in a modest way,
While saluting courteously,   1460
Joyfully, and with a pleasant look.
And he said to her: "My dear lady,
It grieves me greatly that you came forward.
Why did you not remain
Quite demurely in your seat?"   1465
"Very dear sir, so God guide me,
Never should I have done so,
Since I think very much to have erred.
For it is said--and it's something true
Which is easy enough to believe--   1470
That considering the great and the lesser,
All honor should go to every noble lord.
But let's drop the matter;
We ought delay little over it.
Let us rather take our seats on the dais.   1475
There I'd like to see about
Recounting to you an extraordinary thing,
Something quite unlike other wonders.
Go on ahead; I'll follow after,
Keeping quite close to you."   1480
"By God, madam, I'll not do it.
At the very moment I go up
You'll ascend right by me.
You'll never make me agree
That we shouldn't proceed side by side.   1485
I've already been too forward, I think."
On this point they easily concurred
And then mounted up together.
And when they had ascended,
Again through great humility,   1490
They argued much about the seating arrangements.
But finally they did sit down,
And when they were seated,
The lady spoke, her thoughts composed:
"Sir, listen for just a moment,   1495

Et se prenez vostre apetit
A diligenment escouter
Ce que je vous vorray compter.
Vez la Guillaume de Machaut.
C'est uns homs a cui il ne chaut   1500
A tort out a droit soustenir;   xxxiiR
Tout aussi chier s'a il tenir
Vers le tort comme vers le droit,
Si com vous orrez orendroit.
En un debat sommes entré   1505
Dont nous devons de fait outré,
Sire, devant vous plaidïer,
Mais qu'il ne vous doie anuier.
Moy bien meüe et il meüs,
Pour juges estes esleüs;   1510
Dont c'est pour nous belle avenue,
Biau sire, de vostre venue.
Et vous en estes eüreus,
Se de riens estes amoureus.
Car de cause avons nostre plait   1515
Fourmé qui aus amoureus plaist
C'est d'amors, d'amant, et d'amie,
Et de leur noble signourie.
Guillaumes dit, tient, et afferme
Pour vray et que c'est chose ferme   1520
Quant homs qui ha tout son cuer mis
En dame, tant qu'il est amis
Et celle s'amour li ottrie,
Si qu'il la tient pour vraie amie,
Puis est de lui si esprouvée   1525
Qu'il la trueve fausse prouvée,
Qu'il a de ce plus de grieté
Qu'une dame qui loyauté
En son vray ami trouvera;
Et elle aussi tant l'amera   1530
Comme dame puet homme amer,
Entierement, sans point d'amer.
Or avenra il que la mort,
Qui soutilment sus la gent mort,
Torra a son ami la vie.   1535
Et quant elle scet qu'il devie,
Ou qu'il est dou tout devïez,
Il est a la mort marïez,
Lors est finée leur querelle,
Aroit cils aussi grief com celle?   1540
Nennil! Il ne puet avenir;
Cils poins ne se puet soustenir.

1516. A plest

68

And take some pleasure
In attending diligently to
What I wish to say.
You see there Guillaume de Machaut.
He's a man who doesn't concern himself   1500
With upholding either wrong or right;
In fact he'd just as soon sustain
The wrong as the right,
As you will presently hear.
We have entered into a debate   1505
Over an outrageous matter, one that we should,
Sir, plead before you,
If it would not annoy you.
By his desire and my own,
You were chosen as judge;   1510
And so for us this is a happy chance,
Fair sir, that you have arrived here.
And this affair will bring you pleasure
If you have any interest in love.
For our disagreement concerns   1515
An issue that will please the romantically inclined;
It's about love, the lover, and the beloved,
And of their noble regulation.
Guillaume says, holds, and affirms
As a true and unchallengeable fact,   1520
That when a man has given all his heart
To a lady, so intently that he becomes a lover
And she grants him her love,
In such a fashion that he thinks her a true beloved,
But then it happens to him   1525
That he finds her proven false,
He has more grief for this reason
Than a lady who discovers
Faithfulness in her true lover;
And she in turn loves him as much   1530
As a lady can love any man,
Completely, with no bitterness at all.
But then it happens that death,
Which stealthily stings the human race,
Takes the life from her lover.   1535
And when she learns that he has passed away,
That he has been deprived of everything,
That he is bonded to death,
That their affair is finished,
Would that first man grieve as much as this woman?   1540
Not at all! It couldn't happen;
This opinion cannot be defended.

Dont j'ay fait, et fais, et vueil faire
Protestation dou contraire.
C'est auques nostres plaidīez.   1545
Pour ce volons que vous soiez
Juges; si en ordonnerez
Selonc le plait que vous orrez."

                    LE JUGE

"Je vous respons, ma chiere dame,
Par la foy que doy Dieu et m'ame,   1550
Selonc la mienne entention,
Que d'estre en la perfection
De juge est moult noble chose,
Voire qui entrepenre l'ose
Si hautement comme en Amours.   1555
Mais pour les trés douces clamours
Qui y sont, j'entrepren l'office,
Sans mal penser et sans malice.
Se j'ay petit sens, j'apenray
Parmi les parlers que j'orray;   1560
Et s'estre puis bien consilliez,
Je ne seroie pas si liez
D'avoir acquis .v^c mars d'or.
Et pour tant vous dis je desor,
Chiere dame, que j'esliray   1565
Tel conseil, comme je vorray,
De vostre belle compaingnie
Qui a vous est acompaingnie,
Car a .i. bon juge apartient
Qui jugemens en sa part tient   1570
Qu'il ait conseil en tous endrois.
Prenons, qu'il soit ou non soit drois.
Se vous requier je qu'on le face,
Soit par courtoisie ou par grace.
Et d'autre part, quoy que nuls die,   1575
Bons drois a bon mestier d'aīe
Par quoy grace ait adès son cours
Pour aidier droit en toutes cours.

                    LA DAME

"Biau sire, de vostre recort,   xxxiiV
Que ce soit drois, bien m'i acort.   1580
Or prenez cui que vous volez,
Par quoy de riens ne vous dolez."

                    LE JUGE

"Ma dame, je pren Congnoissance

1545. F vostre--1560. A je orray--1564. A omits tant--1573. A
je vous requier je

                          70

And so I've made, and make, and wish to make
A protest to the contrary.
That's the issue our debate concerns.   1545
And we'd like you to be
The judge; thus you would decide this question
According to the disputation you'd hear."

THE JUDGE

"I'll answer you, my dear lady,
By the faith I owe God and my own soul   1550
Just as I see it,
Namely that to be in the privileged place
Of the judge is a very noble thing,
Especially for someone who risks so much
As to take on deciding a question of love.   1555
But because the petitions made here have
Greatly pleased me, I will undertake the office
Without any evil thoughts or malice.
With just a little understanding, I'll learn
From the speeches I'll hear;   1560
And if I can be well counseled,
I'll be much happier than if someone
Gave me five hundred marks of gold.
Moreover, dear lady, I'll make it clear to you
At this point that I'll pick   1565
Whatever advisors I desire
From your splendid entourage,
Which has accompanied you.
Truly it's fitting for a competent judge
Weighing a decision   1570
To take counsel from all sides.
Let us proceed then, and find out if your complaint's a just one.
I request that everything proceed
With courtesy and grace.
Furthermore, despite anyone's opinion,   1575
Real justice needs the good offices of assistance,
So that grace may always have full rein
And thus uphold the right in every court of law."

THE LADY

"Fair sir, concerning your request,
I certainly agree that it's correct.   1580
Choose now whomever you wish,
And no one will oppose you."

THE JUDGE

"My lady, I pick Understanding,

71

Qui est de bon conseil sustance;
Avecques li sera Avis   1585
Li quels n'i sera pas envis,
Pour ce que c'est sa bonne amie;
Volentiers li tient compaingnie.
Et se me plaist, qu'aussi y soit
Raison qui nelui ne deçoit,   1590
Eins est adès en sa partie
De bon conseil apareillie.
Si entendra les parlemens
Pour raporter aus jugemens.
La me sara bien consillier;   1595
Pas ne m'en faurra resveillier.
Avecques li sera Mesure;
Quar qui jugemens ne mesure,
Il ne puelent venir a point
Afin qu'il soient en bon point   1600
Pour les parties delivrer
Et chascune son droit livrer."
La dame bien s'i acorda
Et hautement li recorda:
"Biau sire, bien avez ouvré   1605
D'avoir bon conseil recouvré."

                    LE JUGE

"C'est bon pour moy, ma dame gente;
Dont a mon cuer bien entalente
Que j'en soie einsi bien garnis;
Qui n'est garnis, il est honnis.   1610
Juges sui par commun acort
Espéciaument d'un descort
Qui est ci entre .ii. parties,
Pour atendre droit de parties.
Or est la court garnie et pleinne;   1615
Se puet on bien par voie pleinne,
Ce m'est avis, aler avant.
Dame, vous parlerez devant,
Se fourmerez vostre demande,
Nom pas pour ce que je demande   1620
Que li fais me soit refourmez,
Car j'en suis assez enfourmez;
Mais d'aucuns membres dou procès
Me moustreroient les excès
Qui vous en font doloir et pleindre   1625
Et aussi pour Guillaume ateindre
En son tort, se tort doit avoir;
Autrement ne le puis savoir."

1597. All MSS except B Avec--1598. Other MSS Car--1600. A qui
1617. FBDE Se

                    72

Who is the very substance of good counsel;
Discretion will be at her side,   1585
And he'll not protest at all
Because he's her faithful friend.
Willingly he'll go along.
And I should also be pleased for Reason
To be present, she who deceives no one,   1590
But instead is always for her part
Ready with good advice.
So she'll listen to the testimony
In order to relate it to the judgment.
She'll advise me well about this task;   1595
I'll never need to refresh my mind about what's been said.
Moderation will stand by her;
For whoever does not moderate his judgment
Cannot proceed in the proper and correct fashion,
Coming to the point   1600
Where he can release the parties
And deliver justice to each."
The lady heartily agreed with this
And--quite seriously--said to him:
"Fair sir, you've done well   1605
To obtain such counsel."

THE JUDGE

"It's to my benefit, my noble lady;
For I desire quite fervently in my heart
To have the proper kind of assistance;
For the man who lacks it is shamed.   1610
By common agreement I am now the judge
In the special case of the dispute
That divides these two parties
And awaits a fair decision.
The court is now complete and ready;   1615
And so we may proceed
Without more ado, so it seems to me.
Lady, you will speak first,
And formulate the issue,
Not because I ask   1620
That the details of the case be recounted to me,
For I am already quite adequately informed;
But rather because the parties to this trial
Should explain to me what troubles them
And makes them sorrow and complain,   1625
And also to convince Guillaume
Of his wrongdoing, if his should be the blame;
Otherwise, I'll not be able to recognize it."

"Sire, ceste raison me plait.
Des qu'entamé en avons plait,   1630
Mon fait moustrerai par figure
Selonc les ouevres de Nature,
Tout pour Guillaume qui se tort
De verité dont il ha tort.
Vous savez que la turterelle,   1635
Qui est faitice, gente, et belle,
Cointe, gaie, douce, et jolie
Tant com ses males est en vie,
Et s'il avient qu'elle le pert
Par mort, on scet tout en appert   1640
Que jamais joie n'avera,
Et par signes le moustrera.
Tant est li siens cuers pleins d'ardeur,
Jamais ne serra sus verdeur;
Eins quiert tout adès obscurtez,   1645
Divers lieus et pleins de durtez,
Aubres sès, verseinnes, et trieges;
En tel lieus est souvent ses sieges,
Quant elle se vuet reposer.
Autrement ne vuet disposer   1650
Son cuer qu'en vie dolereuse,
Tant est de son male grieteuse.
Tout autel d'une dame di ge
Qui est rendue a Amours lige:
Quant elle ha son amy perdu   1655
Par mort, le cuer si esperdu   xxxiiiR
Ha que jamais n'avera joie,
Eins quiert lieu, temps, et gens, et voie,
Ou il ait tout adès tristece,
Humble habit en lieu de richesse   1660
Tenebres en lieu de clarté,
Et en lieu de joliveté
Pour porter chapelès de flours
Ist de son chief larmes et plours;
Et s'elle quiert aucun repos,   1665
Il est pris en humble propos.
Einsi la dame se maintient
Que le dueil de son amy tient,
En cas qu'elle soit vraie amie.
Or dirai de l'autre partie.   1670

Quant la secoingne se fourfait,
Et ses males en scet le fait,
Je croy bien que moult s'en aïre

1640. FMBDE ou soit--1647. A rieges

74

THE LADY

"Sir, this plan pleases me.
Since we have begun this discussion,   1630
I will formulate my complaint in a rhetorical figure
That draws on the works of Nature,
And this is for the sake of Guillaume, who has turned
Away from the truth, and therefore erred.
You know the turtle dove,   1635
Which is pretty, noble, and handsome,
Quiet, gay, sweet, and attractive
While her mate is alive,
But if it happens that she loses him
Through death, it's readily apparent   1640
That she'll never find joy,
For she demonstrates this through signs.
Her heart is so filled with passionate burning
That she'll never perch on greenery;
Instead she always seeks out darkness,   1645
Strange places full of misery,
Dead trees, fallow fields, and crossroads;
Her perch is often in such places
Whenever she wishes to rest.
She will not allow herself anything but   1650
A sorrowful life,
She is so grief-stricken for her mate.
It is just the same, I say, for a lady
Who has sworn fealty to Love;
When she's lost her lover   1655
Through death, her heart becomes
So distressed that she'll never find joy,
But rather she'll seek out places, times, people, and directions
Where there is always total sadness;
She chooses a simple habit instead of finery,   1660
Shadows instead of sunlight;
And in place of the gaiety that comes
From wearing chaplets of flowers,
Weeping and tears flow from her face;
And if she looks for any relief at all,   1665
She does it modestly;
Thus the lady conducts herself
Who remains in mourning for her lover,
That is, when she is a true beloved.
Now I'll speak to a second point.   1670

When the swan is unfaithful,
And her mate learns the facts of the matter,
I'm convinced he's greatly upset by it,

75

Et qu'il en ait au cuer grant ire;
Mais trouver en puet aligence   1675
En ce qu'il en atent veingance.
Car il s'en va tantost en serche;
Par les nis des oisiaus reverche
A ceuls qui sont de sa samblance,
Tant qu'il en ha grant habondance;   1680
Puis entour son nif les assamble,
Et quant il sont la tuit ensamble,
Il y tiennent .i. grant concire,
Puis mettent celui a martire
De mort qui l'a, ce dit, forfaite;   1685
La est devourée et deffaite.
Or ha cils ses maus alegiés
Qui en ce point en est vengiés.
Tout autel di je que li homs
Doit estre fiers com uns lions   1690
Contre aucun tort, s'il li est fais.
Et cils puet trouver moult de fais
Aus quels il se puet encliner
Pour son mal faire terminer,
Par pluseurs manieres de tours.   1695
Mais la dame n'a nuls recours
Es quels elle se puist garir,
Qui son amy verra morir.
Dont elle sent pour .i. mal cent
Que cils autres amans ne sent.   1700
Guillaume, après moy respondes;
Se tort avez, si l'amendez."

                    GUILLAUME

Après ces raisons me dressay
Et mes paroles adressay
Au juge qui bien entendi   1705
Ce qu'elle ot dit et que je di.
Et je li dis: "Sire, sans faille
Ma dame a bien, comment qu'il aille,
Son fait moustré, et sagement,
Et de soutil entendement   1710
Bien baillié par vives raisons,
Pour fourmer ses comparisons
Bien faites et bien devisées
Et si justement exposées
Que qui amender y vorroit,   1715
Je croy moult bien qu'on ne porroit.
Et ce qu'elle en a devisé,
Vous l'avez trés bien avisé,

1713. A divisees

                    76

And feels great anger in his heart;
But he can find relief   1675
Because he can expect vengeance.
And so he immediately starts searching;
Through the bird nests he seeks out
Those of his own kind,
Until he finds a multitude of them;   1680
Then he assembles them around his own nest,
And when he has them all together,
They hold a great council,
And afterward make that one suffer
Death who, so they say, has sinned against him;   1685
There she's undone and devoured.
Now this one's lightened the burden of his pain
When he's revenged in this way.
Similarly, I say that a man
Must be as fierce as a lion   1690
In the face of any wrong done to him.
And he could think of many ways
To take action
In order to end his trouble,
Many different tricks to try.   1695
But that lady has no recourse at all,
Nothing that would heal her pain,
She who has witnessed her lover die.
And she suffers a hundred times more misery
Than that other lover.   1700
Guillaume, now respond to this;
If you are wrong, then make amends."

GUILLAUME

After this speech, I drew myself up
And addressed my words
To the judge, who was listening intently   1705
To what she had said and I was saying.
And I said to him: "Sire, without doubt
My lady, whatever the final outcome,
Has stated her case wisely and well,
And with a subtle understanding   1710
Well supplied with lively arguments,
In order to establish her comparisons,
Which are well-developed and nicely thought out,
And so thoroughly expounded
That whoever wished to say more (or better)   1715
Would find it impossible, I believe.
And what she has recounted
You have well remarked,

Oÿ, senti, et entendu.
Car de sa bouche est descendu   1720
En vostre cuer par escouter;
Si ne le faut pas repeter.
Et si croy bien certeinnement
Que c'est de droit vray sentement,
Ce qu'elle en a yci compté,   1725
Gardant sa grace et sa bonté,
Sans point de vainne entention.
Et j'ay une autre oppinion
Qu'elle n'a; s'en dirai m'entente,
S'il li plaist et il vous talente,   1730
Nom pas pour le sien fait punir,
Mais pour ma cause soustenir.
On puet bien sa cause prisier,
Sans autrui fait apetisier."

                        LE JUGE

"Guillaume, ne vueil contredire   1735
Dites ce qu'il vous plaist a dire,
Hastivement ou a loisir;
Ouvrez en a vostre plaisir.
Je vueil bien oïr et entendre,
Et s'ay assez loisir d'atendre."   1740

                      GUILLAUME

"Grant merci, sire! Je diray,
Et croy que point n'en mentiray.
Je vous di que la forfaiture
De dame est si aspre and si dure
En cuer d'amant, et si perverse,   1745
Que, quant elle y est bien aherse,
Jamais jour ne s'en partira.
Or ne scet cils quel part ira
Pour querir son aligement;
Se prendre en voloit vengement   1750
Par mort, et bien le peüst faire,
Il trouveroit tout son contraire
En la fourme de grant folour,
En l'attrait de toute dolour,
Un feu pour toute ardeur ateindre,   1755
Un yaue pour douceur esteindre,
Norrissemens de tous meschies;
Car dou faire seroit pechies.
Et pechiez qui en cuer remort
Est uns commencemens de mort,   1760
De mort qu'on claimme mortel vie.

1723. A certeinnemet--1734. A lacks heading Le Juge--1742.
AME nen; other MSS ne--1752. AFME Y

                          78

Heard, been sympathetic to, and comprehended.
For it has made its way from her mouth   1720
Into your heart as you listened;
And so there's no need to repeat.
Furthermore I believe without question
That this is the result of genuine feeling,
What she has brought up here,   1725
Saving her grace and her goodness,
Devoid of any vain intention.
And I hold to an opinion different
From hers; and I'll state my reasons why,
If it should please and interest you,   1730
Not in order to undermine her viewpoint,
But rather to make my own case.
One can very well value her side
Without belittling a contrary position."

THE JUDGE

"Guillaume, I certainly won't forbid you.   1735
Say whatever you want to say,
Quickly or deliberately;
Work at this as you will.
I would very much like to listen and understand,
And I have the leisure to attend."   1740

GUILLAUME

"Many thanks, sire! I will speak,
And I believe that I'll not say anything false.
I tell you that the unfaithfulness
Of a woman is so bitter and burdensome
To the lover's heart, and such an unnatural thing,   1745
That, when the fact of it has taken firm hold,
It will never release him even for a day.
Now that man knows not where to go
In order to find relief:
If he wishes to revenge himself   1750
Through murder, and is able to accomplish it,
He would be firmly opposed
By the prospect of great folly,
And the power of encompassing grief,
Finding there a fire to afflict all passion,   1755
A water to extinguish sweetness,
Some nourishment for every ill;
Because to kill would be a sin.
And a sin which tortures the heart
Is the beginning of death,   1760
The death of what one calls mortal life.

79

Car qui languist, il ne vit mie.
En mon fait que ci vous present
Maintenant, en vostre present,
Ha plus de griés et plus d'ardure   1765
Qu'en l'autre fait, et trop plus dure.
Dont je vous requier orendroit
Sus ce point ci que j'aie droit."

ATTEMPRANCE

Adont se leva Attemprance
Qui tenoit par la main Souffrance.   1770
Si parla attempréement
En disant: "Guillaume, comment
Droit pour vous demander osastes?
Je me merveil que vous pensastes,
Quant vous en fustes si hastis.   1775
Ou vostres scens est trop petis,
Ou outrecuidiers vous demeinne.
Ne savez vous pas bien qui mainne
Le droit quant parties y tendent
Qui le desirent et attendent?   1780
Je vueil moult bien que vous sachiez
Que Raisons en est li drois chies
Et avec li sa compaingnie;
Chascune y a bonne partie
D'entre nous damoiselles toutes.   1785
De ce ne faites nulles doubtes,
Que drois ne se puet delivrer,
Se toutes ne sont au livrer,
Afin que fait soit bonnement,
Se cils qui fist les drois ne ment.   1790
Je meïsmes y ai office
Pour resister a tout malice,
Qui maintes fois le droit ·destourne;
Et je d'office le retourne.
Quant uns bons procès vient en fourme,   1795
Et je perçoy qu'on l'en deffourme,
J'y puis bien tellement ouvrer
Qu'il puet sa fourme recouvrer.
Se trop ya a, j'en puis oster
(Or vueilliez bien ce point noter!)   1800
Et se po y a , j'y puis mettre,
Quant je m'en vueil bien entremettre.
Et se la chose est en bon point,
Je la puis garder en ce point.
C'est d'Attemprance li mestiers,   1805
Toutes fois qu'il en est mestiers.

1773. FBDE vous oser (D aisier) demandastes--1778. A quil
mainne; other MSS qui meinne--1801. A je y

For whoever languishes so will not live long.
In my case, the one I am presenting
To you now, in your presence,
There's more grief and more burning torment   1765
Than in the other, and something much harder to bear.
And so I ask now if,
For this reason, I might claim victory."

TEMPERANCE

At once Temperance got up,
She who was holding Suffering by the hand.   1770
And she spoke with moderation,
Saying: "Guillaume, how
Did you dare ask for the decision on your behalf?
I wonder why you should even consider this
When you've only offered a brief argument.   1775
Either your intelligence is limited
Or overconfidence rules you.
Don't you know who judges
The right when parties argue
Who desire a decision and await it?   1780
Certainly you should be well aware
That Reason is in charge of this,
And along with her, her entourage;
Each of them holds a place of prominence
Among us other damsels.   1785
Do not be in any doubt about this,
Namely that a decision cannot be rendered
If all of these do not do so together,
In order for everything to be done properly,
Providing that he who decides is honest.   1790
I myself have the task
Of resisting any kind of malice,
Something which many times diverts the right;
And by my efforts I put things back on track.
When a proper trial takes shape,   1795
And I perceive that it's going wrong,
I can do what's needed
For it to be put right.
If there's something irrelevant, I can remove it
(Now please note well this point!)   1800
And if something's lacking, I can add it
Whenever I wish to assert myself.
And if everything's just right,
I can make sure it stays that way.
That's what Temperance does   1805
Anytime it's necessary.

Or vueil je dire d'autre chose
Qui contre vostre fait s'oppose.

Vous avez .i. point soustenu
Dont po d'onneur vous est venu,   1810
En ce que ma dame de pris
Avoit seur la segongne pris,
Comment elle est a la mort traite   xxxivR
Quant envers son male est forfaite.
Cuidies vous qu'elle vosist dire   1815
Qu'on meïst la dame a martyre
De la mort, qui se mefferoit
Envers celui qui l'ameroit?
Nennil! Voir, ce seroit folie.
Ne ma dame ne maintient mie   1820
Qu'il la face tuer ne tue;
Mais elle tient qu'il s'esvertue
Encontre les temptations
Des fausses cogitations
Qui porroient en lui venir.   1825
Encor s'el pooit avenir,
Qu'elle fust de bonne mort morte,
Se vaurroit il miex, drois la porte,
Qu'elle demourast toute vive.
Car tant com la personne vive   1830
Qui se mefferoit par folour,
On n'en a peinne, ne dolour,
Grieté, souffrance, ne meschief,
Dont on ne veingne bien a chief.
Quant il sent aucune grieté,   1835
Il doit penser par verité,
Dès qu'il a loiaument servi,
Qu'il ne l'a mie desservi.
C'est une pensée valable,
Pour lui conforter profitable.   1840
Que vous iroie je comptant?
De remedes ya a autant
En amours, com de griés pointures,
Soient aspres, pongnans, ou dures.
Chascune son remede enseingne.   1845
Or en fait bon querir l'enseigne.
Mais une dame qui verra
Que se trés dous amis morra
En cui en nul jour de sa vie
N'ara trouvé que courtoisie,   1850
Estre porra si fort ferue,
Si griefment, et si abatue,

1821. AFMB facent--1836. FBDE pour--1846. A querre

82

But now I want to bring up something else
That contradicts the view you are defending.

You have made a point
That does you little honor,   1810
And it concerns what my worthy lady
Maintained about the swan,
How she is done to death
When she's proved unfaithful to her mate.
Do you believe that my lady meant   1815
That the woman who did wrong
To the man who loves her
Should be made to suffer death?
Not at all! Truly, this would be madness.
Nor does my lady advise in any way   1820
That he should kill her or have her killed;
Instead she maintains that he should struggle
Against the temptations
Of any false' thoughts
Which might come into his mind.   1825
Furthermore, should it happen
That she die naturally,
He would have been better off--being in the right--
If she had remained alive.
For as long as the person lives   1830
Who sins through mad error,
One does not suffer for it, feels no pain,
Grief, hardship, or misfortune
Because the person does not die.
When pain comes upon him,   1835
He must surely think,
Because he has served her faithfully,
That he has not merited this at all.
He should prize such a thought
Because it helps comfort him.   1840
Should I continue with this?
There are as many remedies
In love as wounds of grief,
However bitter, painful, or enduring these might be.
Each one signals its proper remedy;   1845
One would do well to pay this some attention.
But a lady who experiences
The death of her too sweet lover,
A man in whom on no day of her life
Did she find anything but courtesy,   1850
She can be so terribly stricken,
So grievously, and so far beaten down

83

Que jamais n'en porra garir,
Einsois la couvendra morir.
En l'escripture est contenu   1855
Que pluseurs fois est avenu.
S'en compteray .i. petit compte
Qui vous fera avoir grant honte,
Et a ma dame grant honnour,
Et grant clarté a mon signour,   1860
Dont it verra plus clerement
Comment vous errez folement.

Il n'a pas lonc temps qu'il avint
Qu'une grant dame a Paris vint,
S'amena une sienne fille   1865
Qui, sans penser barat ne guille,
Amoit .i. chevalier gentil,
Sage, courtois, gay, et soutil,
Preus aus armes, fort, et puissant,
De toutes graces souffisant.   1870
De lui nouvelles li venirent,
Qui forment au cuer la pongnirent,
Qu'il estoit a .i. tournoy mors.
'Lasse!' dist elle, 'quel remors
Puis avoir de ceste nouvelle!'   1875
A cest mot cheÿ la pucelle
A la terre, toute estendue.
Adont sa mere y est venue
Acourant moult dolentement;
S'en prist a plourer tenrement   1880
Et la fist porter en .i. lit.
La prist elle povre delit;
Car au cuer estoit fort atainte
Et ou viaire pale et tainte
Et si de son corps amatie   1885
Et de ses membres amortie,
Qu'einc puis ne s'en pot soustenir,
Ne des mains nulle riens tenir;
Et n'ot ainc puis tant de victoire
Qu'elle peüst mengier ne boire.   1890
Fusicien furent mandé,
Et la leur fu il demandé
S'elle averoit de la mort garde,   xxxivV
Et que chascuns y prenist garde,
S'on li porroit donner santé,   1895
Et qu'il demandassent planté
Hardiement de leur avoir,
Tant comme il en vorront avoir.

1869. A Preu--1883. Other MSS ateinte--1884. Other MSS tainte
1889. MBDE se--1898. FMBE vorroient

84

That she'll never be able to recover;
Instead she'll die.
It is written down in books   1855
That such a thing has often happened.
And so I will relate a short tale
Which will cause you great shame
And bring my lady much honor,
Nicely enlightening my lord as well,   1860
So that he will see even more clearly
How foolishly you err.

Not long ago it happened
That a great lady came to Paris,
And she brought one of her daughters with her,   1865
Who, without intending any deception or trouble,
Was in love with a noble knight,
A man wise, courteous, happy, and bright,
Skilled with arms, strong and powerful,
Possessing every grace.   1870
Then news came to her about him
Which greatly afflicted her heart,
Namely that he had been killed in a tournament.
'Alas!' she said, 'what remorse
I'll have from such news!'   1875
With this word the young girl
Fell to the earth and lay still.
Quickly her mother went over to her,
Running with great sorrow;
And she began to cry softly   1880
And had her carried to a bed.
There she found little comfort;
For her heart was so terribly afflicted,
And her face so pale and flushed,
Her body so stricken,   1885
And her limbs so paralyzed
That she could hardly stand
Or even hold anything in her hands;
And she could neither drink nor eat
Much that was nourishing.   1890
Physicians were summoned,
And it was asked of them
If she could be saved from death,
And that each should attend
To bringing her back to health,   1895
And that they should demand without any embarrassment
A great deal of what they possessed,
As much as they desired to have.

Et il en peinne s'en meïrent
Et moult volentiers le feïrent   1900
Pour trouver son aligement,
S'il peüssent, diligenment.
Premiers, s'orine resgarderent,
Et puis après si la tasterent;
Li uns après l'autre tastoient   1905
Partout ou taster la devoient,
Les piez, le pous, et puis les temples;
Et puis si moustroient exemples
Des cures qu'il avoient faites
En pluseurs lieus et bien parfaites.   1910
Et que plus d'exemples moustroient,
De tant plus esbahi estoient.
L'orine la jugoit haitie,
Et li tasters ne jugoit mie
Cause froide, ne de chalour,   1915
En quoy il prenissent coulour
D'ou ne de quoy cils maus venoit,
Ne quel remede y couvenoit,
Pour li un po assouagier
Ou dou tout ses maus alegier,   1920
Fors tant que li uns s'avisa
Et sagement le devisa:
'Signeurs, j'ay veü en s'orine
Einssi comme un po de racine
Qu'elle est en l'esperit troublée.   1925
Or nous est la science emblée
De ce point, s'on ne s'en avise.
Et nous savons une devise
Que li bons philosophes dist;
Il afferme, et je croy son dit,   1930
Que les maladies quelconques--
Et qu'autrement il n'avint onques--
Sont curées par leur contraire.
Or ne pöons a ce point traire
De ceste maladie cy   1935
Tant seulement que par un sy.
Car si hastives maladies
Puelent venir de .ii. parties:
C'est assavoir, se Diex me voie,
De grant dueil ou de trop grant joie.   1940
Et cause de joie desire
Qu'on la courresse et qu'on l'aïre,
Et celle de dueil autrement:
Faire couvenra liement,
Present li, ce qu'elle vorra   1945

1913. A Jugent--1918. A il--1924. AE Aussi--1930. A dist
1931. A quelsconques

86

So then these men diligently applied themselves
And quite eagerly attempted   1900
To devise a cure for her,
If they were able to.
First, they looked at her urine,
And then they felt her with their hands.
One after the other they touched her   1905
At the various places where one should,
The feet, the wrists, and then the temples;
And then they discussed examples
Of the various cures they had brought about
And accomplished in many places.   1910
But the more examples they discussed,
The more they were bewildered.
The urine turned out healthy,
And the examination did not reveal
Any trace of coldness or of heat,   1915
So they were bewildered
About the location of the illness and its cause as well,
Knowing not what remedy was appropriate
In order to soothe her somewhat
Or alleviate her ills altogether;   1920
Until finally one of them took stock
And wisely suggested:
'Colleagues, I've discovered in her urine
Something of what's causing this,
Namely that she's troubled in spirit.   1925
Now our science casts little light
On this point, unless one thinks deeply about it.
For we know a saying
Which the good philosopher devised:
He affirms, and I believe well what he says,   1930
That all illnesses whatsoever--
And there are no exceptions--
Are cured by their contraries.
Now we can infer one thing and one thing alone
From this principle   1935
In regard to this particular illness.
For such sudden maladies
Can arise from two emotional states:
That's to say, so God guide me,
From great sorrow or overwhelming joy.   1940
And as a cause joy requires
That she be made angry and irritated,
And sorrow asks for just the opposite:
One should make merry
In her presence, do whatever would please her   1945

Et quanqu'elle comandera,
Et qu'on li ait admenistres,
Pour faire feste, menestrés.
Or couvenra il qu'elle die
Dou quel li vient la maladie,   1950
Pour li donner certein conseil.
Je le lo einsi et conseil.
Se voit li uns tout simplement
Parler a li secretement.'
Seur ce point furent acordans;   1955
Dont li uns li fu demandans
Ce que devant avez oÿ.
Point n'en ot le cuer esjoÿ,
Eins en respondi moult envis,
Et toute voie vis a vis   1960
Pure verité l'en conta,
Si bien que point n'i arresta.
Lors li fist cils une requeste
Au mieus qu'il pot par voie honneste:
'Fille, respondes moy d'un point   1965
Que je vous dirai bien a point:
Vorries vous de ci en avant
Que vous le veïssiez vivant,
Mais que ce fust par tel maniere
Que jamais ne vous moustrast chiere,   1970
Parole, ne samblant d'ami?'
Et elle respondi: 'Aymi!
Sire, se Diex me doint santé,   xxxvR
Que c'est bien de ma volenté
Que volentiers le reverroie   1975
Vivant, et fust par tele voie
Qu'il heüst fait une autre amie,
La quele fust de moy servie,
Mon vivant, jusqu'au deschaucier.
Ne m'en vueilliez plus enchaucier;   1980
Car tous li cuers de dueil me font
Si aigrement et si parfont
Toutes fois que j'en oy parole.
Si ne vueiľ plus qu'on m'en parole.'
Après ce mot, cils s'en depart   1985
Et s'en ala de celle part
Ou cil estient qui l'atendoient,
Qui desiroient et tendoient,
Savoir quel fin celle feroit.
Et il leur dist qu'elle morroit: 1990
'Je n'i puis vëoir nul retour.
Ses cuers est fermez en la tour

1948. A. menestrels--1950. Other MSS sa--1953. A voist
1983. A os

88

And whatever she asks for,
And also minstrels should be summoned
To entertain her and make her laugh.
At the moment, then, she must reveal
The cause of her illness,   1950
So that what's appropriate may be done for her.
I advise this and suggest we do so for her sake.
So let one of us go very quietly
To speak to her privately.
They were agreed on this point;   1955
And so one went to ask her
What you have already heard.
She was hardly happy in her heart,
But rather answered quite unwillingly,
And nevertheless recounted to him   1960
Face to face the whole truth
Quite fully, without any hesitation.
Then he asked her this,
In the kindest and most gracious way:
'Young lady, answer me one question,   1965
Which I will now put to you.
Would you want from this moment on
To see him alive,
Except that this would happen in such a way
That he would never show you the demeanor,   1970
The speech, the look of a lover?'
And she answered: 'Alas!
Sir, may God grant me health,
Such indeed is my wish,
And willingly I would see him again   1975
Alive, even if it were
That he had taken another beloved,
Who would be served by me,
For all my life, even to taking off her shoes.
I don't want to speak more about this;   1980
For my heart breaks completely with sorrow,
Breaks so bitterly and deeply
Every time anyone speaks of him to me.
So I don't want to hear any more.'
After she finished talking, he left the room   1985
And walked to that place
Where the others were awaiting him,
Those who desired and were anxious
To learn what end she might come to.
And he told them that she would die;   1990
'I don't expect her to recover from this.
Her heart is locked within the tower

89

D'Amour, sous la clef de Tristesse,
Ou elle sueffre grant destresse,
Si que morir la couvenra   1995
Briefment; ja n'en eschapera.
Pour quoy nous nous departirons
De ci; plus n'i arresterons.'
En l'eure de la se partirent,
Et puis a la mere dëirent: 2000
'Ma dame, on n'i puet conseil mettre.
Mais vueilliez vous bien entremettre
De li garder et tenir près.'
Euls departis, tantost après
Elle cria a haute vois: 2005
'Hé! Douce mere, je m'en vois.
A Dieu vous commant, douce dame!'
En droit a ce point rendi l'ame.
Elle fut de la gent criée,
Et sa mere en fut tourmentée.   2010
De ce ne tieng je pas mon compte,
Car a mon propos riens n'en monte.

Guillaume, ou porres vous trouver
Comment vous peüssiez prouver
Qu'uns homs seroit a mort menez   2015
De ce point que vous soustenez,
Dou forfait de sa bien amée,
Et que ce fust chose prouvée
Qu'elle heüst fait la villenie
Et qu'adès demourast en vie?   2020
De la pucelle est chose voire.
Mais ce seroit trop fort a croire
Que plus grans fust li siens meschiez
Que de celle. Bien le sachiez!'

                    GUILLAUME

'Attemprance, moult bel parlez   2025
Toutes les fois que vous volez.
Ci endroit especiaument
Avez parlé moult sagement.
Et quanqu'avez ci dit, je croy,
Ne dou croire point ne recroy.   2030
Car c'est pour moy en aucun point
Qui vient a mon propos a point,
Quant celle damoiselle gente
Ot mis ou chevalier s'entente,
Et il esoit ses vrais amis,   2035
Et puis se fu a la mort mis,

1993. Other MSS Damours--2034. A en--2036. A si

                        90

Of Love, by the key of Sadness,
And in this place she suffers great distress,
And thus she shall die   1995
Soon; she'll never escape.
So we will take our leave
From you here; we won't remain any longer.'
Within the hour they departed,
Saying to the mother: 2000
'My lady, nothing can be done,
But please do your best
To watch over her and keep her close.'
After they left, she cried out
All at once in a loud voice;   2005
'Oh! Sweet Mother, I'm dying.
I commend you to God, sweet lady!'
And just at that moment she gave up her spirit.
She was lamented by the household,
And her mother suffered terribly.   2010
But of this I'll take no account,
Because it is irrelevant to my purpose here.

Guillaume, where will you discover
The proof you need to establish
That a man would meet his death   2015
As a result of the circumstances you suggest,
Namely the betrayal of his dear beloved,
Since it is already well established
That after she sinned so wickedly,
He did in fact remain alive?   2020
The case that concerns the young girl is true,
And it would certainly be too hard to believe
That his misfortune was greater
Than hers. Well you know it!"

                          GUILLAUME

"Temperance, you speak very prettily   2025
Every time you so intend.
On this occasion especially
You have spoken quite wisely.
And whatever you have said here I affirm,
Nor do I shrink from believing any of it in the least.   2030
But, as far as I'm concerned, you've brought up something
Which bears directly on my case,
Namely that when this noble lady
Had granted her devotion to the knight
Who became her true lover   2035
And then was delivered to death,

91

Dont Amours si fort l'atrapa
Que la mort tantost la hapa,
Amours en fist pour li assez;
Car cils cops fu tantost passez.   2040
Aussi a morir avoit elle:
Nuls contre ce point ne rebelle,
Cui la mort ne veingne haper;
Nuls ne li porroit eschaper.
Quant uns homs est grieteusement   2045
Tauxes a mort par jugement
D'un bon juge sans mesprison,
Et il le met en grief prison
D'enfermeté en lieux divers,
Ou estre puet mengiez de vers   2050
Et de planté d'autre vermine,
Et il y est un lonc termine,   xxxvV
Chargié col et les bras de fers
Et les jambes, c'est bien enfers.
La est il de foy en destour,   2055
Pour renoier son creatour;
Volentiers le renieroit
Qui de la le delivreroit.
Mais en celle heure qu'il est pris,
Jugies a mort par juste pris,   2060
Trop miex li vaut qu'on l'en delivre
Par la mort, qu'en tel doleur vivre.
Einsi est il d'un vray amant
Qui est trahis en dame amant,
A tel fin com devant est dit.   2065
J'aferme et se di en mon dit
Que nuls meschies ne s'apartient
Aus grietez que ses cuers soustient,
Tant come il dure et elle dure.
Et si say moult bien que Nature   2070
Ha de son bon droit establi
Qu'on mette celui en oubli
Qui est mors et n'en puet ravoir
Pour grant peinne, ne pour avoir.
Seur ce point droit atenderoie;   2075
Miex estre jugies ne vorroie."

                          PAIS

Après ces mos s'est Pais levée
Et dist, comme bien avisée:
"Guillaume, assez souffissanment,
Selonc le vostre entendement,   2080
Avez vostre propos baillié;

2049. AM Denfermetez--2050. D mengie; other MSS rungiez

                           92

Love held her so close
That death presently struck her in turn.
In this Love showed her great favor;
For this blow passed quickly.   2040
In any case she did have to die:
Not anyone here contests the fact
That there's no one whom death doesn't strike down;
Nobody can avoid it.
When a man is condemned   2045
To a painful death by the sentence
Of a judge in a legal trial,
And that judge sends him to a miserable prison,
Closed within some horrible place
Where he could be eaten by worms   2050
Or by a host of other vermin,
And he's there for a long term,
His neck and arms hung with irons
And his legs as well, that's certainly Hell itself.
There he's turned away from faith,   2055
And so will renounce his creator.
Willingly he would renounce Him
For whoever might deliver him from that place.
Indeed at the time he's taken,
Judged to death in a just decision,   2060
It would avail him much more to be delivered
By death than to live on in such pain.
So it is with the true lover
Who has been betrayed in loving a lady,
The result the same as described above.   2065
I affirm and say in my poem
That no harm's comparable
To the suffering his heart sustains
As long as both he and she do live.
And also I know quite well that Nature   2070
Has established by her proper right
That the person will be forgotten
Who dies and cannot be had back
Either for great trouble or for treasure.
On this point I expect the decision for myself;   2075
I would be judged according to no better issue."

PEACE

After these words Peace got up
And said, like one well schooled:
"Guillaume, you've buttressed
Your argument rather sufficiently,   2080
According to your lights;

93

Mais vous l'avez trop court taillié
Pour avoir droit pour vous si tost;
Car uns autres poins le vous tost.
Vous avez de Nature trait,   2085
Pour prouver, .i. assez biau trait,
Lequel on ha bien entendu.
Mais j'ay un autre las tendu
Contre celui, de plus grant pris,
Par lequel vous serez sourpris,   2090
D'un exemple aucun de fait
Qui bien a ramentevoir fait.
Et pour ceci le vous propos,
Car il sert bien a mon propos.

Dydo, roïne de Cartage,   2095
Ot si grant dueil et si grant rage
Pour l'amour qu'elle ot a Enée
Qui li avoit sa foy donnée
Qu'a mouillier l'aroit et a femme;
Et li faus l'appelloit sa dame,   2100
Son cuer, s'amour, et sa deesse,
Et sa souvereinne maistresse.
Puis s'en ala par mer nagent
En larrecin, lui et sa gent,
Qu'onques puis Dydo ne le vit.   2105
Oiez, comment elle se chevit:
Quant failly li ot dou couvent
Qu'heü li avoit en couvent,
Einsi com pluseurs amans font
Qui l'amant loial contrefont,   2110
La desesperée, la fole,
Qu'amours honnist, qu'amours afole,
L'espée d'Eneas trouva
Et en son corps si l'esprouva
Qu'onques ne se pot espargnier   2115
Qu'en soy ne la feïst baingnier.
Dont elle morut a dolour
Pour amer, et par sa folour.
Mais elle ne morut pas seule,
Einsois a .ii. copa la gueule,   2120
Car d'Eneas estoit enceinte,
Dont moult fu regretée et plainte.
Mais einsois qu'elle s'oceïst,
Elle commanda qu'on feïst
Un ardant feu en sa presence.   2125
Et quant en sa desesperence
S'ocist, si forment s'envaÿ

2090. Other MSS soupris—2091. B ancien—2106. AME comment;
other MSS comme—2108. A Que—2127. FBDE senhay

94

But you've cut it much too short
To gain the judgment for yourself so quickly;
Indeed, another point demands your attention.
You've drawn on Nature   2085
In order to prove your case, a rather nice ploy,
One which has been much appreciated.
But I've laid a trap
For it, a very insidious one,
In which you'll be caught, and it is contained   2090
In a certain exemplum, in fact,
One quite useful to recall.
And so I present it to you
Because it serves my purpose well.

"Dido, queen of Carthage,   2095
Had such great sorrow and terrible anger
For the sake of the love she bore for Aeneas,
A man who had pledged her his faith
That he would have her as his woman and his wife.
And the traitorous one called her his lady,   2100
His heart, his love, and his goddess,
And his sovereign mistress.
Then he sailed off across the sea
Like a thief, he and his followers,
So that Dido never saw him again.   2105
Hear now what she did:
When he had failed her by breaking the promise
He had agreed to make for her sake,
Just as many lovers do
Who play at the role of the loyal lover,   2110
That desperate woman, a person who had lost her wits,
Whom love had shamed, whom love had driven mad,
Found the sword of Aeneas
And tried it out on her own body,
And she didn't spare herself at all   2115
Until she made it bathe in her blood.
So she died painfully
For love's sake, and through her madness.
But she did not die alone;
Instead she cut the throats of two,   2120
For she was carrying Aeneas's child,
And afterward she was much mourned and lamented.
But before she killed herself,
She ordered a blazing fire
To be made in her presence.   2125
And when in her desperation
She was doing herself in, she struck so forcefully

Qu'avec le cop en feu chaÿ,
Dont tantost fu arse et bruïe.
Einsi fina Dydo sa vie.   2130
Bien croy que ce fu chose voire,   xxxviR
Car einsi le truis j'en istoire.

Si que, Guillaume, vraiement,
Il me samble tout autrement,
Veües et considerées   2135
Mes raisons devant devisées.
Car on puet vëoir clerement
Que grieté, peinne, ne tourment
Ne se porroient comparer
Ad ce que celle comparer   2140
Volt pour le grief de son amy.
Et fust uns homs trestout enmy
Grant planté de ses annemis,
Qui tuit li heüssent promis
La mort, et tuer le porroient   2145
A leur plaisir, quant il vorroient,
Lui vivant en celle päour,
Non obstant grieté ne frëour,
Se trouveroit il reconfort.
Encoy y a un point plus fort: 2150
Qui le menroit aus fourches pendre
En celle heure, sans plus attendre,
Si seroit il reconfortez
Et soustenus et deportez
En esperance d'eschaper;   2155
Lors ne le porroient taper
Male errour, ne desesperence,
Tant comme il aroit esperence;
Qu'esperence le conduiroit
Jusqu'a tant qu'il trespasseroit.   2160

Aussi avez vous dit d'un point
Encontre Amour trop mal a point:
C'est que Nature a commandise
Seur la gent d'Amours a sa guise,
Et se Nature le commande,   2165
Nuls n'obeïst a sa commande.
Elle commande qu'on oublie
Et mort d'amant et mort d'amie,
Pour ce qu'on n'i puet recouvrer
Par grant avoir, ne par ouvrer.   2170
Commande; assez nous le volons.
De ce point pas ne nous dolons,

2132. A len   Other MSS histoire--2162. A poit--2170. A par par

96

That with the blow she fell into the fire,
And thus at once was roasted and burned up.
In this way Dido ended her life.   2130
I firmly believe that these things really happened,
For just so did I find them in a written text.

To conclude, Guillaume, truly
My view is just the opposite of yours,
In the light of my consideration of   2135
The reasons I've laid out above.
For it can be clearly seen
That misery, pain, and torment
Cannot be compared
To what she was intent on paying out   2140
Because she grieved for her lover.
And if a man found himself among
Some great horde of his enemies,
All of whom had promised him
Death, and indeed could kill him   2145
At their pleasure, whenever they would,
Though living in this fear
(Disregarding the pain and terror),
Still he might find comfort.
Yet there's an even stronger argument: 2150
Whoever might take him to hang on the gibbet,
At that very hour, without any reprise,
Still he would be comforted
And sustained and heartened
By the hope of escaping: 2155
And neither evil error nor despair
Will be able to strike him
As long as he has hope;
For hope will accompany him
Right until the moment that he dies.   2160

You've also made a point
Against Love which is badly off the mark:
It's that Nature has control
Over the company of Love at her will,
And thus if Nature should command,   2165
No one would disobey that command.
She asks that one forget
The death of both lover and beloved,
Because in this instance nothing can be restored
By great treasure or by deeds.   2170
Let her command; indeed we welcome it!
We don't worry about it,

97

Qu'a ami riens n'en apartient;
Car Bonne Amour en sa part tient
Un cuer d'amant tant seulement   2175
Sans naturel commandement.
Qui ne vuet, nuls n'i est contrains;
Mais on est d'Amours si estrains,
Qu'obeïr y couvient par force;
S'est fols qui contre li s'efforce.   2180
Guillaume, se vous loeroie
A laissier ceste povre voie
De dire que Nature ait grace
Que propre commandement face
En amours, qui soit de valeur,   2185
Nature donne bien couleur
A ami d'un plaisant cuidier
Qui li fait folement cuidier
Acomplir ce qu'Amours desprise.
Et par si faite fole emprise   2190
Sont fait maint incouvenient
Qui valent trop meins que niënt.
Plus desclairier ne m'en couvient
Pour ce que point d'onneur n'en vient.
Pais sui qui volentiers feroie   2195
Adès bien et si defferoie
Le mal; aussi feroit Concorde;
Car quanque je vueil, elle acorde,
Toutes heures, et soit et main.
Pour ce la tien je par la main,   2200
Et pour faire ce qu'il li plait.
Ales avant a vostre plait,
Guillaume, par voie dehüe.
Sans naturel descouvenue.
S'ensieuez d'avis les usages,   2205
Par mon los, si ferez que sages."

                    GUILLAUME

"Pais, damoiselle, pour vous croire
Viennent tous biens, c'est chose voire.
Si me garderay de mesprendre.
Mais je vueil ma cause deffendre   xxxviV   2210
Tant avant, comme je porray.
Dont .i. exemple compteray
Qui s'ensieut, a mon fait prover
Et a vostre tort reprouver."

A Orliens ot .i. cler jadis   2215
Qui estoit renommez et dis

2173. AM Que a moy--2173. A riens rien--2189. FMBDE quamis
2195. A Pas--2202. AF a vostre; other MSS en vostre

                         98

For nothing here pertains to the beloved:
Because Good Love for her part holds onto
A lover's heart by herself alone   2175
Without any command from Nature.
Whoever's against it is hardly forced,
And yet one is so pressed by Love
That he must, feeling its power, obey;
Anyone who struggles against that power is a fool.   2180
Guillaume, I advise you therefore
To drop this unpersuasive argument
Which maintains that Nature has the ability
To enforce her own commands
In matters of love, whatever their value.   2185
Nature lends a good appearance
To a lover's frivolous thought,
And this makes him foolishly intend
To do something that Love hates;
And because such foolishness goes on,   2190
Much misfortune results,
And this is worth much less than nothing.
I need say no more,
Because a point of honor's not involved.
I am Peace, and I would willingly always   2195
Do good and bring down
Evil; Concord wishes the same;
For whatever I desire, so does she,
At all times, both morning and night.
So I hold her by the hand,   2200
In order to do what might please her.
Go on with your argument,
Guillaume, in the way you must,
Without any hindrance from nature.
If, by my advice, you follow the principles   2205
Of discretion, you will do wisely."

GUILLAUME

"Peace, young lady, faith in you
Brings all good things, that's something true.
With it I will guard myself from wrongdoing.
But I wish to defend my opinion   2210
As forcefully as I can.
Therefore I will relate an exemplum,
Which here follows, in order to prove my view
And refute your mistaken opinion.

In Orleans there formerly was a clerk   2215
Who was renowned and said to be

99

Nobles clers, vaillans homs et riches,
Et si n'estoit avers ne chiches,
Sires de lois, et de decrez
Maistres, et uns homs bien discrez   2220
De bien moustrer ce qu'il savoit
Et la vaillance qu'il avoit.
S'avoit esté nez en Prouvence,
Et bien enlignagiez en France
Estoit de princes et de contes   2225
Que veritables soit mes comptes.
De gentils gens estoit servis,
Preus et apers a grant devis,
Et avoit en sa compaingnie
De moult noble chevalerie,   2230
A qui riches robes donnoit.
Cils poins moult bien li avenoit,
Car pour sa grace desservir
Se penoient de lui servir.
Or estoit moult d'amer espris   2235
D'une damoiselle de pris
Qui demouroit vers Montpeslier,
Fille d'un vaillant chevalier,
Attrait de moult noble lignie.
S'estoit la besongne lignie   2240
D'entr'eus .ii. si entierement
Qu'on ne peüst mieus autrement.
Il s'estoient entrepromis,
Il comme ses loiaus amis,
Et elle comme vraie amie: 2245
A tousjours mais, toute leur vie,
Maintenroient en verité
Les courtois poins de loiauté.
Mais si loing devins leur loiens
Qu'il s'en vint manoir a Orliens,   2250
Et elle en Prouvence manoit.
Mais si bien, comme il couvenoit,
Les secrez d'amours maintenoient
Des lettres qu'il s'entr'envoioient
Par leurs especiaus messages,   2255
Honnestes gens, secrez et sages.
Einsi le feïrent grant piece.
Mais Fortune qui tost depiece
Maint honneur aval le païs
Fist tant que cils fu esbahis,   2260
Plus qua perdre .Vᶜ mars d'or,
Si comme je diray des or.

2249. F lons; other MSS loin; other MSS devint--2254. AMD Des;
other MSS De

100

A noble churchman, a valiant man and a powerful one,
And furthermore he was neither miserly nor cheap,
A lord of laws, and of decrees
The master, and a man quite discreet   2220
In the demonstration of what he knew
And the valor that was his.
Now he had been born in Provence,
Though well-connected by blood to princes
And counts in France,   2225
If my story is true.
He was attended by noble people,
The competent and the learned in great number,
And had among his company
Many noble knights,   2230
To whom he would give rich robes.
This quality very well became him,
For in order to merit his thanks
They took pains to serve him.
Now he was very much taken in love   2235
With a worthy damsel
Who lived near Montpelier,
The daughter of a valiant knight,
Descended from a very noble line.
And the relationship had been established   2240
So firmly between these two
That it could not have been better;
They were promised, each to the other,
He as her loyal lover,
And she as a loyal beloved;   2245
And always, moreover, all their life,
They upheld truly
The courtly commandment of faithfulness.
But the distance between them became quite great
When he went to live at Orleans,   2250
And she remained in Provence.
But quite ably, as was necessary,
They maintained their lovers' secrets
With letters they sent to one another
By their special messengers,   2255
Honest men, discreet and wise.
They carried on in this fashion for some time.
But Fortune, who destroys quickly
Many an honorable thing throughout the land,
Saw to it that he had a terrible shock,   2260
One worse than losing five hundred golden marks,
Just as I'll now relate.

Il avint a une journée,
Male pour celui adjournée,
Qu'a lui s'en vint uns messagiers 2265
De Prouvence, preus et legiers,
Qui li aportoit lettres closes,
En .i. petit coffret encloses.
Il les prist, si les resgarda
Et de haut lire se garda; 2270
Car pluseurs secrez devisoient.
Et ou darrein point contenoient
Que s'amie estoit mariée
Au plus vaillant de la contrée
Et estoit ja grosse d'enfant. 2275
'Haro!' dist il, 'li cuers me fent.
Hé! Mors, que ne me viens tu prendre?
A po que je ne me vois pendre!'
Lors prist ses cheveus a tirer,
Et puis sa robe a dessirer. 2280
Quant sa gent einsi le veïrent,
Isnelement avant saillirent,
Dont chascuns forment l'agrapa;
Mais par force leur eschapa.
Aval la ville s'en fuï; 2285
Il devint sours et amuÿ;
Car dès lors qu'il parti de la,
Ainc puis de bouche ne parla
Parole qu'entendre peüst
Homs vivans, tant le congneüst; 2290
Ne dès lors que ce li avint,
Onques puis a li ne revint.
Et ne dormoit que sus fumiers,
Et de ce estoit coustumiers.
Et quant si ami le prenoient 2295
Qui en aucun lieu le lioient,
Jamais n'i beüst ne menjast,
Eins est certein qu'il enrajast,
Si qu'il le laissoient de plain
A son voloir aler a plain. 2300
Mais il ne faisoit a nelui
Nul mal, fors seulement a lui.
En ce point fu .xx. ans tous plains;
S'estoit moult regretez et plains
De la gent qui le congnoissoient 2305
Dont li pluseur forment plouroient.
Si fu bien mis de haut au bas.
Se n'afferoit pas grans debas
A jugier verité certeinne,

2265. A li--2276. A fant--2283. MB lacrappa; FD latrappa
2285. A se--2288. FMBE Eins

102

It happened one day,
Which dawned evilly for him,
That a messenger arrived   2265
From Provence, a man noble and adroit,
Who was bearing to him sealed letters
Closed up in a little chest.
He seized them, then looked them over,
Refraining from reading anything out loud: 2270
For they contained many private things.
And at the very end the letters
Told how his beloved had been married
To the most valiant man of that region,
And was at that time big with child.   2275
'Oh no!' he said, 'My heart is breaking.
Oh Death, why don't you take me now?
I'd almost go and hang myself!'
Then he started to pull out his hair,
And after to tear his robe.   2280
When his company saw him in such a state,
They moved quickly forward,
And each one tried to restrain him by force;
But he was so powerful he escaped them.
He fled down to the town;   2285
He turned deaf and dumb;
And from the time he left that place
He never spoke again with his mouth
A word that any living man
Might understand, however much he knew him;   2290
Nor from the time that this happened to him
Did he ever return home,
Instead he slept only on rubbish heaps,
Becoming accustomed to this.
And when his friends would restrain him   2295
And tie him up in some place,
He would refuse to eat or drink;
Rather he always acted crazy,
And so they let him go free and clear
To roam where he liked across the open country.   2300
But he never did an evil thing
To anyone, only to himself.
He remained like this twenty years altogether;
And he was grieved for and lamented
By the people who knew him,   2305
Many of whom wept bitterly.
So he was pulled down from high to low.
Much discussion is hardly needed
To settle a certain truth,

103

Qu'il ot de grieté et de peinne   2310
Plus que cent dames n'averoient
Qui leurs amans morir verroient.
Quant il vous plaist, si resgardez,
Et de mesjugier vous gardez!"

Adont s'est Foy en piez drecie   2315
Comme sage et bien adrecie
De droit, de coustume, et d'usage;
S'a dit: "Guillaume, le musage
Avez bien paié ci endroit,
Par dehors la voie de droit,   2320
Au mains en aucune partie.
S'en vorray faire departie,
C'est assavoir, devision
Par voie de distinction
Des choses qui ne font a croire   2325
Et d'aucunes qui la victoire
Puelent avoir d'estre creües
Ou pour possible soustenue,
Dont les unes essausseray
Et les autres confonderay,   2330
Au los de m'amie Constance
Qui a tous mes contraires tense
Et me soustient et fortefie
Vers chascun qui en moy se fie.
Que cils clers fust de grant vaillance,   2335
Gentils homs, et de grant puissance,
Renommez de haute noblesse,
Et de temporelle richesse
Trés habondanment assasez,
Espris d'amours et embrasez,   2340
Amis de cuer, amez d'amie,
Et en l'estat de courtoisie
Heüssent fait leur aliance
Par trés amiable fiance,
Si que les secrez garderoient   2345
D'amours, tant comme il viveroient,
Qu'a Orliens fust amainnagiez,
En France bien enlinagiez
De gens si honnourablement
Qu'on ne peüst plus hautement,   2350
Ce sont toutes choses possibles.
Et dou mal qui fu si horribles,
Qui si soudeinnement li vint,
Qu'en lisant lettres li avint,

2324. F distraction--2328. AM possible; other MSS possibles

104

Namely that he felt misery and pain   2310
Which was more than that of any hundred ladies
Who suffered their lovers' deaths.
When it pleases you, take this into consideration,
And thus keep yourself from judging falsely."

FAITH

At this point Faith stood up   2315
Like someone wise and well schooled
In law, custom, and practical matters;
And she said: "Guillaume, you've certainly
Spent your time here foolishly,
Straying far from the path of justice,   2320
At least in some matters.
And I wish to make a discrimination now,
That is to say, a division
By way of a distinction
Between the things which do not enforce belief   2325
And those able to achieve the success
Of being believed,
Or considered possible,
Of which I would prize the latter category
And put little stock in the former   2330
At the urging of my friend Constancy,
Who argues in all my disputes
And supports my side, giving me strength
To uphold those who place their trust in me.
That this clerk was of great valor,   2335
A noble man, and a very powerful person,
Renowned for his great gentility,
And with worldly goods
Provided for quite abundantly,
Seized with love and comforted by it,   2340
A lover from the heart, loved by his beloved;
And further that in all courtliness
They had formed their liaison
Through a most friendly trust,
So that they kept the secrets   2345
Of love, as long as they did live;
Also that he was living in Orleans,
Well connected by blood to people
In France with such honor
That it couldn't be greater,   2350
All these things are possible.
Also, in regard to the illness
Which attacked him so suddenly,
Coming on him while he read the letters,

105

Et si grandement li dura,   2355
Que .xx. ans entiers l'endura,
Encor di je qu'il pot bien estre.
Car Diex en ce siecle terrestre
A mains jugemens si enclos
Qu'estre ne porroient esclos   2360
D'omme mortel par sa science.
Aussi de vostre conscience
Avez vous presentement dit
De cest lettres par vostre dit
Que pluseurs secrez contenoient.   2365
Or ne scet on dont il venoient.
Dont j'ay en droit .i. point trouvé
Que vous n'avez mie prouvé,
Que de s'amie li venist.   xxxviiV
Ceste raison ci defenist   2370
Qu'on n'en puet faire nullement
A vostre profit jugement.
Et se say bien des autres choses
Qui seront, se je puis, escloses,
Pour vous dou tout suppediter,   2375
S'il est qui le sache diter."

                    GUILLAUME

"Damoiselle, vueilliez laissier,
S'il vous plaist, vostre menassier;
Car ce ne vous puet riens valoir,
Et il me fait le cuer doloir."   2380

                    CHARITÉ

Charitez adont s'avisa,
Si a dit: "Foy, entendes sa!
Je vous vueil dire une merveille."
Lors li conseilla en l'oreille
Ce qu'elle volt, secretement.   2385
De quoy Foy debonnairement
Prist un bien petit a sousrire,
Et en sousriant prist a dire:
"Charité, damoiselle chiere,
Liement, de bonne maniere,   2390
Cest besongne conterez.
Trop miex conter la saverez,
Pour certein, que je ne feroie.
Vous en estes ja en la voie;
Car en vous en sentez le fait,   2395
Se vous pri qu'il soit einsi fait."
"Foy, ma trés douce chiere amie,

2381. ABD Savisa; other MSS savanca

                        106

And which lasted so long,   2355
Enduring twenty years all together,
Once again I say that this could well be.
For God in this earthly life
Has ordained many things so secret
That they could not be explained   2360
By the wisdom of mortal man.
But from your own knowledge
You've just now said,
By your own admission, that these letters
Contained much that was secret.   2365
Now it is not established where they came from.
And so I have truly found a point
That you have not proved in the least,
Namely that they were sent by his beloved.
For this reason   2370
No one would be able to make a judgment
For you in this matter.
And this is apparent to me from other issues
Which will be discussed, if I'm able,
In order to defeat you utterly,   2375
If anyone can accomplish this."

GUILLAUME

"Damsel, please stop
Your threatening, if you will,
For this cannot profit you at all,
And it grieves my heart."   2380

CHARITY

Charity then reflected deeply
And said: "Faith, listen to this!
I wish to tell you something marvelous."
Then she whispered in her ear
Secretly what she had in mind.   2385
And at this Faith demurely
Began laughing a little,
And, smiling, started to say:
"Charity, my dear young lady,
You bring this up,   2390
Cheerfully, and in a pleasant manner.
You're better able to address it,
And this is certain, than I.
In fact, you've got a head start
Because you're convinced of its truth,   2395
And so I beg you to go ahead."
"Faith, my very sweet and dear friend,

De ce ne vous faurai je mie,
Eins en diray ce qu'il m'en samble.
Car de .ii. personnes ensamble   2400
Les oppinions en sont bonnes,
Quant loiaus sont les .ii. personnes.
Si qu'a Guillaume en parleray
Et tel chose li moustreray
Qu'il se tenra pour recrëans,   2405
S'il n'est trop fols ou mescrëans.

Guillaume, or entendes, amis:
La puissance qui mâ commis
A estre Charité nommée
Fait que par ouevre sui prouvée,   2410
Dont on en voit les apparans
En tous mes plus prochains parans.
Ce sont li gentil cuer loial
Qui entrent en la court roial
De Bonne Amour qui n'a nul per.   2415
Or entendez en quoy j'aper:
J'aper en souffissans promesses
Et en raisonnables largesses,
Espéciaument par donner
Et d'aucuns meffais pardonner;   2420
Dont eüreus sont cil qui donnent,
Et aussi sont cil qui pardonnent.
Or regardons qu'Amours demande
Qu'on li doint, et plus ne commande:
Elle demande expressement   2425
Les cuers des bons entierement;
Ce demande elle qu'on li doint.
Et se vuet aussi qu'on pardoint
Aucuns fais, selonc le propos
Pourquoy ces raisons ci propos.   2430
Ce le moustreray par figure
Que Bonne Amour en moy figure,
Assés briefment, sans prolongier.

Uns riches homs ha .i. vergier
Ou il a arbres grant planté.   2435
Enseurquetout y a planté
Une moult trés gracieuse ente
Qui au riche homme miex talente
Et li est trop plus avenans
Que ne soit tous li remenans;   2440
Et est einsi de lui amée,
Tant comme elle est ente clamée.

2427. AE Se

108

I will not fail you in this one bit,
But rather I'll make known my view.
For the thoughts of two   2400
Together are useful
When both persons can be trusted.
And so I'll speak to Guillaume,
Demonstrating to him something
Which will make him acknowledge defeat,   2405
If he isn't too foolish or malevolent.

Guillaume, friend, listen to this:
The power which has caused me
To be called Charity
Ordains that I be proved thus in my works,   2410
And what I am is made manifest
In all those closest to me.
They are the noble, faithful hearts
Who enter the royal court
Of Good Love which has no peer.   2415
Now note where I appear:
I am manifest in fulfilled promises
And in reasonable generosity,
Especially in the giving of gifts
And the pardoning of any wrongdoing;   2420
For happy are those who give,
And also those who forgive.
Let's now examine what Love asks
That one give her, and more she doesn't command:
She expressly requests   2425
That the hearts of good people be hers completely;
She demands this be granted her.
And she also desires that one pardon
All deeds, according to the rule
Whose reasons I will here propose.   2430
And I will demonstrate this through a figure
That Good Love images in my own person,
Doing so briefly, without drawing it out.

A prominent man owns a verger
In which there are a great many trees.   2435
Most important he's planted there
A very graceful grafting
Which he, rich and powerful, values highly,
And it pleases him much more
Than all the rest.   2440
And he has loved her
As long as she's had the name of grafting.

109

Or avient que li temps trespasse
Tant que li petis jouvens passe;
Se montent ses branches au vent   2445
Pour entrer en secont jouvent
Qui est moiens temps appelles.   xxxviiiR
S'estent ses branches de tous les,
En eslargissant sa biauté
Et en acroissant sa bonté,   2450
Pour traire a la conclusion
Qui est dite perfection,
Pour li deduire et deporter,
Fleurs, fueilles, et bon fruit porter.
Or di j'einsi qu'il avenra   2455
Que li sires demandera
Comment celle ente se maintient
Et quel qualité elle tient.
Li jardiniers puet dire: 'Sire,
Pour verité, vous en puis dire,   2460
Ce m'est avis, bonne nouvelle.
Ne demandez plus que fait elle,
Mais demandez me bien qu'il fait,
Car vostre ente .i. arbre parfait,
Et en tel guise se deporte   2465
Que flours, fueilles, et bon fruit porte.
Dont perdu a d'ente le nom,
Et d'aubre a recouvré le nom,
Sous qui on se puet ombroier
Plaisanment et esbanoier.   2470
Or vueil je chanter et respondre,
Pour miex m'entencion espondre:
Dont je vueil faire une demande,
Se de la chose qui amende
On doit avoir cuer esperdu,   2475
S'elle a .i. petit nom perdu
Pour .i. plus grant nom recouvrer,
Par nature our par bien ouvrer?
Je respon qu'einsi n'est il mie;
Car ce seroit grant derverie.   2480
Mais ce qu'on aimme chierement
Ou a acheté chierement,
Qui le verroit dou tout perir,
Si que ja ne peüst garir,
Venir en porroit tel meschief   2485
Qu'on y metteroit bien le chief
Et tout le corps entierement.
Je le say bien certeinnement
Que pluseurs einsi l'i ont mis,

2448. A se sent--2470. AF esbanier--2476. MSS Celle; emendation
proposed by Hoepffner--2479. FMBDE repons

110

Now it happens that time passes
Until the little one ends her youth;
Her limbs reach up to the wind   2445
So that she enters into that second age
Called the middle years,
While her branches extend on all sides
To enlarge her beauty,
And, so doing, increase her goodness,   2450
Drawing toward that goal
Which is termed perfection,
In order to delight and amuse him,
By putting forth flowers, leaves, and fine fruit.
At this moment it will happen, I suggest,   2455
That the lord will ask
How the grafting is doing
And what condition she's in.
The gardener might then say: 'Sire,
In truth, I can say this,   2460
Namely good news, or so I think.
No longer ask how she is doing,
But ask me rather what he is doing,
For your grafting is a perfect tree,
And as such takes great delight   2465
In bearing flowers, leaves, and fine fruit.
This means he's lost the name of grafting,
Gaining that of tree,
Under which one can find shade
And relax quite pleasantly.'   2470
Now I'll sing and respond as well
To make clearer my meaning;
And so I'll ask this question,
Namely should one grieve at heart
For that which grows better,   2475
Since she lost an insignificant name
In order to gain a much greater title,
Either by nature's power or her own good works?
I answer no, not at all;
For this would be terribly foolish.   2480
Of course, one loves dearly whatever
One has bought at a high price;
And to witness it perish completely,
So that no recovery could be envisioned,
Would be such a grievous misfortune   2485
That a person might well lose his head,
Indeed his whole self and being as a result.
This I know for certain,
Because many have truly done so,

Tant amie com vrais amis.   2490
Or vueil dou propre fait parler
Pour quoy j'ay meü mon parler:
Celle damoiselle jolie
Qui estoit a ce clerc amie.
C'estoit li ente faitissete   2495
Comme une douce pucelette,
En grant vergier d'Amours plantée.
La pot estre si eslevée
Et de branches si estendue
Et de fueilles si bien vestue,   2500
De fleurs si cointement parée,
Comme estre aus milleurs comparée.
Si me vueil .i. po aviser
Pour les parties deviser:
Branches de bonne renommée,   2505
Fueilles d'estre bel emparlée,
Fleurs d'avoir la condition
D'onneste conversation,
Tant d'abit comme de maintien.
En cest estat dist: 'Amis, tien;   2510
Je te doing, pour toy deporter,
Grace dou fruit d'onneur porter.'
Lors pluseurs pensées li viennent
Qui de neccessité couviennent,
Pour li entrer en mariage   2515
Par le conseil de son linage.
S'elle le fait, ce n'est pas fais
Dont cils doie enchargier tel fais
Comme de lui desesperer;
Eins doit penser et esperer   2520
Qu'elle y a profit et honneur
Quant en la grace d'un signeur
Seroit de droit nommée dame.
Ceste raison bon cuer enflame
D'amer miex assez que devant.   2525
Pourquoy je di d'ore en avant
Que cils ne l'amoit pas pour bien.   xxxviiiV
Vraiement, il y parut bien,
Quant bonne amour li volt souffrir
Son corps a tel martire offrir.   2530
Plus n'en di, Guillaume, biau sire.
Dites ce qu'il vous plaist a dire."

                    GUILLAUME

"Charité, se Diex me doint joie,
Bien avez par soutille voie

2497. AMB En; other MSS Ou--2522. A dou signeur

                        112

Beloveds as well as true lovers.   2490
Now I wish to address the case directly
For whose sake I have altered my speech.
This pretty damsel
Who was the beloved of that clerk,
She was the graceful grafting,   2495
Planted like a sweet young girl
Within the magnificent verger of Love.
There she could grow up,
Extending far her branches,
So finely clothed with leaves,   2500
And so cutely adorned with flowers,
That she compared to the very best.
Now for a moment I wish to reflect upon
The meaning of these different parts:
The branches of good reputation,   2505
The leaves of being well spoken of,
The flowers of having the quality
Of appropriate and truthful dealings with others,
Not just in appearance but in fact.
Thus transformed, she says: 'Friend, it's yours;   2510
I give it to you, so you may enjoy
The favor of bearing the fruit of honor.'
Then many thoughts come into his mind,
And these are born of necessity,
Namely for her to enter into marriage   2515
According to the advice of her family.
If she does so, it's not something
That he should worry so much about
That he starts to despair.
Instead, he ought to wish and hope   2520
That this profits her and gives her honor,
When, through a lord's favor,
She would rightfully be called a lady.
These circumstances encourage the good heart
To love far better than before.   2525
So I maintain from this point on
That he did not love her with a good intention.
Surely it is very apparent
Because good love wants him to suffer,
Offering his body to such torment.   2530
Guillaume, fair sir, I'll say no more.
Speak now whatever you want."

                       GUILLAUME

"Charity, may God give me joy,
You have spoken well and in a subtle

Pluseurs propos par biaus mos dis.   2535
Mais je ne voy pas en vos dis
Que vous m'aiez de riens puny.
J'ay mon procès aussi uny
Comme devant et aussi ferme
En son estat; par quoy j'afferme   2540
Que ja ne sera abatus,
Se d'autres mos ne suis batus.
.I. point y a qui gist en prueve,
Par quoy il convenra qu'on prueve
Le contraire de mes paroles,   2545
Ou je ne tenray qu'a frivoles
Ce que devant avez compté,
Nonobstant vostre grant bonté,
Et que pour grant bien l'avez fait,
Pour auctorisier vostre fait   2550
Et pour le mien suppediter.
Se vueil un petit reciter
De ce clers qui fu vrais amis
Et puis en tel grieté sousmis,
Comme j'ay dit, .xx. ans entiers.   2555
Or prouvez seulement le tiers
Qu'onques nulle dame souffrist,
Tant son corps a la mort offrist;
Prouvez ce point tant seulement.
Mais vous ne porries nullement."   2560

THE AUTHOR

Charitez volt après parler,
Et pour apointier son parler,
Elle avoit ja la bouche ouverte.
Mais Honnesté fu si aperte
Que tantost fu aparillie   2565
Et dist: "Charité, douce amie,
Que je die, mais qu'il vous plaise;
Que je ne seray jamais aaise
Se n'aie dit je mon talent
Pour lui faire le cuer dolent."   2570
Charitez bien s'i acorda,
Et puis Honnesté recorda
S'entention par voie honneste,
Dont toute la court fist grant feste.

HONNESTÉ

S'a dit: "Guillaume, or entendez: 2575
Pour la fin a quoy vous tendez,
Fondez estes petitement;

114

Manner about several points--and in pretty words.   2535
But I do not see that what you've said
Has done me any damage at all.
I've got a brief as consistent
As before and as compelling
In its evidence; and so I maintain   2540
That I will never be defeated,
Unless I am confronted with different arguments.
There's one point which remains proven,
And someone would have to discover how
To prove the opposite of what I say about it;   2545
If not, I will consider only as inconsequential
All that you have just said,
Notwithstanding your great goodness,
And that you have done so in a worthy cause,
Namely to lend authority to your opinion   2550
And denigrate my own.
So I want to say something
About the clerk who was a true lover
And was then plunged into such misfortune
For twenty years, as I have related.   2555
Now prove untrue only the third of these points,
Namely that no lady suffers ever
So terribly that she offers her heart to death;
Refute this point alone.
But you won't be able to do so at all."   2560

THE AUTHOR

After this Charity wanted to say something,
And she had her mouth already open
In order to give shape to her words,
But Honesty was so quick
That she was ready even sooner   2565
And said: "Charity, sweet friend,
Let me speak, if you please:
For I will never be satisfied
If I don't say what I have in mind
In order to trouble his heart."   2570
Charity was in complete agreement,
And so Honesty gave her views
In a very honest fashion,
And this seemed good sport to all the court.

HONESTY

And she said: "Now listen, Guillaume: 2575
You have laid very little foundation
For the point you are trying to make;

115

Se vous dirai raison comment.
Voirs est que grans grief li avint
Et en petit d'eure li vint.   2580
Mais tantost, celle heure passée,
Sa grant grieté fu trespassée.
Car combien que lonc temps dura,
Onques puis grieté n'endura
Qui point fëist a son cuer touche.   2585
Et s'aucuns griés au cuer li touche,
Il n'i a point de sentement,
Dès qu'il n'i a consentement;
C'est chose assez legiere a croire.
Il avoit perdu sa memoire,   2590
Sens, maniere, et entendement;
Dont on puet vëoir clerement
Qu'il n'avoit point de volenté,
Fors que le cuer entalenté
Des grans soties qu'il faisoit.   2595
Quant en .i. fumier se gisoit,
C'estoit sa pais; c'estoit ses lis;
C'estoit de tous poins ses delis,
Ou il dormoit a grant repos.
Encor y a autre propos   2600
Que vous meïsmes dit avez.
C'est certein, et bien le savez,
Que, quant si amy le prenoient
Et en aucuns lieus l'enfermoient,   xxxixR
Jamais n'i beüst ne mengast,   2605
Einsois trestous vis enragast,
Qui le retenist malgré lui;
Il n'en feïst rien pour nelui
Et vivoit a plain comme beste.
C'estoit vie trop deshonneste,   2610
Honteuse, s'il en tenist conte;
Mais point ne congnoissoit de honte.
Dont j'ay assez mon fait prouvé
Et vostre tort bien reprouvé
Par .i. seul point qui me remort.   2615
De dame qui savera mort
Son amy, sera plus cent tans
En .i. jour, que cils en cent ans,
De grieté par .i. si fait trait,
Com ci devant avez retrait.   2620
Guillaume, se vous soufferrez,
Ou d'un autre point parlerez;
Car de cestui estes vaincus,
Ne vous y puet valoir escus."

2579. ADE grief; other MSS gries--2605. A ne ... ne; other
MSS ni ... ne

116

And I'll tell you why.
It's true enough that he experienced
A great misfortune which suddenly came upon him.   2580
But immediately, that moment having passed,
His troubles were gone as well.
Though it may last a long time,
A grief that pierces right to the heart
Will never endure beyond its time.   2585
And if any suffering touches it,
The heart feels nothing
Because it does not acknowledge this.
The point is easy enough to understand.
He had lost his memory,   2590
Reason, bearing, and understanding;
Thus one can see clearly
That he had no will at all,
Except a heart eager for
The mad things he was doing.   2595
When he lay down on a garbage heap,
That was his peace; that was his bed;
That was in every way his delight,
A place where, sleeping, he was quiet and relaxed.
There is yet another matter   2600
Which you yourself have brought up.
It's certain--and well you know it--
That when his friends restrained him
And locked him up in different places,
He never drank or ate,   2605
But, instead, continually raged at
Whoever held him against his will;
He did nothing for anyone
And lived out in the open like an animal.
It was a very disgraceful life,   2610
Shameful, if he had taken account of it.
But he felt no shame at all.
And so I have proved my point sufficiently
And corrected your mistaken opinion
By this single point I have brought up;   2615
Now in regard to the lady who experienced
Her lover's death, her grief would be a
Hundred times greater in a single day than his in a hundred years,
As shown by this particular fact
In what you have rehearsed above.   2620
Guillaume, either suffer the consequences
Or speak to another point;
Because you are defeated in this, and it
Is hardly worth a nickel to you in the debate."

117

"Honesté, pour voir, non feray.   2625
Encor .i. po en parleray,
Car je m'ay bien de quoy deffendre,
Mais que vous le vueilliez entendre.
Quant tout le sens de lui perdi
Pour le mal qu'a lui s'aërdi,   2630
Qui dou tout le deshonnoura,
Plus perdi, meins li demoura.
Vous dites que mal ne sentoit,
Pour ce que desvoiez estoit
De maniere et d'entendement;   2635
Mais il est bien tout autrement:
Car avant que homs son sens perde,
Ne que forsens a lui s'aërde,
Le prent et seurprent maladie
Qui le trait a forcenerie.   2640
Si vueil faire .i. po d'argument
Qui vous moustrera vivement
Comment m'entente prouveray
Dou droit que pour moy trouveray.
Quant .ii. causes sont assamblées   2645
Qui se sont a .i. corps fermées,
Celle qui vient premierement,
Elle attrait le commancement
Dès ce point par la premerainne,
Pour ce que c'est la souvereinne;   2650
Et qui la premiere osteroit,
La seconde s'en partiroit.
Or puelent dire tel y a:
'Guillaume, verbi gracia,
A entendre si comme quoy?'   2655
Vesci en l'eure le pourquoy:
Nous vëons .i. chien qui enrage,
De quel cause li vient la rage?
D'un ver qui la langue li perse.
Or est la cause si desperse   2660
Qu'il pert le boire et le mengier,
Et puis le couvient enragier.
Or est dont li commencemens
De quoy vient li enragemens.
Et quant il en pert l'abaier,   2665
Adont se puet on esmaier
Dès ce point que la gent ne morde.
Et que de ce miex nous remorde,
Je vous en diray qu'il avint
D'un chien qui enragiez devint,   2670

2628. A me vueilliez; other MSS le vueilliez--2629. A de li
2641. A .i. argument--2670. F enrachiez

GUILLAUME

"Honesty, truly I will not do so.   2625
I'll keep on talking,
For I have much to say in my defense,
If only you're willing to listen.
When he lost all his senses
Because of the illness that attacked him   2630
And deprived him of all the honor he had,
He lost much more than what little he kept.
You say that he didn't suffer from the illness
Because he was disoriented
Both in what he did and what he thought;   2635
But it is certainly quite otherwise:
For before a man can lose his senses
Or madness can afflict him,
An illness grips and seizes him
That drives him mad.   2640
Now I will argue this at some length
In order to demonstrate readily to you
What proof I can offer for my view
In order to gain the judgment for myself.
When two causes work together   2645
And manifest themselves within a single body,
The one which comes first
Sets things in motion
Because it's the first to have an effect,
And therefore it's the chief cause;   2650
And whenever the first cause is removed,
The second disappears as well.
There are some who might say:
'Guillaume, thanks for the speech,
But what is your point?'   2655
I'll explain directly:
We witness a dog going mad;
But what brings this madness on?
A worm that pierces his tongue.
Now afterward the cause becomes so dispersed   2660
That he loves the ability to drink and eat,
And then must go mad.
This is then the first cause
Of the madness that assails him.
When afterward the dog can no longer bark,   2665
Then that's the time
To watch out that he doesn't bite anyone.
Now in order to bring this point home,
I'll talk about what happened to
A dog that actually went mad,   2670

119

Amez en l'ostel d'un riche homme.
Or entendez, s'orrez la some.
Li riches homs ot oÿ dire
Dont venoient si fait martire:
S'en volt vëoir l'experience   2675
Pour miex avoir en congnoissance.
Se fist son chien par force prendre,
Loier, bersillier, et estendre
Et sa langue sachier a plain,
Tant qu'on vit le ver tout a plain.   2680
Lors fu li vers fors esrachiez;
Et quant il fu a plain sachiez,
Les mains celui prist a lechier   xxxixV
Cui il ot senti atouchier;
Et fu la garis de tous poins.   2685
Aussi di je que cils clers poins
Fu d'une maladie obscure;
Dont je vous di que la pointure
Dou grant mal que ses corps sentoit
Le tenoit en point qu'il estoit.   2690
Dont mes drois est assez prouvez
Et vostres grans tors reprouvez."

                    THE AUTHOR

Après s'est Franchise levée
Qui ne fu pas trop effraée;
Et s'ot bon vueil et bonne chiere   2695
Et trés gracieuse maniere.
Si encommensa a parler
Et dist einsi en son parler.

                    FRANCHISE

"On a veü generaument
Toudis en amer loiaument   2700
Que les dames se sont portées
Miex et plus loiaument gardées
Que les hommes en tous endrois.
Je le vueil prouver--and c'est drois--
Par exemples que je vueil dire,   2705
Pour ce qu'il font a ma matire.

Quant cil d'Athennes eurent mort
Androgeüs, si grant remort
En ot Minos, li rois de Crete,
Que par voie sage et discrete,   2710
Par force d'armes et de guerre

2674. E martire; other MSS matire--2675. Other MSS vout--2684.
F. arrachier; other MSS esrachier--2688. A repeats this line
2695. AD bon voult; F bon oueil; MB bon vent; E bon veult.
Hoepffner emends to bon vueil.

                    120

One which was well loved in the household of a prominent man.
Listen carefully, and you'll hear what's important.
The rich man had heard about
The cause of this disease,
And he wished to see it for himself,   2675
The better to understand it.
So he had the dog taken by force,
Tied up, rigidly bound, and spread out,
And then its tongue fully extended
So that the worm could be seen quite plainly.   2680
Afterward the worm was extracted;
And when it had been completely drawn out,
The dog began to lick the hands
Of the man he had felt touch him;
And it was completely cured.   2685
I affirm, moreover, that this clear fact
Concerned an obscure malady;
Therefore I maintain that the attack
Of grievous illness which that man's body suffered
Kept him in the state he was in.   2690
And so my point is proved quite adequately,
And your grievous error corrected."

THE AUTHOR

At this Frankness stood up,
And she was hardly afraid;
Her will was good, her appearance pleasing,   2695
And she had a very gracious manner.
Then she started to speak
And made the following remarks.

FRANKNESS

"It has been generally observed
About true loving in all ages   2700
That women have done better with it
And have remained more loyal
Than men in every way.
I intend to prove this--and it's right I do so--
With some exempla that I wish to relate   2705
Because they are relevant to this argument.

When those of Athens had put Androgeus
To death, Minos, the King of Crete,
Felt such remorse on this account
That by wise and prudent means,   2710
Through the force of arms and through war

121

Fist essillier toute leur terre;
Et les mist tous pour cest outrage
Minos en si mortel servage,
Que tous les ans li envoioient   2715
.I. homme; mais il sortissoient,
Et cil seur qui li sors chëoit,
Trop mortelment li meschëoit;
Car li rois Minos devourer
Le faisoit la, sans demourer,   2720
Par un moustre trop mervilleus.
Trop felon, et trop perilleus.
Mais nuls ne se doit mervillier,
Se Minos vout ad ce veillier,
Ne s'il en fu fort esmeüs,   2725
Car peres fu Androgeüs.
Or avint que li sors cheï
Seur Theseüs, qui esbahi
Pluseurs; car il fu fils le roy,
Preuz, vaillans, et de bel arroy.   2730
Mais pour la mort Androgeüs
Ala en Crete Theseüs,
Pour lui faire estrangler au moustre,
Se sa prouesse ne li moustre,
Si qu'envers lui se puist deffendre;   2735
Autrement puet la mort attendre.
Et se Diex li donne victoire,
Il acquerra honneur et gloire;
Car ceuls d'Athennes franchira
Et le servage acquitera.   2740
Mais riens n'i vausist fer ne fust,
Se belle Adriane ne fust,
Qui oublia Minos, son pere,
Et Androgeüs, son chier frere,
Sa terre et ses charnels amis   2745
Pour Theseüs, ou elle a mis
Son cuer, si qu'elle li moustra
Comment occis le fier moustre a
Pour lui delivrer dou servage;
Et li donna son pucelage   2750
Par si qu'a femme la penroit
Et qu'en son païs l'en menroit
Avec Phedra, sa chiere suer,
Qu'elle ne lairoit a nul fuer.
Theseüs qui se parjura   2755
Ses diex et sa loy li jura
Que jamais ne li fausseroit
Et qu'envers li loiaus seroit.

2726. A Endrogeus

122

He made desolate all their land;
And because of this outrage Minos
Put them all into a grievous servitude,
Namely that every year they were to send   2715
A man; but they always cast lots,
And for that man upon whom the lot fell,
It was a very fatal mischance;
Because Minos the king would have him
Devoured there, without delay,   2720
By an all too strange monster,
A too malevolent and dangerous one.
But no one ought to wonder
If Minos wished to arrange all this,
Nor if he were strongly moved to do so,   2725
For he was the father of Androgeus.
Now it happened that the lot fell
On Theseus, something which dismayed
Many, for he was the son of the king,
A noble man, valiant, and of handsome appearance.   2730
But because of the death of Androgeus
Theseus went to Crete,
To have himself be put to death by the monster
If he did not manifest his prowess
And prove able to defend himself against him.   2735
Otherwise he could expect to be killed.
And if God should grant him victory,
He would acquire honor and glory;
For he would free those of Athens
And acquit them of their servitude.   2740
But nothing would have availed him, not wood or iron,
If it hadn't been for beautiful Ariadne,
A woman who forgot about Minos, her father,
And Androgeus, her dear brother,
Her land and her blood relations,   2745
All for the sake of Theseus, in whom she had placed
Her heart, and she showed him
How to kill the proud monster,
In order to deliver himself from bondage;
And she gave him her maidenhood   2750
So that he would make her his wife
And take her away to his own country
Along with Phaedra, her beloved sister,
Whom she would leave behind on no account.
Theseus, perjuring himself,   2755
Swore to her by his gods and law
That he would never prove false
And that he would always be faithful to her.

Il se menti, li renoiez.
Pour quoy ne fu en mer noiez?   x1R   2760
Quant sa besongne ot assevie,
Il les charga en sa navie.
Mais vers li mesprist si forment
Qu'Adriane laissa dormant
Seulette en estrange contrée,   2765
Lasse, dolente, et esgarée,
Et en mena la juene touse,
Phedra sa suer, s'en fist s'espouse.
Ci a trop mortel traïson.
Aussi diray je de Jason   2770
Qui conquist par l'art de Medée
En Colcos la toison dorée,
Et sormonta, li bourdereaus,
L'ardant soufflement des toreaus,
S'endormi le serpent veillable,   2775
Seur toute beste espoventable,
Et desconfist les chevaliers
Armez, a cens et a milliers.
Mais nuls ce faire ne peüst,
Se Medea fait ne l'eüst.   2780
Son païs laissa et son pere,
Et fist decoper son chier frere.
Pelie occist a grant desroy,
Et tout, pour Jason faire roy.
Quanqu'elle ot, li abandonna;   2785
S'amour et s'onneur li donna.
Mais Jason Medea laissa
Pour Creusa, dont moult s'abaissa,
Et mervilleusement mesprist,
Quant la laissa et autre prist.   2790
Et quant elle sot la nouvelle,
Qui ne li fu plaisant ne belle,
Elle fu si desesperée,
Si hors dou sens, si forcenée,
Que .ii. enfans qui sien estoient,   2795
Pour ce que Jason ressambloient,
Occist en despit de Jason,
Puis mist le feu en sa maison.
Après s'en ala la chetive
O ses dragons par l'air fuitive.   2800
Mais puis en estranges contrées
Furent roïnes couronnées.
Car roys d'Athennes Egeüs
Fu de Medée deceüs;
Bacus Adriane honnoura   2805

2764. A Que--2769. FMDE Si--2779. FM uns ce--2795. FMDE siens

124

He lied, the traitor.
Why wasn't he drowned in the sea?   2760
When he had completed his mission,
He embarked them on his ships.
But he grievously betrayed her
When he left Ariadne asleep
And all alone in a strange land,   2765
Abandoned, sorrowing, and deceived,
And led off the young girl,
Her sister Phaedra, and made her his wife.
This was a deadly treason.
And I'll also bring up Jason,   2770
Who captured, by Medea's arts,
The golden fleece of Colchis,
And overcame--that trickster--
The fiery breath of the bulls,
Put to sleep the guardian dragon,   2775
More dreadful than any other beast,
And defeated the armed
Knights in their hundreds and thousands.
But no one could have accomplished all this
If Medea hadn't done it for him.   2780
She deserted her country and her father,
And had her dear brother cut up.
She killed Pelia in great madness,
And all this in order to make Jason king.
Whatever she had, she gave him freely;   2785
She bestowed her love and her honor upon him.
But Jason left Medea
For Creusa, demeaning himself greatly,
And sinning grievously
When he left her and took up with the other.   2790
After she learned the news,
Which was hardly either pleasant or good,
She was so desperate,
So out of her mind, so crazed,
That to spite Jason she killed   2795
The two infants which were hers
Because they resembled him,
And afterward put her own house to the torch!
Then the wretched woman fled
Through the air with her serpents.   2800
But later in foreign lands
Queens were crowned.
For Aegeus, the king of Athens,
Was beguiled by Medea;
Bacchus honored Ariadne   2805

Fort, car en li grant amour a.
Cil dui les dames espouserent
En leur païs et coronnerent.
Si que, Guillaume, c'est la somme,
On ne porroit trouver en homme   2810
Si grant loyauté comme en femme,
Ne jamais d'amoureuse flame
Ne seroient si fort espris,
Comme seroit dame de pris.
Car quant il y a meins d'amour,   2815
Il y a tant meins de dolour,
Puis que ce vient a mal sentir.
Ne je ne me puis assentir
Qu'en endurant les maus d'amer
Qu'homs ait tant com dame d'amer;   2820
Et si a de remedes cent
Li homs tels que fame ne sent."

                          GUILLAUME

"Damoiselle, la traïson
De Theseüs ne de Jason
Ne fait riens a nostre matiere,   2825
Ne ce n'est mie la premiere
Ne la darreinne fausseté
Qui es amoureus ha esté,
Autant es fames comme es hommes.
Ne je ne donroie .ii. pommes   2830
De vostre entention prouver
Par si fais exemples trouver.
Car se mon fait prouver voloie
Par exemples, j'en trouveroie
Plus de .x., voire plus de .xx.   2835
Chascuns scet bien ce qu'il avint
De l'amy a la Chasteleinne
De Vergi: d'amours si certeinne
L'ama qu'il s'ocist sans demour   xlV
Quant morte la vit pour s'amour.   2840

Li bons Lancelos et Tristans
Eurent plus de peinne .x. tans
Que femme ne porroit souffrir,
Tant se peüst a peinne offrir,
Et cent fois furent plus loiaus   2845
Que Jason ne fu desloiaus,
Ne Theseüs qui trop mesprist
D'Adriane, quant Phedra prist.
Encor vueil d'un autre compter,

2821. AD remede

                    126

Greatly, for he dearly loved her.
These two married the women
In their own countries and crowned them.
So Guillaume, that's the most important point;
No man ever is as loyal   2810
As women are,
Nor are men ever so powerfully inflamed
With the spark of love
As any noble lady can be.
So when there's less love,   2815
It follows there's much less suffering,
Because this comes from feeling pain.
Nor can I assent to the view
That, enduring the pangs of loving,
A man might suffer as much bitterness as women do;   2820
In any case the man has a hundred
Remedies unavailable to women."

                        GUILLAUME

"Damsel, the treason
Of either Theseus or Jason
Has nothing to do with the issue we're arguing,   2825
And this is hardly the first,
Nor will it be the last betrayal
To be discovered among lovers,
Both women and men.
I wouldn't give two apples   2830
For proving your point
By the introduction of exempla such as these.
For if I intended to argue my case
With examples, I could find more than
Ten, truly more than twenty of them.   2835
Everyone knows well what happened
To the lover of the Chatelaine
De Vergy; he loved her with a love
So sure that he killed himself without hesitation
When he saw that she was dead for the sake of his love.   2840

Good Lancelot and Tristan
Experienced ten times more pain
Than any woman could suffer,
As much as she could subject herself to it,
And they were a hundred times more loyal   2845
Than Jason was disloyal,
Or Theseus, he who sinned too much
Against Ariadne when he took Phaedra away.
Still I wish to bring up someone else,

                          127

Se vous me volez escouter.   2850
Une dame sans villonnie
D'un chevalier estoit amie,
Si li donna .i. anelet
Trop gent (ne fu villein ne let),
Par si qu'adès le porteroit   2855
Et que jamais ne l'osteroit
De son doy, s'elle ne l'ostoit.
Et li chevaliers, qui estoit
Tous siens, bonnement li promist,
Et la dame en son doy le mist.   2860
Or avint qu'elle avoit mari
Qui ot le cuer triste et mari;
Car l'anel a recongnëu
Pour ce qu'autre fois l'ot vëu.
Si l'ala tantost demander   2865
A la dame et li comander
Qu'elle li baille en la place
Seur peinne de perdre sa grace.
La dame dist qu'elle l'avoit,
Mais ou, pas bien ne le savoit.   2870
Si fist samblant de l'aler querre
Et, en deffermant une serre,
Comme dame avisée et sage,
Dist a un sien privé message:
'Va sans arrest a mon ami   2875
Et si li di que mal pour my,
Se mon anel ne me renvoie.
Et ne demeure pas seur voie,
Car mon signeur le vuet avoir
Sans nul essoinne recevoir.   2880
Di li bien qu'il n'en faille mie;
Car s'il en faut, je sui honnie
Et en peril de perdre honneur
Et la grace de mon signeur.'
Li messages n'atendi pas,   2885
Eins s'en ala plus que le pas
Au chevalier et tout li conte
Ce que devant ay dit en conte.
Quant li chevaliers l'entendi,
A po li cuers ne li fendi,   2890
Car il ot päour que sa dame
Honte pour li n'eüst ou blasme.
Si dist: 'Amis, foy que li doy,
Avuec l'anel ara mon doy,
Car ja par moy n'en partira.'   2895
Si que lors .i. coutel tira,

2896. A. coustel

128

If you'll listen to me.   2850
A lady was loved
By a knight without any baseness,
And she gave him a ring that was
Exceedingly valuable (it was neither cheap nor ugly),
On the condition that he always wear it   2855
And never remove it
From his finger, if she did not take it off.
And the knight, who was
Completely hers, promised this in good faith,
As the lady put it on his finger.   2860
Now it happened that she had a husband
With a heart gloomy and afflicted
For he recognized the ring,
Having seen it before.
So he went at once to ask   2865
The lady and command her
To furnish him with it on the spot
If she didn't want to lose his favor.
The lady said that she had it,
But where, this she didn't know well.   2870
So she made a show of going to look for it,
And, opening a drawer,
Like a woman cunning and sharp,
Spoke this private message to one of her attendants:
'Go directly to my lover   2875
And tell him I'm in for a bad time
If he doesn't return the ring.
Don't delay at all along the way,
For my master wishes to have it
Without hearing any excuses.   2880
Make it clear that he mustn't fail me;
For if he does, I will be shamed
And risk losing the honor
And favor of my lord.'
The messenger didn't hesitate,   2885
But went as fast as possible
To the knight and told him everything
That I mentioned earlier in my story.
When the knight heard,
His heart nearly broke,   2890
For he feared that his lady
Might be shamed or accused on his account.
So he said: 'Friend, by the faith I owe her,
She'll have my finger along with the ring,
For I will never part them.'   2895
Then he drew out a knife,

Son doi copa et li tramist
Aveques l'anel qu'elle y mist.
Puet on faire plus loiaument
Riens, ne plus amoureusement?   2900
Certes, nennil! Ce m'est avis.
Car trop fu loiaus ses amis.
Si que bien oseroie attendre
Vray jugement, sans plus contendre,
Qu'on les doit plus auctorisier   2905
Et en tous estas plus prisier
Que les dames, de qui parole
Tenez que je tien a frivole,
Qu'on dit--et vous le savez bien--
Que par tout doit veincre le bien.   2910
Et cil furent bon et loial
Tenu en toute court roial,
Comment que les dames feïssent
Moult pour leurs amis et souffrissent.
Mais on dit--et c'est veritez--   2915
Qu'adès les .ii. extermitez,
C'est trop et po. Einsi l'enten ge:
Ne doivent recevoir loange;
Mais qui en l'amoureus loien   xliR
Est loiez, s'il tient le moien,   2920
Il ouevre bien et sagement.
Et li sages dist qui ne ment
Qu'adès li bonneüreus tiennent
Le moien partout ou il viennent."

                        L'ACTEUR

A ce Prudence respondi,   2925
Qui riens n'enclot ne repondi
A la matiere appartenant,
Et dist: "Guillaume, maintenant
Voy je bien vostre entention;
Mais j'ay contraire opinion   2930
Qui de la vostre est trop lonteinne.
On scet bien que la Chastelainne
Fu morte pour .i. bacheler,
Pour ce qu'il ne la sot celer.
Car il dist toute leur besongne   2935
A la duchesse de Bourgoingne;
Et la duchesse moult mesprist,
Qu'a une feste li reprist
Qu'elle savoit bien le mestier
Dou petit chiennet affaitier.   2940
S'en morut en disant: aymi!

2905. A auctoriser--2917. A lentens--2924-5. A lacks heading
lacteur--2932. A chastolainne

                          130

Cut off his finger and sent it to her
Along with the ring she had placed there.
Could anyone ever do something more loyal
Than this, or more loving?   2900
Certainly, not at all! This is my view.
For her lover was overly faithful.
And thus I would presume to expect
A correct judgment without any more debate,
For men should have more respect   2905
And in every case be counted superior
To women, whose promises,
You see, I consider frivolous,
Because as one says--and you know it well--
'The good should triumph in everything.'   2910
And the men I've mentioned were considered good
And loyal in every royal court,
Even though the ladies accomplished much
And suffered greatly for their lovers' sakes.
But it's said--and certainly in truth--   2915
That it's always the two extremes,
Either too much or too little--so I understand.
No one ought to be praised,
Except whoever's caught tight
In the snares of love; if he holds to the middle way,   2920
Then he acts wisely and well.
And the sage, a man who does not lie, says
That happy people always keep to the middle
In whatever they do."

THE AUTHOR

Prudence then responded,   2925
Who had not yet engaged in or troubled herself over
The issues being debated,
And she said: "Now Guillaume,
I understand well your point of view;
But I hold a contrary opinion,   2930
One very different from yours.
It is well known that the Chatelaine
Died for the sake of a young man,
Because he did not know how to keep her secret.
Instead he discussed everything about their affair   2935
With the Duchess of Burgundy;
And the Duchess did a terrible thing
When at a feast she let it slip
That she knew about the business
Of dressing up the little dog.   2940
And this put an end to the Chatelaine who, dying, said 'alas!'

131

Par le deffaut de son ami.
Et quant li amis vit s'amie
Par sa gengle morte et perie,
S'il s'ocist, il fist son devoir,   2945
Qu'autre mort deüst recevoir,
N'il ne fist fors meins que justice,
S'il s'ocist pour punir son vice;
Qu'avoir le dehüssent detrait
Chevaus enragiez pour ce trait.   2950
Si m'est vis que la Chastelainne
Ot plus de meschief et de peinne
Quant sans cause reçut la mort,
Que n'ot cils qui se fu la mort
Qui avoit desservi le pendre;   2955
Et pour c'en fu sa dolour mendre.

Et se Tristans ou Lancelos
Furent vaillans, bien dire l'os
Que leur vaillance et leur prouesse
Leur fu gloire, honneur, et richesse;   2960
N'il n'est homs qui peüst acquerre
Tels biens, sans avoir peinne en terre.
Si que, Guillaume, j'ose dire
Que plus de peinne et de martyre
Cent fois les dames soustenoient   2965
Que leurs amis qu'elles faisoient,
Qu'elles avoient les griés pensées
Et les päours desordenées,
Les paroles de mesdisans.
Et s'il demourassent .x. ans,   2970
Ja n'eüssent parfait joie;
Car qui atent, trop li anoie,
N'a cuer humain riens tant ne grieve
Com mesdis et pensée grieve.
Ne autre bienfait n'en portoient   2975
Qu'un po de joie qu'elles avoient.
Einsi est il de pluseurs dames
Qui mettent les cuers et les ames
Et quanqu'elles on en leurs amis,
Et quant tant chascune y a mis   2980
Qu'il sont en vaillance parfait,
Apparent par ouevre et par fait,
Elles n'en ont autre salaire
Fors un petit de gloire au faire.
Il ont le grain; elles ont la paille;   2985
Car l'onneur ont, comment qu'il aille.
Et s'aucune fois leur meschiet,

2967. A lacks les--2969. FDE des--2976. A quelle--2978. Other
MSS corps--2982. A appernt

132

Because of her lover's error.
Now when the lover saw that his beloved
Had been undone and destroyed by his gossiping,
If he then killed himself, he did only what was right,   2945
Since he really deserved to die a different death;
So he did not less than what was just
In killing himself to punish his sin;
For they should have had wild horses
Draw him in pieces for the deed.   2950
So I think that the Chatelaine
Was more unfortunate, suffered more pain,
When for no reason she received her death,
Than the young man who killed himself,
Since he deserved to hang;   2955
And for this reason his torment was less.

And if Tristan and Lancelot
Were valiant, I dare well say
That their valor and prowess
Meant glory, honor, and riches to them,   2960
Since there's no one on this earth who could acquire
Such goods without undergoing some difficulty.
Yet, Guillaume, I would maintain
That the ladies in question endured
A hundred times more trouble and torment   2965
Than the lovers they were joined to;
They suffered from the mournful thoughts,
And confusing fears,
The backbiting of scandal-mongers.
And if these men had waited around ten years,   2970
Never would they have found perfect joy;
Because whoever waits is too much annoyed,
And nothing grieves the human heart so much
As slander and nagging thoughts.
Nor did the ladies desire any benefit from all this,   2975
Except what little joy they received.
And so it is with many ladies
Who surrender both heart and soul
And whatever is theirs to their lovers,
And when each woman has given so much   2980
That their men acquire knightly honor,
Something manifest in word and action,
The women have no reward at all in turn,
Except a little glory in the deed itself.
The men get the kernel; the women have the chaff.   2985
Whatever might happen, men find honor in some way.
But if something turns out wrong at any time,

133

Tout premiers seur les dames chiet.
Certes, c'est mauvais guerredon,
Quant pour bien ont de guerre don.   2990
De l'autre qui son doy copa,
Vraiement fait .i. let cop a.
Car Guillaume, quoy que nuls die,
Je le tien a grant cornardie,
Se m'en pense po a debatre.   2995
Car il y avoit .iii. ou .iiii.
Voies qui deüssent souffire,
Et il prist de toutes la pire.
Et d'autre part, je ne croy mie   xliV
Que celle qui estoit s'amie,   3000
S'elle l'amoit d'amour seüre,
N'eüst trop plus chier l'aventure
De son mari et son courrous,
Et deüst estre entre'eaus .ii. rous
Li festus jusqu'a une piece,   3005
Qu'oster de son ami tel piece,
Qu'a tous jours fu desfigurez,
Meins prisies et plus empirez."

                       GUILLAUME

"Certes, Franchise, vous avez
Bien dit, que bien dire savez.   3010
Mais je say sans nulle doubtance
Que c'est contre vo conscience,
Et que dit avez le contraire
De ce qui en vo cuer repaire.
Mais je vous requier, s'il vous pleist,   3015
Que nous abregons nostre plet,
Car trop esloingnons la matiere
Qui meüe a esté premiere.
Il est certein--et je l'afferme--
Qu'en cuer de femme n'a riens ferme,   3020
Rien seür, rien d'estableté.
Fors toute variableté.
Et puis qu'elle est si variable
Qu'elle en rien n'est ferme n'estable
Et que de petit se varie.   3025
Il faut que de po pleure et rie.
Dont grant joie et grant tourment
N'i puelent estre longuement,
Car sa nature li enseingne
Que tost rie et de po se pleingne;   3030
Tost ottroie, tost escondit;
Elle a son dit et son desdit,

3015. Other MSS plaist--3016. Other MSS plait--3017. A alongons
followed by an indecipherable word. Other MSS esloingnons

                          134

The ladies are the first to suffer.
Surely their recompense is hardly just,
When for good, they get strife in return.   2990
Concerning the other man who cut off his finger,
Truly he struck a stupid blow.
For Guillaume--and I don't care what anyone might say--
I consider his action terribly foolish,
And I'll explain why.   2995
For there were three or four
Other things to do,
But he chose the worst of all.
Moreover, I don't believe one bit
That the woman who was his beloved,   3000
If the love she felt for him had been loyal,
Would have considered more important the question
Of her husband and his anger,
And so the bond ought to have been
Broken between those two right at that moment,   3005
Rather than for her lover to lose a finger,
And thus always be disfigured,
Less worthy and much impaired."

GUILLAUME

"Frankness, there's no doubt that you have
Spoken well, and you are someone quite well-spoken.   3010
But I know for certain
That what you said's against your own conscience,
And that you have argued the opposite
Of what really lies in your heart.
But I ask you, and please agree,   3015
To narrow our debate,
For we have moved much too far from the question
Which was broached at the beginning.
It is indisputable--and so I affirm--
That nothing's stable in a woman's heart,   3020
Nothing's certain, there's no constancy,
But rather complete instability.
And since she is so changeable
That she stands firm on or is convinced of nothing,
And since she alters for the slightest reason,   3025
It follows that she cries or laughs over trifles.
This means that great joy and immense suffering
Cannot remain with her for very long,
Because her nature convinces her
To laugh quickly and lament nothing;   3030
She grants readily, refuses easily;
She has her say but then denies it,

135

Et s'oublie enterinement
Ce que ne voit, legierement.
Et puis qu'elle ne puet ravoir   3035
Jamais son ami pour avoir,
Pour pleindre, ne crier, ne braire,
Ne pour chose qu'elle puist faire,
Et aussi que de sa nature
Oublie toute creature   3040
Legierement quant ne la voit,
On puet bien penser, s'elle avoit
De ses amis damage ou perte,
Que briefment seroit si aperte
Que d'un perdu .ii. retrouvez   3045
Li seroit encor reprouvez.
Mais cuers d'omme est fermes et seürs,
Sages, esprouvez, et meürs,
Vertüeus et fors pour durer,
Et humbles pour mal endurer.   3050
Et quant de l'amoureuse ardure
Est espris, tellement l'endure
Qu'einsois morroit dessous l'escu
Qu'on le veïst mat ne veincu.
Ce que je di n'est past contrueve,   3055
Car chascuns le dit et apprueve;
Et pour ce que chascuns le dit,
L'ai je recordé en mon dit.
Si di en ma conclusion
Que, vëu la condicion   3060
D'omme et de feme, nullement
Feme ne puet avoir tourment,
Tant braie ne se desconforte,
Comme uns homs en son cuer le porte,
Qu'estre ne puet en sa nature.   3065
Raison s'i acorde et droiture.
Et aussi li maus qui termine
Est mendres que cils qui ne fine,
Einsois dure jusqu'a la mort,
Tant qu'il a son malade mort."   3070

                    LARGESSE

Largesse qui après sëoit
Parla, car moult bien li sëoit,
Et dist: "Guillaume, vraiement,
Je sui mervilleuse, comment
Vous osez des dames mesdire: 3075
Car ce ne deüssiez pas dire.
Et de ce qu'avez dit, li blames   xliiR

3033. Other MSS certainement--3045. FBDE recouurez--3047. Other
MSS omit et--3050. FMBDE humbles; A humble

And forgets utterly
And swiftly what she does not see.
Now since she cannot ever have her lover   3035
Back for money,
For tears, or moaning, or lamentation,
Or for anything she might do,
And since by her nature
She forgets quite readily   3040
Any creature out of her sight,
It would well seem that had she
Suffered hurt or loss on her lover's account,
She'd be so ready again in such a short time
That 'for the one lost two recovered'   3045
Would be proved again and by her.
In contrast, a man's heart is firm, secure,
Wise, experienced, and mature,
Virtuous and strong enough to endure,
But humble in suffering adversity.   3050
And when it is all aflame
With amorous burning, it suffers
But would rather die behind the shield
Than be seen beaten down or vanquished.
What I maintain is hardly fiction,   3055
For everyone says and agrees with it;
And because it's the common view,
I have recorded it in my poem.
So I say in conclusion
That, considering the nature   3060
Of men and women, no woman
Can suffer as much torment,
However much she screams and carries on,
As any man can bear within his heart,
For it simply is not in her nature.   3065
Reason and justice concur with this.
In any case, the misfortune which ends
Is less than that which doesn't,
But rather endures to death itself,
Having killed its victim."   3070

LARGESSE

Largesse, who was sitting nearby,
Then spoke up, for she was pleased to do so,
Saying: "Truly Guillaume,
I am astounded
How you dare malign women;   3075
For you should not talk like this.
And any blame in what you have said

137

Est plus seur vous que seur les dames.
Vous avez dit en vostre dit--
Dont, certes, vous avez mal dit--   3080
Que chascuns tient pour veritable
Que toute dame est variable,
Et que ce n'est de leur couvent
Nès que d'un cochelet au vent.
Mais toute ceste compaingnie   3085
Tient le contraire et le vous nie.
Et pour ce bien dire pouez
Que vous n'estes pas avouez;
Si devez paier la lamproie.
De ce plus dire ne saroie,   3090
Qu'on ne puet bon argüement
Faire seur mauvais fondement."

DOUBTANCE

"Et je ne m'en porroie taire,"
Ce dist Doubtance de meffaire,
"Eins en diray ce qu'il m'en samble;   3095
Car tous li cuers me frit et tramble
Quant einsi sans cause blamer
Oy les dames et diffamer.
Or entendez a ma demande:
Biau Guillaume, je vous demande,   3100
Se celle change ne varie
Qui est tous les jours de sa vie
Loial amie, sans fausser,
N'en fait, n'en desire, n'en penser?"

GUILLAUME

"Certes, damoiselle, nennil!   3105
Mais je croy qu'entre .Vͨ mil
N'en seroit pas une trouvée;
Car tel greinne est trop cler semée."

DOUBTANCE

"Mon biau sire, se Diex me gart,
Moult avez estrange regart,   3110
Et s'avez diverse parole;
Et s'avez esté a l'escole,
Si com je croy, d'aler en change;
Et pour ce que li cuers vous change,
Vous cuidiez que chascuns le face   3115
Si com vous; mais ja Dieu ne place;
Car je prouverai le contraire
De fait, cui qu'il doie desplaire."

138

Falls more on you than on women.
You have said in your poem--
And surely you have gotten it wrong--   3080
That everyone believes
All women are fickle,
With no more to their word
Than there is in a weathercock blown by the wind.
But this entire company   3085
Believes the opposite and opposes your view.
So for this reason you can certainly say
That you are not endorsed;
Thus you must pay the piper.
I need not say anything more.   3090
For no one can make a valid
Argument with a faulty premise."

FEAR

"Nor can I keep silent about this,"
Declared Fear of misdoing,
"Rather I'll say what's on my mind;   3095
For all my heart shakes and trembles
When for no reason I hear
Ladies maligned and defamed.
Listen well to my question:
Fair Guillaume, I ask you,   3100
If that woman proves fickle or changes her mind,
She who is all the days of her life
A loyal beloved, never betraying
In deed, in desire, or in thought?"

GUILLAUME

"Surely, damsel, not at all!   3105
But I believe that not one such would be found
Among five hundred thousand,
For this seed is too thinly sown."

FEAR

"My fair sir, may God preserve me,
Your expression is very strange,   3110
And your words amaze me;
Thus you must have been to the school
Of constant change, or so I believe;
And because your heart changes within,
You think that everyone else does the same   3115
As you; but may it never please God;
For I will prove the contrary
In fact, whomever it might displease."

139

"Damoiselle, ne vous desplaise,
Se je vous resgarde a mon aaise,   3120
Car pas ne vous hé si forment
Come je vous regart laidement;
Et se ma parole est diverse,
Bons cherretons est qui ne verse.
Mais je cuide verité dire,   3125
Comment que m'en vueilliez desdire;
Si me sui ci mal embatus,
Se pour voir dire sui batus."

SOUFFISSANCE

Adont se leva Souffissance
Et dist: "Guillaume, sans doubtance,   3130
Vous estes or mal emparlez.
Resgardez coment vous parlez;
Car nuls homs qui vueille voir dire
Ne porroit des dames mesdire,
Qu'en elles est, ce scet on bien,   3135
Tant quanqu'on puet dire de bien.
Si que je vous lo et conseil
Que plus ne parlez sans conseil;
Car vous estes trop juenes homs
Pour dire si faites raisons."   3140

GUILLAUME

Lors entroÿ une murmure,
Que chascune d'elles murmure
De ce que si fort soustenoie,
Ce que des dames dit avoie;
Et vi que chascune faisoit   3145
Samblant, qu'il li en desplaisoit.
Et quant j'aperçu la maniere
De leur parler et de leur chiere,
Et que meües furent toutes
Pour bouter le feu es estoupes,   3150
Au juge fis une requeste   xliiV
Qui me sambloit assez honneste,
Et humblement li depriay
Et requis en mon depri ay
Qu'elles parlassent tout a fait,   3155
Si averoient plus tost fait.
Si firent elles, ce me samble;
Qu'elles parloient tout ensamble.
Dont li juges prist a sousrire
Qui vit que chascune s'aïre.   3160

3136. AFBE Tout; other MSS Tant--3127. FBE ja perceu

GUILLAUME

"Damsel, do not be dismayed
If I look at you in a friendly way,   3120
For I do not dislike you so much
That I would stare at you rudely;
And if what I've said is wrong,
It's a good cart that never turns over.
But I believe I'm speaking the truth,   3125
Despite how much you'd like to deny it;
So if for speaking the truth I'm beaten down,
I'm truly very badly treated."

SUFFICIENCY

And then Sufficiency rose to her feet,
Saying: "Guillaume, without doubt   3130
You have been severely talked to.
So be careful what you say;
For no man who wishes to speak the truth
Can defame women,
Or their particular qualities (this is well known),   3135
Because so much good can be said.
Thus I advise and counsel you
To say nothing more without reflection;
For you are too young a man
To support such an opinion."   3140

GUILLAUME

Then I heard a murmuring,
For each of them was whispering
About what I had so forcefully declared,
About what I had said about women;
And I saw that each was giving the impression   3145
Of being displeased,
And when I perceived the manner
Of their discussion and the look on their faces,
That all were excited
To add fuel to the fire,   3150
I made a request to the judge,
Who seemed fairly honest to me,
Begging him humbly,
And appealing in my request
That they should speak out all together,   3155
And thus have done more quickly.
For so they were doing, it seemed to me,
Namely talking all at once;
The judge started to smile at this,
For he saw that each of them was getting angry.   3160

141

Et certes, j'en eus moult grant joie,
Quant en tel estat les vëoie.
Mais li juges qui sagement
Voloit faire son jugement
Tantost leur imposa silence,   3165
Fors seulement a Souffissance
Et a Doubtance de meffaire.
Et lors prist Doubtance a retraire
.I. conte proper a sa matiere,
Et commensa par tel maniere.   3170

                    DOUBTANCE

"Que fist Tysbé pour Piramus?
Quant elle vit que mors et nus
Estoit pour li, sans nul retour,
A doloir s'en prist par tel tour,
Que d'une espée s'acoura   3175
Seur le corps et la demoura;
Car après li ne volt pas vivre,
Eins fina s'amour et son vivre
En pleins, en plours, et en clamours.
Certes, ce fu parfaite amours;   3180
Car il n'est dolour ne remort
Qu'on puist comparer a la mort.
Ne nuls ne me feroit entendre
Que nuls homs vosist son cuer fendre
Si crueusement, n'entamer,   3185
Comme Tysbé fist pour amer.
Et qui diroit uns homs est fors
Pour souffrir d'amours les effors,
Et s'a cuer plus dur qu'aÿmant
Ou que ne soit .i. dÿamant,   3190
Je ne donroie de sa force
Le quart d'une pourrie escorce,
Ne je ne pris riens sa durté,
Sa vertu, ne sa mëurté,
Ne chose qu'il endure aussi.   3195
Mais quant une dame a soussi
Qu'en son cuer secretement cuevre,
Par tel guise le met a ouevre
Qu'elle y met le corps et la vie.
Mais, Guillaume, je ne croy mie   3200
Que on veïst onques morir
Homme par deffaut de merit
Et qui tost ne fust confortez,
Tant fust ses cuers desconfortez;
N'il n'est doleur qui se compere   3205

3183. Other MSS riens--3203. Other MSS fu

                    142

Now, of course, I had great joy
In seeing them in such a state.
But the judge, who wished
To make a wise judgment,
Immediately imposed silence on them,   3165
With the exception only of Sufficiency
And Fear of misdoing.
And then Fear began to tell
A story relevant to her opinion,
Beginning just like this: 3170

FEAR

"What did Thisbé do for the sake of Pyramus?
When she saw him naked and dead
Because of her, without any recourse,
She became so grief-stricken
That she ran herself through with a sword,   3175
Through her own body and left it there;
For she would not live after him,
But instead put an end to her love and life
With laments, tears, and wailing.
Surely this love was perfect,   3180
For there is no pain or grief
Which can be compared to death.
Nor would anyone make me admit
That any man's heart could break
So cruelly, or he could injure himself   3185
As did Thisbé for love.
It is said that a man is strong
In suffering the hardships of loving,
With a heart stronger than adamant
Or any diamond;   3190
But I wouldn't give for such strength
A bit of rotten apple,
Nor do I consider his endurance to be anything much,
Or his virtue or maturity,
Or what he suffers through.   3195
But when a woman suffers some pain
That she conceals in her heart,
She acts on it in such a way
As to give it substance and expression.
But Guillaume, I don't believe at all   3200
That a man was ever seen
To die from a lack of reward,
Nor was there ever any who wasn't quickly comforted,
However much his heart had been troubled;
Nor is there any pain which compares   3205

143

A mòrt, com grieve qu'elle appere,
Ne que li feus, fais en peinture,
Encòntre le feu de Nature.
Car Nature ne puet pas faire,
Tant soit a corps humein contraire;   3210
Ne cuers ne puet riens endurer
Qu'on peüst a mort comparer."

                    SOUFFISSANCE

"Doubtance, laissiez le plaidier,
Car .i. petit vous vueil aidier,
Pour mettre nostre entencion   3215
A plus vraie conclusion,
Comment qu'aiez si bien conclus
Selonc raison, qu'on ne puet plus.
Adont commensa Souffissance
Et dist ainsi en audiance: 3220

Leandus, li biaus et li cointes,
D'une pucelle estoit acointes
Qui bele Hero fu nommée;
N'avoit en toute la contrée
Nulle si cointe damoiselle,   3225
De trop si gente, ne si belle;
N'en en Abidois n'avoit, n'en Crete
Nulle amour qui fust si secrete,
Car nuls ne savoit leur couvine,   xliiiR
Fors seulement une meschine   3230
Qui belle Hero norrie avoit;
Celle seulement le savoit.
De moult parfaite amour s'amoient;
Mais a grant peinne se vëoient,
Qu'entre Hero et Leandus   3235
Fu un bras de mer espandus
Qui estoit larges et parfons,
Si qu'on n'i preïst jamais fons;
Et ce leur faisoit trop d'anuis.
Mais Leandus, toutes les nuis,   3240
Passoit le bras de mer au large,
Tous nus, seuls, sans nef et sans barge.
Belle Hero au gent atour
Ot en sa maison une tour
Ou toutes les nuis l'atendoit,   3245
Et .i. sierge ardant la tendoit,
Auquel Leandus se ravoie
Souvent, quant la mer le desvoie.
Or avint que la mer s'enfla

3212. A heading reads souffrance--3215. Other MSS vostre
3228. AM fust; other MSS fu--3249. A tourbla; other MSS senfla

                    144

To death, however grievous it may seem,
Any more than fire fashioned in a painting
Can be compared to real fire.
For Nature cannot produce anything similar,
However much it might torment the body,   3210
Nor can the heart endure any pain
That might be likened to death."

SUFFICIENCY

"Fear, stop your arguing
For I wish to afford you a little help,
In order to bring your point   3215
To an even truer conclusion,
Although you've developed it quite well,
In a reasonable way, and no one could do better."
Sufficiency began in this way,
Speaking then for all to hear: 3220

"Leander, that handsome and clever man,
Was friendly with a young girl
Who was named Hero the beautiful;
In all the land there was not
Another damsel so attractive,   3225
None so noble by far, or so pretty;
Nor was there in Abidos or in Crete
Any love affair so secret,
For no one knew of their bond,
Except a serving woman   3230
Who had raised beautiful Hero;
She alone did know.
They loved each other with a quite perfect love;
But they could see each other only with great difficulty,
For between Hero and Leander   3235
Extended an arm of the sea
So wide and so deep
That no bridge could be built over it;
And this circumstance troubled them greatly.
But Leander, every night,   3240
Passed over that arm of the sea in the open,
Completely naked, alone, without any boat or barge.
Beautiful Hero of the noble appearance
Had a house with a tower
Where she waited every night for him,   3245
Keeping a candle burning
Toward which Leander directed himself
Often when the sea threw him off course.
Now it happened that the seas rose high

145

Pour le fort vent qui y souffla   3250
Si qu'elle en devint toute trouble
Pour le vent qui l'esmuet et trouble.
Leandus se tient a la rive,
Qui fort contre son cuer estrive;
Qu'Amours li enjoint et commande   3255
Et ses cuers, qu'a passer entende,
Et la plus belle de ce mont
Voit d'autre part qui l'en semont;
Si que li las ne sot que faire,
N'il ne voit goute en son affaire.   3260
Car il voit la mer si orrible
Que de passer est impossible;
Et de sa tempeste et son bruit
Toute la region en bruit.
Mais finalment tant l'assailly   3265
Amours, que en la mer sailli,
Dont briefment le couvint noier;
Car a li ne pot forsoier.
Et certes, ce fu grans damages,
Car moult estoit vaillans et sages.   3270

Bele Hero ne scet que dire;
Tant a de meschief, tant a d'ire,
Qu'en nulle riens ne se conforte.
Elle vorroit bien estre morte,
Quant son dous amy tant demeure.   3275
Dou cuer souspire, des yeus pleure;
La nui ot plus de mil pensées,
Par .V^c. mille fois doublées.
Elle ne fait que reclamer
Nepturnus, le dieu de la mer,   3280
Et li promet veaus et genices,
Oblations et sacrefices,
Mais que la mer face cesser,
Par quoy Leandus puis passer.
Einsi toute nuit se maintint   3285
Et l'ardant sierge en sa main tint,
Jusqu'a tant qu'il fu adjourné.
Mais mar vit pour li ce jour né,
Qu'entre les flos vit Leandon
Qui floteloit a abandon.   3290
Et quant de près le pot vëoir,
Seur le corps se laissa chëoir
Au piet de sa tour droitement;
Si l'embrassoit estroitement,
Forcenée et criant: 'Haro!'   3295

3251. AM tourble--3275. Other MSS amis--3289. AB leandont
3293. Other MSS pie

146

Blown by a strong wind,   3250
And they became all troubled
Because the wind disturbed and moved them.
Leander kept back on the shore,
Struggling mightily against his heart;
For Love enjoined and commanded him,   3255
As did his heart, to make the decision to cross,
And on the other side, summoning him,
He saw the most beautiful woman in the world;
So the miserable man didn't know what to do,
Nor could he see a way out of his fix.   3260
For the sea, he saw, was so threatening
That it was impossible to traverse;
And all the region was in an uproar
With storm and thundering.
But at last Love   3265
So provoked him that he jumped in the water,
And shortly afterward did drown;
For he could not make the crossing.
And surely, this was a great loss,
For he was a very valiant and wise man.   3270

Beautiful Hero couldn't speak at all;
Her grief and anger were so great
That she could find no comfort.
She wished very much for death herself
When her lover was so delayed.   3275
She sighed from the heart, cried with her eyes;
That night she had more than a thousand thoughts,
Multiplied some five hundred thousand times.
All she could do was call upon
Neptune, god of the sea,   3280
Promising him calves and heifers,
Oblations and sacrifices,
If only he would make the seas stop moving,
So that Leander might cross them.
She continued all night with this,   3285
Holding the burning candle in her hand
Until the dawn came.
But with ill fortune she saw this day come,
For in the waves she spied Leander,
Floating aimlessly.   3290
And when she could see him close up,
She threw herself upon his body
Right at the foot of her tower;
And she held him close,
Crazed and crying out: 'Alas!'   3295

Einsi fina belle Hero,
Qui de dueil fu noïe en mer
Avec son ami, pour amer.
Si qu'il n'est doleurs ne meschies
Dont cuers d'amans soit entechiez,   3300
Qui soit de si triste marrien
Com celle qui n'espargna rien
Que Hero ne meïst a mort
Pour son amy qu'elle vit mort,
Ne nuls n'en porroit par raison   3305
Faire juste comparison,
Ne que de fiel encontre baume.
Et pour ce je vous lo, Guillaume,
Que cils debas soit en deport;   xliiiV
Car vraiement, vous avez tort."   3310

                    GUILLAUME

"Damoiselle, se tort avoie,
Bien say que condempnez seroie
Nom pas par vous; car l'ordenance
Ne doit pas de ceste sentence
Estre couchie en vostre bouche,   3315
Pour ce que la chose vous touche;
Eins la doit prononcier le juge
Qui a point et loyaument juge.
Mais j'ay le cuer moult esjoÿ
De ce que j'ay de vous oÿ;   3320
Car c'est tout pour moy, vraiement."

                    SOUFFISSANCE

"Pour vous, biau Guillaume? Et comment?"

                    GUILLAUME

"Damoiselle, or vueilliez entendre,
Et je le dirai sans attendre;
Quant Amours si fort enlassoit   3325
Leandus, que la mer passoit
A no, sans batel n'aviron,
A la minuit ou environ,
Li fols qui tant y trespassa
Que d'amer en mer trespassa,   3330
Il fist trop plus et plus souffri
Que Hero qui a mort s'offri,
Consideres les grans peris
Ou il fu en la fin peris,
Que ne fist Hero pour s'amour,   3335
Non contrestant mort ne clamour.

3300. A entichiez; other MSS entechiez--3215. FMDE touchie
3328. A mienuit

148

Beautiful Hero came to her end in this way,
Drowned in the sea from grief,
Along with her lover, for love's sake.
So there's no pain or misfortune
That might afflict the lover's heart   3300
Which brings such grievous pain
As that which spares nothing,
Putting Hero to death
For the sake of the lover she saw dead,
Nor could anyone reasonably make   3305
A true comparison of this to anything else,
No more than bitterness set against salve.
So for this reason I tell you, Guillaume,
That this debate's a joke;
Doubtless you are wrong."   3310

GUILLAUME

"Damsel, if I am wrong,
I certainly know that I will be condemned,
But hardly by you; for the passing
Of such a sentence ought not
To come from your mouth,   3315
Since the issue concerns you;
Instead the judge will be the one to say.
He will decide fittingly and truthfully.
But my heart greatly rejoices
In what I have heard you say;   3320
For it certainly helps my case."

SUFFICIENCY

"Helps yours, fair Guillaume? How so?"

GUILLAUME

"Damsel, now please listen carefully,
And I'll explain it to you straightaway:
When Love so tightly snared   3325
Leander, who would swim across
The sea, without boat or oar,
At midnight or thereabouts,
That foolish man who made the terrible mistake
Of crossing the sea for the sake of love,   3330
He did more and suffered worse
Than Hero, who offered herself to death,
If one considers the great perils
Which destroyed him in the end;
For the sake of her love he did more than Hero,   3335
Notwithstanding both death and lamenting.

149

Car cils qui fait premierement
Honneur, on dit communement
Qu'il a la grace dou bien fait,
Nom pas cils a qui on le fait;   3340
Et plus va a amour tirant
Cils qui preste que cils qui rant.
Einsi est il de tous services
Et aussi de tous malefices:
Car qui d'autrui grever se peinne,   3345
Certes, il doit porter la peinne.
Si que, ma chiere damoiselle,
Qui moult amez honneur la belle,
Vous devez bien, a dire voir,
De ce cop ci honneur avoir.   3350
Car bien et bel et sagement
L'avez dit; et certeinnement,
Diex pour moy dire le vous fit,
Car j'en averai le profit.

Si que, gentils dame de pris,   3355
Je croy que bien avez compris
L'entention des .ii. parties.
Et se celles qui ci parties
Sont contre moy vuelent plus dire,
Ce ne vueil je pas contredire   3360
Mais j'en ay dit ce qu'il m'en samble,
Present elles toutes ensamble,
Et tant, que je ne doubte mie
Que n'aie droit de ma partie."

                    LA DAME

Adont la dame souvereinne,   3365
Des .xii. droite cheveteinne
Qui avoient parlé pour li,
Dont au juge moult abely,
Prist a dire tout en oiant;
"De riens ne me va anoiant   3370
Ce qui est fait de nostre plait,
Mais moult souffissanment me plait,
Et bien m'en vueil passer atant.
Sires juges, jugiez atant
Que sentence sera rendue.   3375
Je suis de moult bonne attendue
Pour attendre vostre jugier,
Quant il vous en plaira jugier.
Bon conseil avez et seür,
Bien attemré et bien meür.   3380

3338. A dist

150

For the one who first does something
Honorable is commonly said
To get the grace from the good deed,
Not the one benefitted by it;   3340
And in the order of love the one who bestows
Advances farther than the one who gives in return.
So it is of all kinds of service,
And likewise of mistreatment as well;
For whoever troubles himself to hurt another   3345
Ought surely bear some pain himself.
Thus, my dear damsel, you
Who very much love to honor the beautiful lady,
You ought well, if the truth were spoken,
Bear off the honor from this encounter.   3350
For you have spoken well,
Prettily, and wisely; but surely
God made you do so for my sake,
Since I'll take the advantage from it.

And so, noble and worthy lady,   3355
I think you understand quite well
The opinions of the two parties,
And if those ladies who have here sided
Against me wish to say something more,
I will not protest.   3360
But I've said what I think on this subject
In the presence of these assembled ladies,
And it's sufficient, I think,
To win the debate for me."

                    THE LADY

And then the sovereign lady,   3365
True leader of the twelve
Who had spoken on her side,
And this pleased the judge greatly,
Began saying in the hearing of all:
"Nothing of what has come to pass   3370
In our debate displeases me;
Instead I am quite well satisfied,
And I certainly wish to leave it behind at this point.
Sir judge, make your decision now
That the sentence can be passed.   3375
I have very high hopes
In regard to the judgment I attend from you,
Whenever it pleases you to decide.
Your counselors are competent and assured,
Cool-headed and quite mature.   3380

S'alez, s'il vous plaist, a conseil,
Je le lo einsi et conseil,
Et vous conseilliez tout a trait.
Faire ne pouez plua biau trait
Que de traitablement attraire   xliiiiR   3385
Bon conseil, et puis de retraire
Les articles dou jugement,
Selonc le nostre entendement,
En gardant toudis nostre honneur.
Faire le devez, mon signeur.   3390
Et vous estes bien si vaillans
Que point n'en serez defaillans."

L'ACTEUR

Li juges qui bien l'escouta
Ses paroles si bien nota
Qu'a entendre pas ne failly.   3395
Tantost son conseil acueilly,
Et puis de la se departirent.
Or ne sceus je pas qu'il deïrent
En leur secret quant ad present,
Mais assez tost m'en fist present   3400
Uns amans qui tant bien m'ama
Que de tous poins m'en enfourma,
Nom pas par favourableté,
Mais de sa debonnaireté,
Afin que point ne variasse   3405
Et que de riens ne m'esmaiasse,
Par quoy je preïsse maniere
Uniement toudis entiere;
Qu'autel samblant devoie faire
Dou droit pour moy com dou contraire.   3410
Or me fonday seur ce propos;
S'en fu mes cuers plus a repos.
Quant a conseil se furent mis,
Li juges dist: "Je suis commis
A estre bons juges fïables,   3415
Aus .ii. parties amïables
Justement a point, sans cliner.
Si doy moult bien examiner
Trestout le fait par ordenence
Qui appert en nostre audience,   3420
Afin que loiaument en juge.
Einsi doivent faire bon juge.
Et vous vous devez travillier
De moy loyaument consillier.

3386. A le contraire; other MSS de retraire--3388. Other MSS
vostre--3389. AB nostre; other MSS vostre--3392-3. AFMBE heading reads le juge--3401. ABD amans; other MSS amis--3420. Other
MSS vostre

152

So proceed, if you please, to deliberate.
I advise and recommend
That you take this matter under consideration at once.
You could do no better
Than to request, in a fitting way,   3385
Some good advice and then rehearse
The issues which bear on the judgment,
As you understand them,
Preserving at all times your honor.
This you ought to do, my lord.   3390
For you certainly are so competent
That you will not be found wanting in any way."

THE AUTHOR

The judge, listening closely to her words,
Took such good notice
That he did not fail to understand them.   3395
He assembled his advisors at once,
And then they retired.
Now for the moment I didn't know
What they said in private,
But soon after a lover   3400
Who was very fond of me
Came and told me, so that I learned everything,
Not through any favoritism on his part,
But because of his good breeding,
So that I wouldn't disagree at all   3405
Or be surprised by anything,
And could thus assume an attitude
Of complete composure and firmness;
For I was obliged to react the same
To a decision for me as one against,   3410
And so I set myself upon this course;
Thus my heart was put more at ease.
When they arrived at the place of deliberation,
The judge said: "I have been commissioned
To be a competent and trustworthy judge,   3415
Amicable toward the two parties
To the same degree and without bias.
Thus I must examine quite carefully
All the evidence as it was presented
To us as we listened,   3420
So that we can judge it fairly.
This is what a competent judge should do.
And you must do your best
To advise me in good faith.

153

S'en die chascuns son plaisir,   3425
Tandis com nous avons loisir."
Dont Avis dist tantost après,
Qui fu de Congnoissance prés:
"Avis sui qui doy bien viser
Comment je vous puisse aviser.   3430
Car on puet faire trop envis
Bon jugement sans bon avis.

Je vous avis que bien facies
Et que le contraire effacies.
S'il vient par devant vostre face,   3435
Afin que point ne se parface,
En avisant seur .iiii. choses
Qui ne sont mie si encloses
Qu'on ne les puist assez vĕoir,
Qui un po s'en vuet pourvĕoir: 3440
Se jugement avez a rendre,
Premierement devez entendre
De savoir quels est li meffais
Et a qui il a esté fais.
Et si devez aussi savoir   3445
Et enquerir, par grant savoir,
Quant vous saverez le forfait
Et a cui cils l'avera fait,
Que vous sachiez dou tout l'affaire,
Quel cause l'esmuet ad ce faire.   3450
Or avez de .iiii. les trois.
Et li quars est li plus estrois
Auquel on doit bien regarder,
Comment on le puist bien garder:
C'est que vous metez vostre cure   3455
En sieuir les poins de nature
Ou coustume attraite de droit;
Si jugerez en bon endroit.
Plus n'en di. Qui vuet, si en die.
J'en ay assez dit ma partie."   3460

                    CONGNOISSANCE

Congnoissance qui avisa
Les poins qu'Avis bien devisa
Dist en haut: 'Avis, mes amis,
Ha orendroit en termes mis   xliiiiV
Aucuns poins qu'il a devisé,   3465
Les quels j'ay moult bien avisé,
Pour quoy dont je sui Congnoissance
Qui donne a bon Avis substance

3426. AB Toudis com non--3435. A Si bien--3441. ADE Ce
3456. Other MSS droiture

So everyone should say what he wants,   3425
Because we have the time for it."
And immediately afterward Discretion said,
He who was near Understanding:
"Because I'm Discretion I must attend carefully
To how I should advise you.   3430
For someone might very well be rather hesitant to attempt
A fair judgment without good advice.

I counsel you to do what's good
And undo what's wrong.
So it is your task,   3435
Before you come to a conclusion,
To attend to four things
Which are not so cut and dried
That they can be examined completely,
Whoever might wish to attempt it: 3440
If you have a judgment to render,
First you must undertake
To learn what the wrong is
And against whom it has been done.
After you should go on to discover   3445
And learn, with great wisdom,
Having already found out what the crime is
And who was injured by it,
What you should know about the matter as a whole--
Namely what was his motive for doing it.   3450
Now you have three things out of four.
And the fourth is the one which
Must be attended to most strictly and competently,
In whatever way it can best be seen to:
And that's to pay attention   3455
To following the rules of nature
Or of custom related to law;
In this way you'll judge from a firm basis.
I'll say no more; whoever wishes to, let her speak.
I've said enough here for my part."   3460

UNDERSTANDING

Understanding, having paid attention
To the points which Discretion has so well developed,
Said loudly: "Discretion, my friend,
Has just mentioned several points
In a suitable fashion, calling them to mind,   3465
The which I have taken very good note of
Because I am Understanding,
Who lends good Discretion the substance

155

Pour deviser ce qu'il devise,
De quoy la bonne gent avise.   3470
Je fais le scens d'Avis congnoistre,
Et il fait Congnoissance croistre
Par le courtois avis qu'il donne
De son droit a mainte personne.
Juges, se vous apointerez   3475
Comment seürement tenrez
D'Avis les poins et les usages.
Faites le, si ferez que sages.
Et de moy qui sui sa compaingne
Entendez que je vous enseingne;   3480
On a ci ce plait demené
Tant qu'on l'a par poins amené
Jusques au jugement oïr.
Resgardez qui en doit joïr.
Jugiez selonc le plaidïé   3485
Qu'on a devant vous plaidïé.
Par ce point ne poez mesprendre;
Car s'on vous en voloit reprendre,
Li plaïdiers aprenderoit
Le scens qui vous deffenderoit.   3490
Jugiez einsi hardiement
Et le faites congnoissanment
Au condempné bien amender;
Vous le pouez bien commander.
Je, Congnoissance, m'i acort;   3495
Et s'en preng aussi le recort
De Mesure qui la se siet
Lez Raison, et moult bien li siet,
Et Raison aussi en dira
Ce qui bon li en semblera."   3500

                        MESURE

Adont s'est Mesure levée,
En disant: "Ma trésbien amée
Congnoissance, dire ne vueil
Riens qui soit contre vostre vueil,
Eins sui moult trés bien acordans   3505
Ad ce qu'estes ci recordans.
S'en parleray a vostre honneur
Au juge, ce noble seigneur,
Qui est courtois et amïables,
Sages, vaillans, et honnourables."   3510
Lors tourna devers li sa chiere
De si amoureuse maniere,
Qu'il ne s'en pot tenir de rire.

3475. AF Jugiez

156

To devise what he devises,
So that he may counsel this good company.   3470
I make acknowledged the meaning of Discretion,
While he makes Understanding increase
With the courtly advice he gives,
By his right, to many a person.
Judge, please make plain   3475
How closely you will hold
To the terms and customs of Discretion.
If you do so, you'll act wisely.
And as for me, his companion,
Do attend to what I will teach you: 3480
This debate has continued,
Proceeding through its different stages
Until the time has come to hear a decision.
Let's see who'll be happy with it.
Judge according to the testimony   3485
Which has been presented to you.
In this way you cannot go wrong;
For if anyone wished to fault you,
The plaintiff would understand
The rationale which would justify you.   3490
Judge, therefore, with confidence,
And knowledgeably too,
So that you may correct the condemned party well.
You have the right to command him.
I, Understanding, am in agreement;   3495
And I am of the same opinion
As Moderation, seated there
By Reason's side--and well this suits her--
For now Reason will speak, in turn,
What she deems appropriate."   3500

                          MODERATION

Then Moderation stood up,
Saying: "My very well loved friend
Understanding, I'll now say nothing
That might be objectionable to you;
Instead I very much agree   3505
With what you've here maintained.
And I will talk about it to your credit
With the judge, this noble lord,
A man courteous and friendly,
Wise, courageous, and honorable."   3510
Then she turned her face toward his
In such a loving fashion
That he could not refrain from smiling.

Et Mesure li prist a dire:
"Biau sire, bien eüreus fustes   3515
Dou conseil que vous esleüstes.
Vous avez tout premierement
A Avis si bel commencement,
Qu'on faurroit bien en court roial
D'avoir conseil aussi loial.   3520
Je ne di pas qu'aucune gent
Ne moustrassent bien aussi gent
Conseil et aussi bien baillié
Et d'aussi bel parler taillié.
Mais vëons la condition   3525
D'Avis selonc s'entention:
Il donne conseil franc et quitte
Et n'en attent autre merite,
Fors ce que li juges tant face
Qu'il en ait pais, honneur, et grace.   3530
Et Congnoissance, sa compaingne,
A tel salaire s'acompaingne,
Sans demander nulle autre chose.
Dont loiaus juges se repose
Qui de tels gens est consilliez.   3535
Sire, s'en devez estre liez.
Comment qu'il aient dit a point,
Se passerai je outre d'un point
Qu'Avis avoit bien avisé--
Et se ne l'a pas devisé--   3540
Et Congnoissance congnëu.
Mais il s'en sont en cas dëu
Pour moy porter honneur, souffert;   xlvR
Dont de moy vous sera offert,
Pour ce que j'ay bien entendu   3545
Qu'il s'en sont a moy attendu.
Mais einsois averai ditté
D'un petit de ma qualité.

Je suis Mesure mesurée,
En tous bons fais amesurée,   3550
Et aussi sui je mesurans,
Ferme, seüre, et bien durans
A ceuls qui vuelent sans ruser
Justement de mesure user;
Et qui non, aveingne qu'aveingne,   3555
De son damage li souveingne.
Dont uns maistres de grant science
Et de trés bonne conscience
A un sien deciple enseingne

3518. A si; other MSS lack si--3538. Other MSS joutre
3553. All MSS Et

158

And Moderation began, saying to him:
"Fair sir, you have been very fortunate   3515
In the advisors you have chosen.
In the beginning you
Started out well with Discretion,
For one assuredly should, in a royal court,
Have advice as trustworthy as this.   3520
I don't say that another company
Would not proffer advice
As genteel and as well considered,
Fittingly furnished with pretty speech.
In any case, let us examine the nature   3525
Of Discretion as he himself understands it:
He provides counsel free and clear,
Expecting in return no reward at all,
Except that the judge might do what
Would bring him peace, honor, and thanks.   3530
Now Understanding, his companion,
Accompanies him for the same salary,
Without demanding anything else.
And so a trustworthy judge, one counseled
By such advisors, may rest easy.   3535
Sire, you ought to be happy
Because they have said what's appropriate;
But I will treat an issue
Which Discretion has certainly recognized--
And yet not discussed in detail--   3540
Though Understanding has taken note of it as well.
In any case, they have struggled, as obliged
In this matter, to bring me honor;
Therefore I offer this to you
Because I have certainly noticed   3545
The attention they've paid me.
And so I'll go ahead and explain
Something of my nature and purpose.

I am Moderation moderated,
Temperate in all good deeds,   3550
And also I am moderating,
Firm, stable, and filled with endurance
For all of those who wish, without trickery,
To make proper use of moderation;
And whoever does not, what will be will be;   3555
Let him be mindful of his own hurt.
In this regard, a master of great wisdom,
A man of great conscience,
Was instructing his disciple

159

Et li moustre de moy l'enseingne,   3560
Disant; 'Amis, je te chastoy;
Se tu ne mès Mesure en toy,
Elle s'i mettra maugré tien.
Ceste parole bien retien.
S'elle s'i met, tu és peris;   3565
Se tu l'i mès, tu és garis.'
Or vueil passer les poins tout outre
Qu'Avis et Congnoissance moustre.
Il ont servi courtoisement
De leur bon conseil largement,   3570
Si comme on sert a un mengier,
Sans rien d'especïal jugier;
Et de ce qu'il ont bien servi,
Dont il ont grace desservi,
J'en vorray l'escot assener,   3575
Et a chascun son droit donner.
Guillaumes qui en ses affaires
Soloit estre si debonnaires,
Si honnestes et si courtois,
Enclins aus amoureus chastois,   3580
A attenté contre Franchise,
Et tout de sa premiere assise,
Quant ma dame a point l'aprocha
Dou fait qu'elle li reprocha,
Et il s'en senti aprochiez   3585
A juste cause et reprochiez.
Il ala avant par rigueur,
Et se mist tout sa vigueur
Pour lui deffendre encontre li.
Cils poins fort me desabeli,   3590
Pour ce qu'il se desmesura:
Par ces raisons de Mesure ha
Les regles et les poins perdus,
Dont il sera moult esperdus
Quant a moy le retourneray;   3595
Car d'onneur le destourneray
Quant Congnoissance li dira
Le meffait que fait avera.
Il deüst avoir mesuré
L'estat dou gent corps honnouré   3600
De celle dame souvereinne;
Qu'en tout le crestïen demainne
N'a homme, s'il la congnoissoit,
—C'est bon a croire qu'einsi soit—
Qui hautement ne l'onnourast   3605
Et qui de lui ne mesurast

3590. A poins ci me—3606. A de li

And demonstrating my meaning   3560
In these words: 'Friend, I admonish you:
If you do not acquire Moderation yourself,
She'll make herself felt in you anyway.
Remember this saying well:
If she comes to you, you're done for;   3565
But if you welcome her, you'll be all right.'
Now I would like to review all the issues
Which Discretion and Understanding have brought up.
They have served courteously
And generously with their good advice,   3570
Just as one serves at a meal,
But without passing judgment on particulars;
And since they have served well,
They have earned thanks,
But now is the time to add up the bill,   3575
And give everyone his due.
Guillaume, who used to be
So well mannered in all he did,
A man so honest and courtly,
Bending to the warnings of love,   3580
Wronged Frankness
And all of her high rank
When my lady, as was proper, approached him
About the deed she chastized him for,
And he felt himself upbraided,   3585
For just cause, and reprimanded as well.
He then forcefully went about
Defending himself against her,
Putting all his strength in the effort.
And this very much distresses me   3590
Because he acted immoderately;
For these reasons he's left behind the rules
And principles of Moderation,
And as a result he'll be very much troubled
When I return him to me;   3595
For I will take away his honor
When Understanding informs him
About the error he has made.
He should have taken into account
The standing of the gentle, honored person   3600
Of the sovereign lady here;
For in all the Christian realm,
There's no man, if he recognized her
--And it's pleasing to believe it would be so--
Who would not honor her highly   3605
And who would not consider himself

161

Humble et courtoise petitesse
Au resgart de sa grant noblesse.
Dont Guillaumes est deceüs
Quant il ne s'en est perceüs.   3610
Car trop hautement commensa,
Dont petitement s'avansa.
Pour bien sa cause soustenir;
Eins est assez pour lui punir.
Or vëons au fait proprement   3615
Dès le premier commencement,
Pour bien deviser les parties,
Comment elles sont departies,
A savoir la quele se tort:
Je di que Guillaumes a tort;   3620
Car de tous les crueus meschiez
La mort en est li propres chies;
A dire est que tous meschies passe,   xlvV
Et pour ce que nuls n'en respasse;
Car on se puet trop miex passer   3625
De ce dont on puet respasser.
Plus de vueil de ce fait espondre,
Car j'ay assez, pour lui confondre,
D'autres choses trop plus greveinnes,
Simples, foles, vuides, et veinnes.   3630

Sires juges, or m'entendez;
Pour la fin a quoy vous tendez,
De rendre loial jugement,
Je vueil un po viser, comment
On a alligué de ce plait.   3635
Et vous meïsmes, s'il vous plait,
.I. petit y resgarderez,
Si que miex vous en garderez
De jugier autrement qu'a point.
Car vous congnoisterez le point   3640
De quoy justice est a point pointe
Quant juges sus bon droit s'apointe.
Je vueil que vous soiez certeins
Que Guillaumes doit estre attains
De son plait en celle partie   3645
Ou sa cause est mal plaidoïe,
Non obstant ce qu'en tous endrois
Par tout est contre lui li drois;
Dont ma dame a tout sormonté,
Tant dou plait com de la bonté   3650
De sa querelle qui est toute
Mise en clarté et hors de doubte,

3614. A li

162

Of much lower estate in regard to courtliness
When faced by her great nobility.
And so Guillaume was wrong
When he did not understand this.   3610
For he began in too haughty a fashion,
Advancing himself little
In regard to the competent presentation of his case;
On the contrary, there's enough here to condemn him.
Now let us examine the issue itself   3615
From its very beginning,
In order to distinguish between the parties,
To see what divides them,
So that we can discover which one is wrong.
In my view, Guillaume has erred: 3620
For of all cruel misfortunes,
Death is the absolute worst;
Which is to say that it surpasses all miseries,
And that's because no one recovers from it;
For a person can endure much better   3625
What he can recover from.
I don't wish to develop this point further,
For, in order to condemn him, I have plenty
Of evidence which is much more grievous,
Things which are stupid, foolish, empty, and vain.   3630

Sir judge, now listen to me:
For the sake of the goal you're aiming at,
Namely the rendering of an honest judgment,
I wish to consider how
This debate has been conducted.   3635
And you as well, if you please,
Look into this a little,
So that you may the better keep yourself
From passing anything but the appropriate judgment.
For you recognize the point   3640
On which justice is rightly fixed
When a judge establishes himself on true justice.
I want you to make certain
That Guillaume is reproached
For that part of his argument   3645
Which has badly furthered his case,
Notwithstanding the fact that in every way
And in everything the law is already against him;
Thus my lady has been completely successful,
As much in her debating as in the rightness   3650
Of her complaint, which has been completely
Clarified and put beyond doubt.

Ma dame, par ses damoiselles,
A alligué raisons trés beles
Et toutes choses veritables,   3655
Fermes, seüres, et estables,
Toutes traites de l'escripture
Et ramenées a droiture.
Mais qui tout vorroit deviser,
Trop y averoit a viser.   3660
Et, d'autre part, chose est certeinne,
Que la court en est assez pleinne
De tout ce qu'on a volu dire
De par ma dame, sans mesdire;
Si que de ma dame me tais.   3665
Et de Guillaume, qui entais
A esté d'alliguer s'entente,
Parleray--car il me talente--,
De son plaidïé seulement,
Et se m'en passerai briefment,   3670
Foy que devez tous vos amis.
Vëons qu'il a en terme mis:
Dou clerc qui hors dou scens devint,
A il prouvé dont ce li vint,
Que ce li venist de sa dame?   3675
Sires juges, foy que doi m'ame,
Il n'en a nulle riens prouvé;
Se li doit estre reprouvé.
Et dou chevalier qui par ire,
Pour ce qu'il ne se volt desdire,   3680
Copa son doi a tout l'anel,
Il fist en s'onneur .i. crenel
De honte pleinne de sotie
Avec trés grant forcenerie
Quant a sa dame l'envoia.   3685
Car bien croy qu'il li enuya;
Au mains li dut il ennuier
D'un si fait present envoier.
Car quant dame son ami aimme,
Dou droit d'Amours pour sien le claimme   3690
Et puet clamer, ce m'est avis.
Or resgardons sus ce devis,
Comment li chevaliers meffist:
Ce qu'elle amoit, il le deffist,
Qui estoit sien dou droit d'Amour.   3695
Dont je fais ci une clamour
Contre Guillaume de ce fait,
Que avis m'est qu'il n'a riens fait,
Car cils poins qu'il a mis en prueve

3687. FMBDE deust

164

My lady, through her damsels,
Has alleged very appropriate reasons
And facts which were all true,   3655
Firm, unassailable, and unwavering,
All justly drawn and adduced
From the written tradition of the law.
But whoever would care to recount all of it
Would have too much here to consider.   3660
And furthermore, one thing is certain,
Namely that the court has been sufficiently filled
With everything one might want to say
On my lady's behalf, and this is no lie;
So I won't say anything about my lady.   3665
But in regard to Guillaume, who has been
Intent on arguing his case,
I will speak--for I want to do so--,
But only in regard to his arguments,
And I will be brief about it,   3670
By the faith which you owe all your friends.
Let's see what he has brought up:
Concerning the clerk who went out of his mind,
Has he proved how this happened to him,
That it was caused by his lady?   3675
Sir judge, by the faith I owe my soul,
He has proved nothing of the kind;
And so he ought to be chastized.
And about the knight who through his anguish,
Because he would not break his word,   3680
Cut off his finger with the ring still on it,
He erected a monument full of shame
And madness in her honor,
When, in a terrible fit of craziness,
He sent it on to his lady.   3685
For I believe that it surely upset her;
At least it ought to have upset her
To have such a thing sent her as a present.
For when a lady loves her lover,
She claims him for her own by the law of Love,   3690
And can claim him rightfully as such, so I think.
Now, in regard to this principle, let us consider
How the knight erred:
He harmed what she loved,
What was hers by the law of Love.   3695
So I make a protest
To Guillaume on this point,
Because it seems to me he's done nothing with this,
For the fact he has presented as evidence

Sa cause punist et reprueve.   3700
Et aussi de la Chastelainne
De Vergi, a petite peinne
Assez reprouver le porray   xlviR
Par les raisons que je diray:
Li fais que Guillaumes soustient,   3705
Sire, vous savez qu'il contient
Qu'amans, garnis de loiauté,
Truist en sa dame fausseté.
Et sus ceste devision
Il fait une allegation,   3710
Pour prouver par .i. fait contraire:
La Chasteleinne debonnaire
N'avoit son ami riens meffait;
Mais il meïsmes fist le fait
Pour quoy elle se mist a mort.   3715
Quant il le sceut, il se remort
Et se mist en la congnoissance
Qu'il y apartenoit vengence;
Dont il meïsmes se juga,
Punist dou tout et corriga.   3720
Dont Guillaumes a par son dit
Pour son profit meins que nient dit.
Plus n'en di; mais Raisons dira
Ci après ce qu'il li plaira.'

                    L'ACTEUR

A ces mos s'est Raison drecie,   3725
Comme sage et bien adrecie,

                    RAISON

Disant: "Ralons en consistoire.
La porrons par parole voire,
Ce m'est vis, bon jugement rendre,
S'il est qui bien le sache entendre."   3730
Atant de la se departirent.
Es propres lieus se rasseïrent
Ou il avoient devant sis.
Lors dist Raisons par mos rassis:
"Sire juges, certeinnement   3735
Chose n'a sous le firmament
Qui ne tende a conclusion:
Les unes a perfection
Pour pluseurs cas de leur droit tendent;
Et si a autres qui descendent   3740
De haut ou elles ont esté
En declinant d'un temps d'esté

3703. A li--3735. ABDE Sire; other MSS Sires

                         166

Damages and undermines his case.   3700
And also concerning the Chatelaine
De Vergy, with only a little trouble
I can refute his claim satisfactorily
Using the reasons I'll here rehearse;
The view Guillaume supports,   3705
You know, Sire, that it holds
That the lover, filled with loyalty,
Found falseness in his lady.
Now, beginning with this assumption,
He made an allegation   3710
In order to offer proof by a contrary fact:
The Chatelaine of noble birth
Did not wrong her lover in any way;
Rather it was he himself who did what
Caused her to kill herself.   3715
When he learned about it, he had remorse
And came to the realization
That vengeance was appropriate;
So he passed judgment on himself,
Punished and corrected himself for all he had done.   3720
Thus Guillaume, with what he has said,
Has spoken nothing here that profits him.
I'll say nothing more; but Reason will speak
Here afterward whatever she wishes."

THE AUTHOR

With these words Reason got up,   3725
Like someone wise and well schooled,

REASON

Saying: "Let's go back to the courtroom.
There with truthful speech we can
Render an appropriate judgment, or so I think,
If there's anyone well able to understand it.'   3730
And then they left that place.
And they seated themselves again in their own seats,
Just where they had sat before.
Reason with measured words then said:
"Sir Judge, certainly   3735
There's no body under heaven's vault
That doesn't seek its proper end:
Some tend toward perfection
For various reasons pertaining to their own laws;
And there are yet others which descend   3740
From the height where they've been,
Declining from the summer season

167

En l'iver qu'on dit anientir.
Dont cils plais desire a sentir
De droit conclusions hastive   3745
Par sentence diffinitive,
Pour ce qui est bien pris parfaire
Et ce qui est mal pris deffaire.
Et il est temps, bien le savez,
Que desormais dire en devez,   3750
Ou ordener qu'on en dira."

                     LE JUGE

"Raison, dame, ne m'avenra
Que j'en die, quant ad present.
Mais je reçoy bien le present
D'ordener. Et de m'ordenance,   3755
Mais qu'il soit a vostre plaisence,
Dites en et tant en faciez
Que le tort dou tout effaciez,
Et metez le droit en couleur
De toute honnourable honneur,   3760
Qui savez en tels couleurs teindre
Ou nuls, fors vous, ne puet ateindre."

                   GUILLAUME

Lors Raisons .i. po s'arresta
Et puis sus destre s'acota,
En regardant devers senestre,   3765
Pour miex aviser de mon estre.

                    RAISON

Se me dist: "Guillaume, biaus sire,
Vous avez piessa oÿ dire
Que c'est folie d'entreprendre
Plus que pooirs ne puet estendre.   3770
Et toute voie, s'on emprent
Aucun fait de quoy on mesprent,
S'on s'en repent au moien point,
Encor y vient il bien a point.
Mais qui son forfait continue   3775
Et dou parfaire s'esvertue
Jusqu'a tant qu'il vient au darrain,
Et a ce point ne trueve rien   xlviV
Fors que son dueil et son damage.
Se lors recongnoist son outrage,   3780
Il vient trop tart au repentir.
Guillaume, sachiez sans mentir,
Qu'ensement avez vous ouvré.

3749. Other MSS vous le--3751. A qui; other MSS quon
3767. AF biaus; other MSS biau--3776. A parfaire continue
3777. A darrain; other MSS derrien

                      168

Into the so-called winter of destruction.
Similarly, this debate is moving toward
A correct and quick conclusion   3745
By means of a definitive sentence,
In order to perfect what has been well undertaken
And undo all that has been unfortunately begun.
Now, as well you know, the moment has come
When you must address this   3750
Or command that it be spoken of."

THE JUDGE

"Reason, madam, it's not appropriate for me
To speak, at least for the present,
But I receive gladly the notion
Of a decision. And in regard to my judgment,   3755
So that it may be to your liking,
Say and do enough here
In order to efface everything wrong,
Restoring the right to the shade
Of every honorable honor,   3760
You who know how to paint in such hues
Which no one, save you, can manage."
Then Reason halted a little,

GUILLAUME

Leaning then toward the right,
While glancing to her left   3765
In order to take better account of the state I was in.

REASON

And she said to me: "Guillaume, fair sir,
You've just now heard it said
That it's madness to take on
More than ability can compass.   3770
And certainly, if anyone does
Something that gives offense,
If, in the middle of doing so, he repents,
Then he'll still make out all right.
But whoever persists in his error   3775
And exerts himself to see it through,
Until he comes to the very end itself,
At this point he will find nothing
But his own grief and harm;
If then he recognizes his outrage,   3780
He comes too late to repentance.
Guillaume, be sure--and it's no lie--
That you have carried on in this way.

169

S'en avez un dueil recouvré
Qui vous venra procheinnement, 3785
Et se vous durra longuement,
Voire, se ne vous repentez.
Mais je croy que vous estes telz
Que vous ne le deingneries faire.
Car trop fustes de rude affaire, 3790
Quant la dame vous aprocha
D'un fait qu'elle vous reprocha
Que fait avies ou temps passé.
Se vous heüssiez compassé
En vous aucune congnoissance 3795
Qui fust signes de repentence
De ce que vous aviez mespris
Contre les dames de haut pris,
Vous heüssiez fait moult que sages.
Car d'Amours est tels li usages 3800
Que s'aucuns des dames mesdit,
S'il ne s'en refreint et desdit,
Amender le doit hautement
Ou comparer moult chierement.
Or de ce meffait premerein 3805
Vous di de par le souverain
Amours, qui est maistres et sires,
Des plaies amoureuses mires:
Jugemens en est ordenez
Dou quel vous estez condempnez. 3810
Si qu'amender le vous couvient;
Hastivement li termes vient.
Encor vous puis je commander
Si qu'il vous couvient amender
Un autre fait qui me desplait, 3815
De ce que vous prenistes plait
Contre dame de tel vaillance
Et de si trés noble puissance,
Que je ne say haute personne,
Tant com li siecles environne, 3820
Prince ne duc, conte ne roy,
Qui osast faire tel desroy,
Guillaume, comme vous feïstes
Dou plait qu'a li entrepreïstes,
Et meïstes force et vigueur 3825
En aler avant par rigueur.
Einsi l'avez continué;
S'avez vostre sens desnué
De courtoisie et d'ordenance.
Se ce ne fust la pacience 3830

170

Thus you have deserved some sorrow,
And it will shortly be yours,
To last a long time,
Truly, if you do not repent.
But I believe you are the kind of man
Who will not deign to do so.
For you were much too stupid   3790
When the lady approached you
About the deed she then censured you for,
One which you committed some time ago.
If you had shown
Any sign in your manner   3795
Which would have indicated repentance
For the wrong you did
To ladies of great worth,
You would have been acting wisely.
For the custom of love is such   3800
That if anyone defames women,
And does not recant doing so, afterward refraining,
He must make severe amends
Or pay quite dearly.
Now about this first misdeed,   3805
I tell you, on the part of sovereign
Love, who is lord and master,
The physician of the wounds of loving,
That the judgment here has been made
That you are to be condemned.   3810
So it's necessary for you to make amends;
The time for this quickly approaches.
Furthermore, I am empowered to order you
To make amends--and you must do so--
For another deed that displeases me,   3815
Namely that you undertook a debate
Against a lady of such worth
And of such noble power
That I know of no high personage,
So far as the world extends,   3820
No prince or duke, no count or king,
Who would dare perpetrate such an outrage,
Guillaume, as did you,
When you entered into a debate against her,
A debate in which you put force and energy   3825
And proceeded aggressively.
Now you have continued to do so;
And thus you have stripped your mind
Of courtesy and due respect.
But if she didn't have the patience   3830

171

Qui est en li, vous perdissiez
Tant qu'a meschief le portissiez."

GUILLAUME

Quant j'oÿ ce, je fui dolens;
Mais je ne fui feintis ne lens
De li demander humblement   3835
Qu'elle me devisast briefment
De la dame la verité
D'un petit de sa poësté.

RAISON

Lors dist: "Guillaume, volentiers.
Mais je n'en dirai hui le tiers,   3840
Non mie, par Dieu, le centisme.
Car dès le ciel jusques en bisme
Ses puissances par tout s'espandent,
Et de ses puissances descendent
Circonstances trop mervilleuses,   3845
Et sont a dire perilleuses,
Qui s'apruevent par leur contraire.
Par ces raisons s'en couvient taire
Pour les entendemens divers
Qui sont aucune fois pervers.   3850
La dame a nom Bonneürté,
Qui tient en sa main Seürté
En la partie de Fortune;
Car il n'est personne nesune
Cui Fortune peüst abatre,   3855
Se la dame le vuet debatre.   xlviiR
Et quant elle vuet en Nature
Ouvrer par especial cure,
La la voit on sans nul moien,
Voire, li astronomien   3860
Qui congnoissent les nations
Parmi les constellations,
C'est assavoir ès enfans nestre
De quel couvine il doivent estre.
Dont, quant la chiere dame regne   3865
Et uns enfes naist en son regne,
Se Bonneürtez l'entreprent,
Nature point ne l'en reprent,
Eins l'en laist moult bien couvenir,
Comment qu'il en doie avenir.   3870
Voirs est que Nature norrit
Par quoy li enfes vit et rit;
Et Bonneürtez le demeinne

3841. FMBDE la centisme

172

Which she does, you would have lost so much
That you'd have been ruined by it."

GUILLAUME

When I heard this, I was distressed;
But I was neither too abashed nor hesitant
To ask her humbly   3835
If she would briefly explain to me
The truth about the lady,
And something of her power.

REASON

Then she said: "Guillaume, willingly.
But I won't describe even a third of it today,   3840
Not even, by God, a hundredth part.
For from the sky down to the pit
Her powers extend through things,
And these powers cause things
To happen which are too wondrous   3845
And even too dangerous to speak of,
For they show this by their contrary.
So it's necessary to pass over them in silence
Because of the unusual meaning they have,
Something which would be perverse at any time.   3850
The lady's name is Happiness,
And she holds Security, from among
The company of Fortune, by the hand;
For there is no person at all
Whom Fortune can bring low   3855
If the lady wishes to oppose it.
And when she wishes to intervene in Nature
Because of some special concern,
She can be observed there without any difficulty,
That is, by the astrologers   3860
Who interpret births
By the constellations,
Which is to say divining through the birth of infants
What condition they are to live in.
Thus when the dear lady is in the reigning position   3865
And a child is born during that reign,
If Happiness takes charge of him,
Nature does not sorrow at all;
Instead she very much lets her do what she will,
However it may be destined to turn out.   3870
It is true that Nature looks to
How the child lives and laughs;
And Happiness leads him into

Tout parmi l'eüreus demainne,
Tant qu'il est temps qu'en lui appere   3875
Que de Bonneürté se pere.

Or sont celle gent si parent,
Dont elle est en euls apparent
Parmi le bien qu'il en reçoivent,
Afin que ne lui n'en deçoivent.   3880
Or vous vueil je dire en appert
En quels manieres elle appert,
En aucunes, nom pas en toutes;
Et si ne faites nulles doubtes
Des paroles que j'en diray;   3885
Car de riens ne vous mentiray.
Elle appert en prosperité
Et en issir de povreté;
Elle appert en acquerre amis
Et en punis ses anemis   3890
Par victoire, sans nul tort faire;
Elle appert en tout bon affaire;
Et quant elle appert en amours,
C'est quant amans, par reclamours,
Par servir ou par ses prieres   3895
Et en toutes bonnes manieres,
Puet en pais de dame joïr
Dou droit especial joïr
Qu'amours donne de sa franchise.
La est Bonneürtes assise   3900
Entre ami et loial amie
Qui ne vuelent que courtoisie
Et ont par certeinne affiance
Li uns a l'autre grant fiance.
La les tient elle en moult grant point.   3905
Elle est a tous biens mettre a point;
S'en est moult plus gaie et plus cointe;
Elle est de tous les bons acointe.
Elle appert en mains esbanois,
Tant en joustes comme en tournois,   3910
Pour chevalerie essaucier
Et les fais des bons avancier
A la congnoissance des dames.
La croist honneur; la chiet diffames.
Car tels a esté diffamez   3915
Qui puis est chieris et amez
De ceuls qui ains le diffamoient,
Pour ce qu'apertement vëoient

3887. MSS I1; emendation suggested by Hoepffner--3889. MSS
I1; emendation suggested by Hoepffner--3891. Other MSS sans
nul tort; A accort--3897. A dames--3908. A les biens--3911. A
cevalerie--3913. A des des--3914. A crois bonneur

174

The domain itself of good fortune,
Until it's time for it to show   3875
That he's being glorified by Happiness.

Now these people are quite remarkable
Because she is manifest in them
Through the benefits they receive from her,
Unless they deceive her in some way.   3880
Now I'll tell you specifically
About the different ways she manifests herself,
About some, but not all.
And have no doubt about
The words I'll speak here;   3885
For I will lie to you in no way.
She appears in prosperity
And in the leaving behind of poverty;
She's there in the making of friends
And the punishment of enemies   3890
In victory, without any quarter given;
She appears in every good deed,
And when she's present in love,
It's that the lover, through his demands,
Through his service and his pleading,   3895
Or by any suitable means at all,
Is able to enjoy his lady in peace,
To take pleasure in the special privilege
That love grants in her generosity.
There Happiness sits   3900
Between the lover and loyal beloved,
Those who wish for only what's courtly
And who have by an explicit pledge
Placed great trust in one another.
She sustains them in a quite grand state.   3905
All goods are hers to grant properly;
And she is much more gay and pleased because of them.
She's the acquaintance of all good people.
She appears in many pleasurable things,
In jousts as much as in tourneys,   3910
In order to exalt chivalry
And advance the deeds of good men
In the recognition of women.
There honor grows; there infamy falls away.
For such a man who has been ill spoken of   3915
Is afterward cherished and loved
By those who, before, had defamed him,
Because they see openly

Qu'il met son corps en aventure;
Dont tels fois est qu'il aventure   3920
Dou fait d'armes qu'il a empris,
Tant qu'il vient au souverein pris.
Einsi Bonneürtez avance
Les siens de sa haute puissance.

Se Bonneürtez par nature,   3925
Par fortune ou selonc droiture,
Appert en la chevalerie,
Elle appert aussi en clergie:
La tient elle honneur en ses mains.
A l'un plus et a l'autre mains   3930
En fait ses larges departies;
S'en donne les plus grans parties
A ceuls qui tiennent miex l'adresse
Ou Bonneürtez les adresse.
Aussi appert elle en science,   3935
Et se s'enclot en conscience,   xlviiV
Pour garder ceuls aucune fois
En cui est pais et bonne fois,
Qui n'ont pas par voie autentique
Mis leur scens en fourme publique,   3940
Eins sont sage secretement.
La se tient elle closement;
La li tiennent grant compaignie
Loiaus secrez et bonne vie.
La se vuet elle reposer   3945
Et les cuers a point disposer
En la vie contemplative.
Or revient par la voie active
Pour esmouvoir ceuls de parler
Qui tiennent volentiers parler   3950
Des biens de contemplation;
Dont maint, par bonne entention,
S'enlcinent si a sa doctrine
Que chascuns par soy se doctrine
D'estre diligens et hastis   3955
De devenir contemplatis.
Que vous iroie je contant?
En Bonneürté a de biens tant
Que jamais n'aroie compté
Le centisme de sa bonté.   3960
Dont au monde n'a grant signeur
Ne dame, tant aient d'onneur,
Qu'il ne leur fust et bel et gent,
S'estre pooient de sa gent.

3948. A la vie--3958. Other MSS omit En

176

That he risks his life;
And so the time comes when he takes his chance   3920
In the trial of arms he's engaged in,
Until at last he rises to the highest rank.
Thus Happiness advances
Her own with her great power.

Though Happiness by nature,   3925
By fortune or according to custom,
Is evident in the deeds of chivalry,
She appears also in learning:
There she holds honor in her hands,
More to the one and to the other less   3930
She makes her generous distribution;
And she gives out the greatest shares
To those who keep better to the summons
Happiness directs to them.
She is also manifest in knowledge,   3935
Enclosing herself within the conscience
In order to safeguard at all times those
In whom there's peacefulness and good faith,
Those who have not in any accustomed way
Put their wisdom into a public form,   3940
But rather are secretly wise.
There she keeps herself hidden;
And there faithful secret and good living
Afford her good companionship.
There she wishes to remain,   3945
Appropriately turning those hearts
Toward the contemplative life.
Then by the active path she returns
To encourage those to speak
Who willingly hold discussion   3950
About the benefits of contemplation;
And so many, with good intentions,
Incline themselves in this way to her teaching,
So that each teaches himself, through his own impulse,
How to be diligent and eager   3955
To become a contemplative.
Should I go on speaking about it to you?
Happiness possesses so many goods
That never would I be able to relate
The hundredth part of her goodness.   3960
So in the world there's no great lord
Nor lady, however much honor they possess,
For whom it would not be pleasing and noble
To be of her company.

Atant m'en tais; je n'en di plus,   3965
Mais que venir vueil au seurplus
Des .ii. poins dont condempnés estes;
Et s'ay mes raisons toutes prestes
Dou tiers point que je vous diray,
Dou quel je vous condempneray.   3970

Il est bien veritable chose
Que, s'aucuns a .i. plait s'oppose,
S'il se trait a production
Et il vient a probation,
Se s'entention bien ne prueve,   3975
Verité de droit li reprueve
Qu'il en doit estre condempnez.
Cils drois est de si lonc temps nez
Qu'il n'est memoire dou contraire.
Or vëons a quoy je vueil traire,   3980
Et s'entendez bien a mon dit:
De quanque la dame vous dit
De son fait, vous vous opposastes
Et dou prouver vous avansastes.
Mais vous avez si mal prouvé   3985
Qu'il vous doit estre reprouvé
A vostre condempnation,
Selonc la mienne entention.
Vous n'avez ci dit que paroles
Qui sont aussi comme frivoles.   3990
Belles sont a conter en chambre,
Mais elles ne contiennent membre
Dont pourfis vous peüst venir
Pour vostre prueve soustenir.
Et si avons si bien gardé   3995
Com nous poons, et regardé,
Pour querir loyal jugement.
S'il vous plaist a savoir comment,
On vous en dira les parties,
Comment elles sont departies.   4000
Et de vostre erreur tous les poins.
Et se vous veëz qu'il soit poins
Qu'on vous die vostre sentence,
Se nous dites que vos cuers pense;
Qu'il vous en plaist, on le fera   4005
Si a point que bien souffira."

                    GUILLAUME

"Dame, bien vous ay entendu,
Et s'ay bonne piece attendu

3984. A dou premier

                    178

Now I'll be silent; I'll say no more about her,   3965
But rather I'd like to see to what remains
Concerning the two counts for which you are condemned.
Now I'll speak about the third count,
For my arguments are all ready,
And it's something I condemn you for as well.   3970

It's certainly an indisputable fact
That, if someone opposes a complaint,
Busies himself with producing evidence
And comes to the test,
Yet fails to prove his view adequately,   3975
True justice reprimands him
And he must be condemned.
This legal principle came into being so long ago
That there is no memory of its contrary.
Now let's attend to what I wish to explain;   3980
Listen carefully to my words.
Whatever the lady told you
About your opinions you contradicted,
And you tried to offer proof for your view.
But you have so badly failed to prove it   3985
That you ought to be reprimanded
And, as a consequence, condemned;
At least that's my thought.
The words you've uttered here
Are nothing but frivolity.   3990
They are pretty to mouth in private,
But they contain no substance
That might help you
In sustaining the proof you require.
Furthermore, we have considered this issue   3995
And examined it as ably as we might
In order to reach an impartial verdict.
And if it pleases you to know the particulars,
You will be told about its different parts,
Just as they are divided up,   4000
And also all the aspects of your error.
And since you see that it's time
For your sentence to be pronounced,
Tell us what you think in your heart;
If you like, this may be done   4005
Thoroughly enough to satisfy."

GUILLAUME

"Lady, I understand you quite well,
And have waited some time

179

Que je fusse sentenciez.
Se vous pri que vous en soiez   4010
Diligens de moy delivrer,
Quant a ma sentence livrer.
Dès que mes fais est si estrois
Que je doy des amendes trois
Et qu'autrement ne puet aler,   xlviiiR   4015
Je n'en quier plus faire parler."

"Guillaume, soiez tous certeins
Que de droit y estes ateins;
Se n'en serons point negligens.
Or soiez aussi diligens,   4020
Et puis maintenant vous levez
Pour faire ce que vous devez
Vers celui qui pour juge siet.
S'en fera ce que bon l'en siet.
Dès or mais a lui appartient,   4025
Car tout le droit en sa main tient."

A ce mot au juge en alay
Et d'un genouil m'agonouillay.
La li presentai je mon corps
Par si couvenable recors,   4030
Comme je peus et li sceus dire;
Dont it prist un petit a rire.
Lors pris mes gans, si li tendi;
Dont il qui bien y entendi
Les prist, et puis si les laissa;   4035
Après .i. po se rabaissa,
Si que secondement les prist,
Puis les laissa, puis les reprist,
En signe de moy moustrer voie
Que troie amendes li devoie.   4040
Moult bien le me signefia,
Et pour verité m'affia
Qu'il les me couvenroit paier.
Lors me dist il, sans delaier,
Que je me ralasse sëoir,   4045
Car il se voloit pourvëoir
Quel penitence il me donroit,
Et que brief m'en delivreroit.

Lors près de la dame se trait,
Et Raison aussi, tout a trait,   4050

                    180

To be sentenced.
So I beg you to be diligent   4010
In delivering me to this,
That is, in granting me my sentence.
Since what I did is so serious
That it requires three compensations,
And since things cannot be different,   4015
I don't wish any further discussion."

REASON

"Guillaume, be completely assured
That you've received justice here;
And that we will not be negligent in any way.
But now you should be just as diligent;   4020
So get on your feet
To do what you should do
For that man who sits as judge,
And then he'll do what he thinks right.
From now on the matter rests with him,   4025
For he holds all the legal power in his hands."

GUILLAUME

After she said this I went over to the judge
And got down on one knee.
There I offered my person to him
In as appropriate a speech   4030
As I was able and knew how to make;
At this he began to smile a little.
Then I removed my gloves, tendering them to him;
And he who understood quite well
Took them and then dropped them;   4035
In a moment he leaned down again,
Taking them up a second time,
Then letting them go; and he took them up once more
As a sign to demonstrate to me
That I owed three compensations.   4040
He signified this to me quite well,
Assuring me in truth
That I would have to pay them.
Then he told me, without any hesitation,
That I should go back and sit down,   4045
For he wished to consider
What penance he would give me,
Something he would shortly deliver.

Then he drew up close to the lady,
And Reason did as well, quite demurely,   4050

181

A leur secret conseil se mist
Et de bas parler s'entremist.
Mais a leur parler bassement
Pris un petit d'aligement,
Pour ce que je bien percevoie   4055
Que leurs consaus estoit de joie;
Car d'eures en autres rioient,
Et a ce droit point qu'il estoient
Au plus estroit de leur conseil,
Avis me dist: "Je vous conseil   4060
Que ceste dame resgardez
Et songneusement entendez
Aus drois poins de sa qualité.
La verrez vous grant quantité
De sa grace et de son effort.   4065
S'en averez le cuer plus fort
Pour endurer et pour souffrir
Ce que drois vous vorra offrir."
Lors li dis je: "Biaus dous amis,
Mais vous m'en faites le devis   4070
Qui congnoissez de moult de choses
Les apparans et les encloses;
Souvent en estes a l'essay,
C'est une chose que bien say."
Adont dist Avis: "Ce vaut fait.   4075
Or entendez bien tout a fait:
Quant aus parties deviser,
Se bien vous volez aviser,
Elle a vestu une chemise
Qui est appellée Franchise   4080
Pour secrés amans afranchir
Et de Sobreté enrichir
En la partie de Silence
Parmi l'acort de Congnoissance.
Car pour tant qu'elle n'est venüe,   4085
Sa cause doit estre teüe.
Et sa pelice, c'est Simplesse
Si souef que point ne la blesse,
Car elle est de Beniveillance,
Orfroisie de Souffissance,   4090
A pelles de douce Plaisance
Qui bon cuers en tous biens avance.
Et li changes qu'elle a vestu   xlviiiV
Par trés honnourable vertu
Fu fais de loial Acointance   4095
Et ridez de Continuance
A pointes de Perseverance

4089. A bniveillance--4091. FMBDE Appelles; A Appelle

And he counseled privately with them,
Being careful to speak softly.
But in their whispering
He found some enjoyment,
For I readily perceived   4055
That their meeting was a happy one
For from time to time they laughed.
And just at that moment when they were
Most seriously deliberating,
Discretion said to me: "I advise you   4060
To look at this lady
And attend carefully to
The rightful aspects of her character.
There you'll see a great deal
Of her grace and power.   4065
And in this way your heart will be much stronger
To endure and suffer
Whatever justice she'll offer you."
Then I said to him: "Dear sweet friend,
Do you give me the key to this,   4070
You who know the obvious and hidden details
Of so many things.
Often you take on such a task;
That's something I know well."
Discretion said then: "This merits doing.   4075
Now pay quick attention:
As far as describing the elements is concerned,
If you wish to mark this well,
She's wearing a blouse
Called Frankness   4080
In order to liberate secret lovers
And enrich them with Seriousness
On behalf of Silence,
According to the agreement of Understanding.
For in as much as she's not seen,   4085
Her purpose may be kept secret.
And her fur wrap, that's Simplicity,
So soft that nothing may injure her,
For it comes from Good Will,
Gilt-edged by Sufficiency,   4090
With the pelts of Sweet Pleasure,
Who moves all good hearts toward every good.
And the robe which she wears
With very honorable virtue
Was made by loyal Friendship,   4095
Pleated by Steadfastness
With the marks of Perseverance

Egalment, sans desordenance.
Or est cils changes biaus et les
Et est de son droit appellez   4100
Pour certeine condition
Honneste Conversation.
Et la sainture qu'elle ha sainte
N'est pas en amours chose fainte,
C'est propre loial Couvenance,   4105
Cloée de ferme Fiance.
Car qui couvenances affie,
Necessitez est qu'on s'i fie.
Et li mordans, pour ce qu'il poise,
Sert d'abaissier tençon et noise,   4110
Si que jusqu'a ses piez li bat.
Et si piet deffont maint debat
Entre amie et loial amy,
Quant aucuns amans dit: 'Aimy!
De ma dame sui refusez;   4115
Mais mes drois n'est pas abusez,
Car je croy bien qu'elle le fit
A s'onneur et a mon profit.'
Einsi si piet la gent demainne,
Cui elle tient en son demainne;   4120
Car il sont chaucié d'Aligence,
Lacié a laz de Diligence.
Et s'a mis blans gans en ses mains,
Li quel sont fait ne plus ne mains
Entre Charité et Largesse,   4125
Dont elle depart la richesse
D'Amours qu'on ne puet espuisier
Ne par nul jour apetisier.
Plus en prent on, plus en demeure
De jour en jour et d'eure en heure.   4130
Dou mantel vous vueil aviser
Comme il est biaus a deviser,
Et mieudres que biaus qui s'en cuevre
Par dit, par maintieng, et par oeuvre.
Lainne de bons Appensemens   4135
Avecques courtois Parlemens,
Scienteuse Introduction,
Et amiable Entention
Furent ensamble compilées,
De Bonté proprement drapées;   4140
Et de ses choses asamblant
Fu fais li dras de bon samblant,
Tains en une gaie couleur
De trés honnourable valeur

4107. A Qu--4121. A chauciet--4124. A son--4129. A prent et
plus--4141. AFMBE ses; other MSS ces

184

Neatly, without disorder.
Now this robe is both beautiful and flowing
And is by proper right called,   4100
Because of its special status,
Honest Familiarity.
And the belt she's girded herself with
Is hardly insignificant as far as love's concerned,
For it's properly loyal Promise,   4105
Studded with stable Accord.
For whoever makes promises
Must then carry them out.
And the belt medallion, because it is heavy,
Serves to beat down dissension and discord,   4110
And thus it hangs to her feet.
And her feet prevent many an argument
Between beloved and loyal lover,
Whenever a lover cries: 'Alas!
I have been refused by my lady;   4115
But my rights have not been abused,
For I believe that she's done so
For my profit and in accord with her honor.'
Thus her feet keep this company in line,
Whomever she holds in her domain;   4120
For they are shod with Relief,
Laced with cords of Diligence.
And she's put white gloves on her hands,
Which have not been made more or less
By both Charity and Generosity,   4125
With which she shares out the riches
Of love that cannot be exhausted,
Nor at any time reduced.
The more that's taken, the more remains
From day to day and hour to hour.   4130
I'd like to tell you about the mantle
Since it is handsome to describe,
And better than handsome for whoever uses it as a cover
By words, by demeanor, and by deeds.
The linen of good Reflection,   4135
Along with courtly Speech,
Knowledgeable Introduction,
And friendly Intention
Were pieced there together,
Properly fabricated by Goodness;   4140
And the wrap of good appearance
Was made of her things together,
Dyed with a merry color
Of most honorable worth

Qui est appellée Noblesse,   4145
Et est fourrez de Gentillesse.
Or est Bonneürtez couverte
Dou mantel, et est chose aperte
Que par dessous tous biens enclot.
Mais veritablement esclot   4150
Quanqu'il a sous sa couverture
Li apparans de sa figure,
Si comme, en sa fisonomie,
Li bien de toute courtoisie
Trés souffissanment y apperent,   4155
Dont ses damoiselles se perent.
Et elle est aussi bien parée
D'elles, sans estre separée
D'elles et de leur bon arroy;
Car elles souffissent pour roy   4160
Et pour souvereinne roÿne.
Pour ces raisons vous determine
Que Bonneürtez dou tout passe
Toutes roÿnes et trespasse.
Se je voloie sa coronne   4165
Deviser qui est belle et bonne,
Trop longuement vous en tenroie;
Car je voy bien la droite voie
Que leur consaus va a declin.
Atant pais de ce vous declin."   4170

                        GUILLAUME

Quant leur consaus fu affinez,
Li juges s'est vers moy tournes,   xlixR

                        LE JUGE

En disant: "Guillaume, par m'ame,
Ytant vous di de par ma dame
Et de par raison ensement,   4175
Et je sui en l'acordement,
Que de .iii. amendes devez
Devisées, et eslevez,
Lesqueles vous devez sans faille
Par jugement, comment qu'il aille.   4180
Il vous couvient, chose est certeinne,
Faire .i. lay pour la premereinne
Amiablement, sans tenson;
Pour la seconde une chanson
De .iii. vers et a un refrein   4185
--Oëz, comment je le refrein--
Qui par le refrein se commense,

4151. AMBDE sa; other MSS la--4155. A apperet--4185. A aa un

                          186

Which is called Nobility, 4145
And it was ornamented with Gentility.
Now happiness is covered
With the mantle, and it's an apparent fact
That she encloses all good things therein.
But certainly on the outside, 4150
Whatever's under cover,
Is the appearance of her face,
So that the goods of total courtesy
Appear quite sufficiently
In her features, 4155
And her damsels glorify themselves with them.
And she is in turn well graced
By those damsels, and is not separated
From them and their noble array.
For they would suffice a king 4160
And a sovereign queen.
For these reasons I put it to you
That Happiness completely surpasses
And is of higher status than all queens.
If I wished to describe 4165
Her crown, which is beautiful and good,
I would detain you too long;
For I readily see--and there can be no doubt--
That their council is ending.
And so I say 'peace' to you in this." 4170

GUILLAUME

When their council had ended,
The judge turned to me,

THE JUDGE

Saying: "Guillaume, by my soul,
Now I'll tell you on my lady's behalf,
And on behalf of Reason as well, 4175
And I agree with them about it,
What three compensations you must make,
As these have been considered and laid out,
Which you must accomplish without fail
In accordance with the sentence, whatever might come of it.
You must--the thing is certain--
Compose a lay for the first,
And agreeably, without resisting;
For the second, a song
Of three stanzas and a refrain 4185
--Listen how I qualify this--
A song which begins with the refrain

187

Si comme on doit chanter a dance;
Et pour la tierce, une balade.
Or n'en faites pas le malade,   4190
Eins respondez haitiement
Après nostre commandement
De tous poins vostre entention;
Je fais ci ma conclusion."

                    GUILLAUME

Et pour ce que trop fort mespris,   4195
Quant a dame de si haut pris
M'osay nullement aastir
De plait encontre li bastir,
Je, Guillaumes dessus nommez,
Qui de Machau sui seurnommez,   4200
Pour miex congnoistre mon meffait,
Ay ce livret rimé et fait.
S'en feray ma dame present,
Et mon service li present,
Li priant que tout me pardoint.   4205
Et Diex pais et honneur li doint
Et de paradis la grant joie
Tele que pour moy la voudroie.
Mais pour ce que je ne vueil mie
Que m'amende ne soit païe,   4210
Pour la paier vueil sans delay
Commencier .i. amoureus lay.

Explicit le Jugement le Roy de Navarre contre le Jugement dou
Roy de Behaingne.

Explicit. A le roy; other MSS dou roy

Just like the ones sung at a dance;
And for the third, a ballade.
Now don't act like you're sick about this,   4190
But respond happily,
As we have commanded,
About your views on all these issues;
I make here an end."

GUILLAUME

And because I so grievously erred,   4195
When I dared to make trouble
For a lady of such high station
By attempting to debate her,
I, the Guillaume named above,
Who has the surname de Machaut,   4200
In order the better to understand my fault,
Have composed and rhymed this little book.
And I'll make my lady a present of it,
Offering her my service,
And begging her to pardon me for everything.   4205
And may God grant her peace and honor
And the great joy of paradise,
Just as I would wish it for myself.
But because I don't want in any way
Not to accomplish my amending,   4210
I am eager to do so by beginning work
Without delay on a lay about love.

Here ends the Judgment of the King of Navarre against the Judgment of the King of Bohemia.

APPENDIX: Le Lay de Plour (text from Hoepffner, I, pp. 283-291)

I

Qui bien aimme a tart oublie,
Et cuers qui oublie a tart
Ressamble le feu qui art
Qui de legier n'esteint mie.
Aussi qui a maladie   5
Qui plaist, envis se depart.
En ce point, se Dieus me gart,
Me tient Amours et maistrie.
Car Plaisence si me lie
Que jamais l'amoureus dart   10
N'iert hors trait, a tiers n'a quart,
De mon cuer, quoy que nuls die.
Car tant m'a fait compaingnie,
Que c'est niant dou depart,
Ne que jamais, par nul art,   15
Soit sa pointure garie.

I

Whoever loves well forgets slowly,
And the heart that slowly forgets
Is like the fire that burns
But cannot easily be put out.
And whoever suffers an illness   5
That pleases unwillingly recovers.
In such a state, so God give me help,
Love restrains and commands me,
For Pleasure has me so snared
That the arrow of loving   10
Will never be drawn out, not even a little,
From my heart, whatever anyone might say,
For it's been with me so long
That there's no question of its leaving,
Nor ever, by any art,   15
Will that wound be healed.

Qu'envis puet on deraciner
Un grant arbre, sans demourer
   De la racine,
Qu'on voit puis flourir et porter   20
Et ses branches croistre et geter,
   En brief termine.
Certes, einsi est il d'amer:
Car quant uns cuers se vuet enter
   En amour fine,   25
Envis puet s'amour oublier,
Einsois adès, par ramembrer,
   A li s'encline.

A huge tree can hardly be
Uprooted, without leaving behind
   Some of its roots,
And so in a short time it is seen   20
Bearing flowers and fruit, its branches
   Growing and spreading.
Surely, it's the same with love;
For when a heart's bent on
   A noble love affair,   25
It can hardly forget its loved one,
Rather, always, through memory
   Inclines toward him.

Car l'iaue qui chiet desseure
La racine qui demeure   30
Fait renverdir et florir
    Et porter fruit:
Tout einsi mes cuers qui pleure
Parfondement a toute heure
Acroistre mon souvenir   35
    Fait jour et nuit.
Et c'est ce qui me deveure;
C'est ce qui mon vis espleure;
C'est ce pour quoy je soupir;
    A ce me duit   40
Vraie Amour qui me court seure
Et Bonté qui l'assaveure:
Qu'en moy ne puissent venir,
    Ce me destruit.

III

For the water flowing down
To the root that remains   30
Makes it green again and flourish,
      Bearing fruit:
Just the same, my heart, weeping
Bitterly all the time
Makes my memory grow   35
      Both day and night.
And this drives me mad;
This covers my face in tears;
This is the reason I cry out;
      True Love   40
Drives me to it, assaulting me,
And Goodness finds it sweet:
But they cannot enter in me,
      And I am destroyed.

Raisons et Droiture,   45
Plaisence et Nature
Font par leur pooir
Toute creature
De volenté pure
Tendre a mieus valoir.   50
Et je m'asseüre.
Que, tant com je dure,
Ne porray vĕoir
Amour si seüre,
Bonté si meüre   55
N'a tant de savoir.

IV

Reason and Justice,   45
Pleasure and Nature,
Create by their power
All that lives
Through pure will
To incline toward greater worthiness.   50
And I console myself,
For, as long as I endure,
I'll never see
A love so certain,
A goodness so well grown,   55
Nor so much wisdom.

V

Aussi voit on clerement
Que li cuer qui loyaument
    Et sans folour
Aimment de trés fine amour   60
    Cuident souvent
Qu'en milleur et en plus gent
    Aient sejour;
Car plaisence et sa rigour
    Ce leur aprent: 65
Or say je certeinnement
Que mienne estoit ligement
    La droite flour
De ceaus qui ont plus d'onnour;
    Car toute gent   70
Disoient communement,
    Et li millour,
Qu'il avoit toute valour
    Entierement.

V

And more, it is obvious
That the hearts which loyally
    And without madness
Love with a quite noble love   60
    Often think
To find a relief that's better
    And more noble;
For pleasure in its insistence
    Suggests this to them: 65
Now I know for sure
That my lover, without doubt,
    Was the rightful flower
Of those men with the greatest honor:
    For everyone   70
Says this everywhere,
    And the best in fact,
That his alone was complete
    Worthiness.

Et quant si bon ne millour ne plus cointe   75
N'est, ne si bel, ne d'onneur si acointe,
    A droit jugier,
    Mervillier
    Ne se doit
Nulz, se ne vueil par l'amoureuse pointe   80
Nouvellement d'autre amour estre pointe.
    Pour ce changier
    Ne me quier,
    Et j'ay droit;
Qu'en mon cuer est si trés ferme et si jointe   85
L'amour de li qu'estre n'en puet desjointe;
    Car cuer entier
    Qui trichier
    Ne saroit
Par souvenir vuet que dou tout m'apointe,   90
Si qu'autre amour n'entrepreingne, n'acointe;
    Qu'autre acointier
    Empirier
    Me feroit.

VI

And since there's none better, more genteel,   75
None more handsome, so familiar with honor,
 No one,
 To judge truly,
 Should wonder
If by the shaft of love, I don't wish   80
To be wounded with another lover.
 I don't want
 To change this,
 And I'm right;
For my love for him is so implanted, so firm   85
In my heart, that it cannot be removed;
 For a heart undivided
 Which cannot
 Be false
Intends that I spur myself on through memory   90
To never undertake a new love, or meet with one;
 For to take up with another
 Would do
 Me harm.

Dont le bon recort   95
Que de li recort
Fait qu'a ce m'acort
Que ja ne soie en acort
D'avoir autre amy;
Mais en desconfort,   100
Sans nul reconfort
De tout mon effort
Vueil pleindre et plourer sa mort,
En disant einsi:
'Amis, mi confort,   105
Mi joieus deport,
Ma pais, mi ressort,
Et tuit me amoureus sort
Estoient en ty.
O ray un remort   110
De toy qui me mort
Et point si trés fort
Qu'o toy sont tuit mi bien mort
Et ensevely.'

VII

For the beautiful memory   95
That recalls him to me
Makes me determined
Never to agree
To have another lover;
Rather in misery,   100
With no relief,
But with all my strength
I intend to lament and weep over his death,
Saying this:
'Lover, my comfort,   105
My joyous pleasure,
My peace, my refuge,
And all my loving destiny
Were in you.
O I'll have pain again   110
To tear at me on your account,
Wounding me so terribly,
For all my goods died with you
And were put in the ground.'

Dous amis, tant fort me dueil;   115
  Tant te plaint,
  Tant te complaint
  Le cuer de moy,
Tant ay grief que, par may foy,
  Tout mal recueil;   120
  Dont mi oueil
  Que souvent mueil,
  Et cuer estreint,
Viaire pali et taint,
  Garni d'effroy   125
  Et d'anoy,
  Sans esbanoy;
  Moustrent mon dueil.
Dous amis, seur ton sarcueil
  Sont mi plaint   130
  Et mi complaint;
  La m'esbanoy,
Par pensée la te voy;
  Plus que ne sueil
  La me vueil;   135
  La sont mi vueil;
  La mes cuers maint.
La mort pri que la me maint,
  Car la m'ottroy.
  La, ce croy,   140
  De la mort doy
  Passer le sueil.

Sweet love, I grieve so hard;   115
        My heart
    Mourns you so much,
    Laments you so much,
My grief's so great, by my faith,
    I reap all ills;   120
        Whence my eyes
    Are so often wet,
    My heart so anguished,
My face pale, tear-stained,
    Full of troubles,   125
        And pain,
    Lacking comfort;
    These show my sorrow.
Sweet lover, on your bier
    Lie my laments,   130
    And all my weeping;
    There I find pleasure,
Seeing you in my thoughts;
    More than my custom
        I wish to be there.   135
    There lie my desires.
    My heart remains there.
I beg for the death that leads me there,
    For there I offer myself.
        There, I believe,   140
    I ought pass over
    Death's threshold.

IX

La souspire,

La s'aire

Mes cuers qui tant a martire   145

  Et de mortel peinne

    Et tant d'ire,

    Qu'a voir dire

Son mal ne porroit descrire

    Creature humeinne.   150

    La s'empire

    Tire a tire;

La ne fait que fondre et frire:

  La son dueil demeinne;

    La, sans rire,   155

    Se martire;

La se mourdrist; la desire

  Qu'il ait mort procheinne.

IX

My heart
Sighs there
Grows angry there, suffers so much,   145
    Feels such deadly pain
        And so much regret,
        That to tell the truth
No person alive could even
        Describe it.   150
        There my heart grows worse
        Without stopping;
There it can only tremble and burst;
    There it manifests its grief;
        There, hardly laughing,   155
        It suffers;
There it kills itself; there it wishes for
    A death that's soon to come.

Dous amis, tant ay grevance,
    Tant ay grief souffrance,   160
Tant ay dueil, tant ay pesance,
Quant jamais ne te verray,
Que doleur me point et lance
    De si mortel lance
Au cuer qu'en desesperance   165
Pour toy mes jours fineray.
En toy estoit m'esperance
    Toute et ma fiance,
Ma joie, ma soustenance.
Lassette! Or perdu les ay.   170
Bien pert a ma contenance
    Et a ma loquence,
Car maniere ne puissance
N'ay, tant me dueil et esmay.

X

Sweet lover, my grief's so great,
    My suffering so terrible,   160
I feel such pain, worrying so much,
Since I never will see you,
And so sorrow stabs and wounds me
    With such a deadly lance
In the heart that despairing   165
For you I'll end my days.
All my hope was in
    You, my trust as well,
My joy, my nourishment.
Sorrowful one! Now I've lost them.   170
It's readily apparent in my look
    And in my speech,
For I've no strength or direction,
So much do I sorrow and grieve.

A cuer pensis   175
Regret et devis
    Ton haut pris
    Que tant pris.
Einsi le couvient;
  Et vis a vis   180
Te voy, ce m'est vis,
    Dous amis,
    Et toudis
De toy me souvient.

  Mes esperis   185
Et mes paradis
    Estient mis
    Et assis
En toy; s'apartient
  Que soit fenis   190
Mes cuers et peris,
    Qu'est chetis
    Et remis,
Quant vie le tient.

With a heavy heart 175
I mourn and recall
 Your great worthiness
 Which I prized so much.
It must be so;
 And I see you 180
Face to face, so I think,
 Sweet lover,
 And always
I remember you.
 My soul 185
And my paradise
 Were placed
 And set
In you; and so it follows
 That my heart 190
Is finished and done for
 For it is wretched
 And brought to nothing,
While life clings to it.

Amis, je fusse moult lie,   195
S'eüsses cuer plus couart;
Mieus vausist a mon esgart
Que volenté si hardie.
Mais honneur, chevalerie
Et tes renons qui s'espart   200
Par le monde en mainte part
Ont fait de nous departie.
Ta mort tant me contralie
Et tant de maus me repart,
Amis, que li cuers me part;   205
Mais einsois que je devie,
Humblement mes cuers supplie
Au vray Dieu qu'il nous regart
De si amoureus regart
Qu'en livre soiens de vie.   210

EXPLICIT LE LAY DE PLOUR

XII

Lover, I would have been quite happy   195
If you had had more the coward's heart;
This would have been worth more to me
Than a will so hardy.
But honor, chivalry,
And your renown, spreading   200
Throughout the world in many places,
Have brought us to an end.
Your death does trouble me so much,
And so much ill comes upon me,
Lover, that the heart goes out of me;   205
But before I do die,
My heart humbly begs
The True God to look upon us
With such a loving countenance
That in a book we'll find life.   210

HERE ENDS THE LAY DE PLOUR

Line 9 -- The term *hoquès* is interestingly ambiguous here since
its two commonly attested senses, a lyric form and
a musical rest, each give good meaning here. In
the *Prologue* Machaut uses the term to denote a kind
of lyric poem, so I have translated with that sense
in mind here. But the line could alternately be
rendered: "held their service with notes and rests."

Lines 119-136 -- The reference to the Book of Ecclesiastes is
a commonplace element in the topos *mundus senescit*
or "the world grows old." Machaut's pessimism and
worldweariness here are thoroughly conventional.

Lines 151-180 -- The astrological and meteorological events
mentioned here are attested in the various chronicles
of the period. Machaut is likely following one of
them closely. See further lines 214-256.

Line 391 -- The other MSS give good sense here as well. Perhaps read "often one saw it happen."

Lines 437ff -- If this part of the poem is accurate autobiog-
raphy, then Machaut is probably referring to his
residence in Rheims as the "house" where, secluded
from the rest of the city, he sat out the ravages
of the epidemic.

Line 485 -- The other MSS give good sense here as well. Perhaps read "so that I went out of that prison."

Lines 508ff -- Rabbit-hunting in the courtly texts of the period is often a slyly oblique way of referring to
the pursuit of women (based on an obscene double
entendre). Machaut does not reproduce the double
entendre here, so it is not certain whether he meant
the passage to be read in other than a literal sense.
It is known from other sources that he did possess
a horse named Grisart and owned some hunting dogs;
this means that a literal, autobiographical meaning
may well be here intended.

Line 585 -- The monosyllabic *pour*, attested by a number of
MSS, would be more metrically regular here. A disyl-
labic form, however, is attested to by some of the
most reliable MSS.

Lines 611-612 -- The meaning of these lines is very obscure.
The translation offered here is not certain, hardly
more than an educated guess.

Line 721 -- MS A is very inconsistent in its treatment of in-
tervocalic "st," sometimes recording the change to
"t" and sometimes retaining the older form.

Line 737 -- The other MSS give a slightly better reading here.
Perhaps read with them "and so, talking, we rode
along so much that."

Line 902 -- MSS FMB give an interesting reading here, one particularly appropriate to the tone of the passage.
Perhaps read with them and translate either "that
the thought which annoys you" or "that your annoying
thought."

Line 1151 -- The literal translation here is "there was no
Maggie or Agnes present."

Line 1302 -- The other MSS have *siecles* here, the more learned
or ecclesiastical word for "world." Its connotations
fit the context better.

Line 1395 -- MS A's reading here is possible but gives inferior
sense. If retained, the line would translate: "Lift
up your eyes, it pleases us."

Lines 1750-1762 -- While its general meaning is fairly clear,
the specific ideas in this passage are somewhat obscure and confusing, perhaps deliberately so. The
translation offered is provisional.

Lines 2055-2058 -- The meaning of these lines is fairly clear,
but the relevance of the ideas contained therein is
questionable. This may well be another example of
Guillaume's "ineffective" argument. See lines 1750-
1762 for a similar lapse of good rhetoric.

Line 2381 -- It is tempting to read with the MSS other than
ABD here. In that case we would translate "Then
Charity moved forward."

Line 2476 -- As it stands this line does not make good gram-
matical sense without an introductory conjunction.
Hoepffner's emendation supplies the necessary conjunction and also offers an acceptable reason for
the textual corruption in the first place (*s'elle*
understood as its homonym *celle*).

Line 2628 -- It is difficult to decide between the reading of
          MS A here and that offered by the other MSS since
          both make good sense. Reading with MS A here we
          would translate: "If only you would listen to me."

Line 2695 -- This line is obviously corrupted in all MSS; the
          diversity of inadequate readings attests to this.
          Hoepffner's emendation, adopted here, reasonably
          explains the corruption and offers good sense.

Lines 3112-3113 -- The meaning here is somewhat obscure, per-
          haps a confusing reference to the stereotypical an-
          tifeminist of the late Middle Ages, the university
          scholar.

Line 3249 -- MS A's reading here is possible, but that of the
          other MSS gives a better rhyme.

Line 3389 -- MSS AB read *nostre* here, while the other MSS read
          vostre. Both readings give good sense. Perhaps
          read with the other MSS and translate: "preserving
          always your honor."

Line 3401 -- I have retained the reading of MSS ABD though
          that of the other MSS gives slightly better sense.
          Perhaps read with them and translate: "a friend who
          was very fond of me."

Line 3590 -- MS A's reading is possible here, but definitely
          weaker than that of the other MSS.

Line 3749 -- The reading of the MSS other than A gives good
          sense here as well. Perhaps read with them and
          translate: "and it is time, as you know."

Line 3776 -- The reading of MS A gives satisfactory sense,
          but that of the other MSS is somewhat stronger. If
          we read with A, then translate: "and continues to
          work at it."

Lines 3868-3870 -- The sense of these lines is somewhat ob-
          scure. The translation is not certain.

Line 3887, Line 3889 -- The change in gender for pronoun ref-
          erences to Lady Good Fortune in all the MSS is puz-
          zling. Hoepffner emends the masculine forms to fem-
          inine ones, and I have followed his lead.

Line 3891 -- MS A's reading makes only weak sense here. If
          we retain it, then translate: "through victory, with-
          out coming to terms."

217

The Garland Library
of Medieval Literature

Series A (Texts and Translations); Series B (Translations Only)

1. Chrétien de Troyes: *Lancelot,* or *The Knight of the Cart.* Edited and translated by William W. Kibler. Series A.
2. Brunetto Latini: *Il Tesoretto (The Little Treasure).* Edited and translated by Julia Bolton Holloway. Series A.
3. *The Poetry of Arnaut Daniel.* Edited and translated by James J. Wilhelm. Series A.
4. *The Poetry of William VII, Count of Poitiers, IX Duke of Aquitaine.* Edited and translated by Gerald A. Bond; music edited by Hendrik van der Werf. Series A.
5. *The Poetry of Cercamon and Jaufre Rudel.* Edited and translated by George Wolf and Roy Rosenstein; music edited by Hendrik van der Werf. Series A.
6. *The Vidas of the Troubadours.* Translated by Margarita Egan. Series B.
7. *Medieval Latin Poems of Male Love and Friendship.* Translated by Thomas Stehling. Series A.
8. *Barthar Saga.* Edited and translated by Jon Skaptason and Phillip Pulsiano. Series A.
9. Guillaume de Machaut: *Judgment of the King of Bohemia (Le Jugement dou Roy de Behaingne).* Edited and translated by R. Barton Palmer. Series A.
10. *Three Lives of the Last Englishmen.* Translated by Michael Swanton. Series B.
11. Giovanni Boccaccio: *Eclogues.* Edited and translated by Janet Smarr. Series A.
12. Hartmann von Aue: *Erec.* Translated by Thomas L. Keller. Series B.
13. *Waltharius* and *Ruodlieb.* Edited and translated by Dennis M. Kratz. Series A.
14. *The Writings of Medieval Women.* Translated by Marcelle Thiébaux. Series B.
15. *The Rise of Gawain, Nephew of Arthur (De ortu Waluuanii Nepotis Arturi).* Edited and translated by Mildred Leake Day. Series A.

16, 17. *The French Fabliau:* B.N. 837. Edited and translated by Raymond Eichmann and John DuVal. Series A.

18. *The Poetry of Guido Cavalcanti.* Edited and translated by Lowry Nelson, Jr. Series A.

19. Hartmann von Aue: *Iwein.* Edited and translated by Patrick M. McConeghy. Series A.

20. *Seven Medieval Latin Comedies.* Translated by Alison Goddard Elliott. Series B.

21. Christine de Pizan: *The Epistle of the Prison of Human Life.* Edited and translated by Josette A. Wisman. Series A.

22. *The Poetry of the Sicilian School.* Edited and translated by Frede Jensen. Series A.

23. *The Poetry of Cino da Pistoia.* Edited and translated by Christopher Kleinhenz. Series A.

24. *The Lyrics and Melodies of Adam de la Halle.* Lyrics edited and translated by Deborah Hubbard Nelson; music edited by Hendrik van der Werf. Series A.

25. Chrétien de Troyes. *Erec and Enide.* Edited and translated by Carleton W. Carroll. Series A.

26. *Three Ovidian Tales of Love.* Edited and translated by Raymond J. Cormier. Series A.

27. *The Poetry of Guido Guinizelli.* Edited and translated by Robert Edwards. Series A.

28. Wernher der Gartenaere: *Helmbrecht.* Edited by Ulrich Seelbach; introduced and translated by Linda B. Parshall. Series A.

29. *Pathelin and Other Farces.* Edited and translated by Richard Switzer and Mireille Guillet-Rydell. Series A.

30. *Les Cent Nouvelles Nouvelles.* Translated by Judith Bruskin Diner. Series B.

31. Gerald of Wales (Giraldus Cambrensis): *The Life of St. Hugh of Avalon.* Edited and translated by Richard M. Loomis. Series A.

32. *L'Art d'Amours.* Translated by Lawrence Blonquist. Series B.

33. Giovanni Boccaccio: *L'Ameto.* Translated by Judith Serafini-Sauli. Series B.

34, 35. *The Medieval Pastourelle.* Selected, translated, and edited in part by William D. Paden, Jr. Series A.

36. Béroul: *Tristan.* Edited and translated by Norris J. Lacy. Series A.

37. *Graelent* and *Guingamor:* Two Breton Lays. Edited and translated by Russell Weingartner. Series A.

38. Heinrich von Veldeke: *Eneit.* Translated by J. Welsey Thomas. Series B.

39. *The Lyrics and Melodies of Gace Brulé.* Edited and translated by Samuel Rosenberg and Samuel Danon; music edited by Hendrik van der Werf. Series A.